Spoken English, TESOL and Applied Linguistics

Spoken English, TESOL and Applied Linguistics

Challenges for Theory and Practice

Edited by

Rebecca Hughes
University of Nottingham

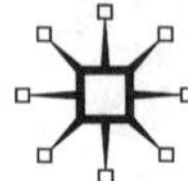

First published 2006 by
PALGRAVE MACMILLAN
Houndmills, Basingstoke, Hampshire RG21 6XS and
175 Fifth Avenue, New York, N.Y. 10010
Companies and representatives throughout the world

PALGRAVE MACMILLAN is the global academic imprint of the Palgrave
Macmillan division of St. Martin's Press, LLC and of Palgrave Macmillan Ltd.
Macmillan® is a registered trademark in the United States, United Kingdom
and other countries. Palgrave is a registered trademark in the European
Union and other countries.

ISBN 13: 978–1–4039–3632–5
ISBN 10: 1–4039–3632–3

This book is printed on paper suitable for recycling and made from fully
managed and sustained forest sources.

A catalogue record for this book is available from the British Library.

Library of Congress Cataloging-in-Publication Data
Spoken English, TESOL, and applied linguistics : challenges for theory and
practice / edited by Rebecca Hughes
    p. cm.
  Includes bibliographical references and index.
  ISBN 1–4039–3632–3 (cloth)
  1. English language–Study and teaching–Foreign speakers. 2. English
language–Spoken English–Study and teaching. 3. English language–
Pronunciation–Study and teaching. 4. English language–Pronunciation by
foreign speakers. I. Hughes, Rebecca, 1962–
  PE1128.A2S643 2005
  428′.0071–dc22
                                               2005050963

10 9 8 7 6 5 4 3 2 1
15 14 13 12 11 10 09 08 07 06

Printed and bound in Great Britain by
Antony Rowe Ltd, Chippenham and Eastbourne

Contents

PART I　ATTITUDES AND IDEOLOGIES

**1　Uncovering the sociopolitical situatedness of accents
in the World Englishes paradigm**　　　　　　　3
Jasmine C.M. Luk and Angel M.Y. Lin

**2　What the other half gives: the interlocutor's role in　23
non-native speaker performance**
Stephanie Lindemann

List of Tables and Figures

Acknowledgements

I would like to acknowledge the help of several people in the creation of this collection. First, I would like to thank Christopher Candlin and Ronald Carter for their many helpful conversations, comments and suggestions in the early stages of the conception of the book, and Jill Lake at Palgrave-Macmillan for her efficient, intelligent and humane approach to the commissioning and editing process. Joanne Rajadurai offered valuable support with mid-stage proofreading and insightful comments from the perspective of a speech researcher, and my thanks go to Julie King, Martha Jones, Ann Smith, Neil Taylor and others in the Centre for English Language Education for further read-throughs and for offering their more class-room informed perspectives. My particularly warm thanks to Beatrice Szczepek Reed for giving me well-organized editorial support in the closing strait (and for all her insightful comments in our recent conversations about speech research generally).

Primarily, of course, the people whom I should most like to thank are the contributors of the chapters making up this volume. Their good humoured, patient, and professional approach throughout made the putting together of this collection an enjoyable and intellectually stimulating task for me.

My thanks to all those who have supported me in the process. Any remaining errors or omissions should be ascribed to me.

REBECCA HUGHES

Notes on the Contributors

Wallace Chafe was educated at Yale University and was then employed in the Smithsonian Institution in Washington as a specialist in Native American languages before moving in 1962 to the University of California at Berkeley, USA. In 1986 he moved to the Santa Barbara campus, where he is now Professor Emeritus. He has worked extensively with Native American languages, and has studied differences between speaking and writing and applications of linguistics to literature as well as various functions of prosody. Among his many writings have been the books *Meaning and the Structure of Language* (1970) and *Discourse, Consciousness, and Time* (1994).

Joan Cutting is Senior Lecturer in TESOL, University of Edinburgh, UK. She has taught EFL, English for Business, and English for Medicine, and teacher-training on MA TESOLs in Havana, Cuba, and Sunderland and Edinburgh, UK. Her research interests are pragmatics, the codes of academic discourse communities, spoken grammar, teacher training and TEFL. She is currently engaged in a European Community funded research project on the language of airport ground staff. She is editor of *The Grammar of Spoken English and EAP Teaching*, and author of *Analysing the Language of Discourse Communities* and *Pragmatics and Discourse*.

Fiona Farr is a lecturer in EFL/ELT and course director of the MA in ELT at the University of Limerick, Ireland. She is part of the research group IVACS (Inter-varietal applied corpus studies) and is co-manager of the Limerick Corpus of Irish English (L-CIE). Her professional interests include language teacher education, spoken language corpora and their applications, discourse analysis and language variety. She has published in journals such as *TESOL Quarterly* and the *Journal of English for Academic Purposes*, and also has chapters in books on corpora and language variety, as well as Irish-English pragmatics and teacher education.

Rebecca Hughes is a Senior Lecturer at the University of Nottingham, UK, and Director of the Centre for English Language Education. She has published and presented widely, including *English in Speech and Writing: Investigating Language and Literature*, *Exploring Grammar in Context* (co-authored with Ronald Carter and Michael McCarthy), *Teaching and Researching Speaking*, *Exploring Grammar in Writing*.

Marysia Johnson Gerson is Associate Professor in the department of English, Linguistics/TESL Program, Arizona State University, USA. She is the author of *A Philosophy of Second Language Acquisition* and *The Art of Nonconversation: A Reexamination of the Validity of the Oral Proficiency Interview*.

John M. Levis teaches in the TESL/Applied Linguistics program at Iowa State University, USA. He is interested in how NSs and NNSs use intonation in discourse and in the role of pronunciation in judgments of speech intelligibility. He has published articles about pronunciation in *TESOL Quarterly, World Englishes, ELT Journal, TESOL Journal, PASAA, Applied Linguistics* and *Speak Out*.

Angel M.Y. Lin is Associate Professor in the Department of English and Communication, City University of Hong Kong. She has published research articles in *Curriculum Inquiry, TESOL Quarterly, Linguistics and Education, the International Journal of the Sociology of Language, Journal of Pragmatics, Journal of Language, Identity, and Education, Canadian Modern Language Review*, and *Language, Culture and Curriculum*. She serves on the Editorial Advisory Boards of *Linguistics and Education, Critical Discourse Studies,* and *Critical Inquiry in Language Studies* and she started the publication of *TESL-HK* (http://www.tesl-hk.org) in 1997.

Stephanie Lindemann is Assistant Professor of Applied Linguistics at Georgia State University, USA. She received her PhD in 2000 from the University of Michigan. Her research interests include language ideologies, native-nonnative communication, and speech perception; publications include articles in *Language in Society* and *English for Specific Purposes*.

Ee Ling Low is Sub-Dean of Degree Programmes at the National Insitute of Education, Singapore, where she is an Assistant Professor with the English Language & Literature Academic Group. She obtained her PhD in Linguistics specializing in Phonetics from the University of Cambridge in 1998. She has published widely in the area of speech rhythm and her articles have appeared in *Language & Speech, TESOL Quarterly* and *Laboratory Phonology 7*. In addition, she has published four textbooks with McGraw-Hill, Education (Asia), on the topic of English in Singapore.

Jasmine C.M. Luk is a Lecturer in English at the Hong Kong Institute of Education. She obtained her doctoral degree from Lancaster University,

UK. She has been researching classroom interactions between native-English-speaking teachers and Hong Kong students. She is an experienced English teacher and teacher educator for both primary and secondary levels. Her research interests include cross-cultural dialogic interaction practices, culture and second and foreign language learning, and World English intelligibility issues.

Anna Mauranen is Professor of English at the University of Helsinki, Finland. Her recent research and publications focus on corpus linguistics, speech corpora, applied linguistics and translation studies. Her major publications include *Translation Universals–Do They Exist* (co-ed.), *Academic Writing. Intercultural and Textual Issues* (co-ed.) and *Cultural Differences in Academic Rhetoric*. She is currently running a research project on English as lingua franca, and compiling a corpus on spoken academic English used as a lingua franca (the ELFA corpus).

Beatrice Szczepek Reed is a Research Fellow in the Centre for English Language Education at the University of Nottingham, UK. She received a PhD in Linguistics form the University of Potsdam, Germany, and an MA in Music from the University of York, UK. Her current research is into the teaching of conversational turn-taking to learners of English. Other research interests include the prosody of natural conversation, and the interface between speech and singing. Publications include *Prosodic Orientation in English Talk-in-Interaction* and contributions to *InLiSt* and *Zeitschrift für germanistische Linguistik*.

Steve Walsh is Head of External Relations and Lecturer in Education in the Graduate School of Education, Queen's University Belfast, Northern Ireland. He directs the MSc TESOL programme and a teacher education programme for newly appointed university lecturers. He has worked on British Council projects as a teacher, teacher trainer and assistant director in Spain, Hong Kong, Hungary, Poland, the Republic of Ireland and China. He has ELT project experience in the areas of teacher education, curriculum renewal, materials development, testing and evaluation. Research interests include teacher language awareness, discourse analysis and teacher development.

Ann Wennerstrom teaches Applied Linguistics and English as a Second Language at the University of Washington in the United States. She is author of *The Music of Everyday Speech: Prosody and Discourse Analysis* and *Discourse Analysis in the Language Classroom: Genres of Writing.* Her research interests include intonation, discourse analysis, language learning, and cognitive linguistics.

Introduction

This collection of essays by leading researchers in the field of spoken discourse and language teaching pursues two aims. Its first aim is to present an issues-led discussion of the present state of research into spoken language. Contributors address issues concerning, for example, the extent to which new data regarding the nature of spoken discourse challenge existing language theories, models or paradigms; and the question whether there is a 'paradigm-shift' taking place due to the weight of evidence that spoken discourse is a distinctive form in its own right, or whether this evidence will be absorbed into existing models and theories.

The collection's second aim is to address some of the complex and rewarding opportunities offered by these emerging insights for language teaching. Can the insights of current research on spoken language easily be accommodated into existing language teaching, whether at the level of pedagogic grammars, or methods; or do they present challenges which break new ground? Is there such a thing as a 'spoken genre', and how can this concept inform materials production or language teaching? Will current research on spoken forms have an impact on the assessment of speaking? And what weight should be given to the phonetic and paralinguistic meaning-bearing elements of the spoken form, either in language description or in the curriculum?

The chapters

The following chapters contribute to research into the connection between spoken language and language teaching in four basic ways: by uncovering underlying attitudes towards language learners, and the ideologies embedded in the teaching of foreign languages and their pronunciation; by highlighting the prosodic aspect of second language acquisition; by focusing on aspects of spoken discourse in the pedagogy of language teaching; and by addressing the problem of how to assess pronunciation in an examination environment.

In Part I, Angel Lin and Jasmine Luk analyze the practices of TESOL in postcolonial Hong Kong. They find that learners are strongly encouraged to acquire native-like pronunciation of British English, rather than a Hong Kong variety. The authors call for an attitude of acceptance in the field of TESOL of World Englishes as varieties of, rather than deviations from, the English language.

Stephanie Lindemann's contribution focuses on the native interlocutor's part in native/non-native interactions. She finds that a variety of difficulties in such interactions is rooted within the interlocutor's behaviour, rather than that of the language learner. Her chapter also discusses ways in which native speakers' attitudes influence their judgement of good or bad linguistic competence in co-participants. The chapter calls upon the language teaching community to bring issues of prejudice and discrimination against non-native speakers to the foreground at various levels of education.

Prosody is the overall focus of the contributions grouped together in Part II. Wallace Chafe reports on the difference between the prosody of natural talk and that of reading aloud. His analyses of two instances in which both natural and reading prosody occur within one stretch of talk from the same speaker show the marked differences between the two forms of delivery, and their potential motivations. The chapter also discusses the interdependency of punctuation and prosodic breaks in a read-out text.

Ann Wennerstrom makes a strong plea for practitioners of TESOL to incorporate into their teaching the intonation of naturally occurring speech, and the various layers of meaning it communicates in context. She argues that, as intonational meaning is fundamental to the comprehension and the comprehensibility of speech, language learners must be taught the skills of interpreting and using intonation. Her analyses of several natural instances of native/non-native interactions show that learners' discourse can provide a basis for teaching intonational meaning.

Ee Ling Low's contribution reviews current research on speech rhythm and its implications for TESOL and second language acquisition. In particular, the chapter discusses a variety of rhythmic indexes as a form of investigation into speech rhythm, and their applications in the fields of language acquisition, language disorders and language teaching.

Rebecca Hughes and Beatrice Szczepek Reed explore the kind of knowledge required by native and non-native speakers in order to accomplish turn-taking in everyday conversation. They find that in addition to knowledge of local prosodic and syntactic signalling cues, speakers must be familiar with other aspects of interaction, such as the genre they are engaging in, and their co-participant's individual way of employing prosodic forms. The authors call for research into turn-taking to broaden its perspective from a micro level of prosody and syntax to a macro level which includes areas such as conversational genre and speaker idiolect.

Part III focuses on the pedagogic aspect of language teaching and spoken discourse. Anna Mauranen's chapter highlights the priority of the spoken over the written mode, and the benefit of using spoken corpora in research and language teaching. Her chapter calls for descriptions of linguistic domains such as grammar, lexis and pragmatics to draw upon speech rather than writing. Furthermore, Mauranen pleads for TESOL to include spoken language data in which English is used as a lingua franca between non-native speakers into their teaching practice, alongside native varieties of English.

Joan Cutting's contribution reviews the literature on grammatical, lexical and discourse structural vagueness. She explores implicit meaning among speakers in an in-group environment, and then goes on to call for TESOL practitioners to include implicit meaning into their curriculum in order to prepare students for informal conversational settings.

Fiona Farr's chapter contributes to current research into language teacher education, in particular self-reflection of professional practice. Her analyses of extracts from a corpus of ELT trainers and trainees highlight a variety of feedback strategies used by teacher trainers, and shows how spoken language corpora can be used in teacher training in order to raise teachers' self-awareness.

Steve Walsh analyzes research on second language classroom discourse within the framework of different approaches, such as interaction analysis, discourse analysis, and conversation analysis, and calls for a variable approach in analyzing L2 classroom interaction. He shows how a flexible approach is better able to accommodate different patterns of interaction, which vary according to teachers' and students' goals and backgrounds.

Issues concerning the assessment of spoken language are the focus of the contributions in Part IV. John M. Levis's chapter explores the complex issues involved in the assessment of students' speaking and pronunciation skills. He argues that, rather than testing for pronunciation accuracy, it is more effective to assess learners' intelligibility and comprehensibility, and calls for language teacher education to place more emphasis on teaching future practitioners how to teach pronunciation.

Marysia Johnson Gerson presents Vygotsky's sociocultural theory and Bakhtin's dialogized heteroglossia as a framework in which to view second language acquisition. As implications of this perspective, Johnson Gerson calls for language classrooms to reflect sociocultural and institutional realities, and to take into account students' potential for development. Based on these demands, she presents a model for second language testing, which situates language competence within a student's given sociocultural setting.

Part 1
Attitudes and Ideologies

1
Uncovering the Sociopolitical Situatedness of Accents in the World Englishes Paradigm

Jasmine C.M. Luk and Angel M.Y. Lin

Introduction: Englishes in a world tug-of-war

The emergence of the 'World Englishes' paradigm over the last two decades has boosted the morale and confidence of many ESL/EFL users in the outer and expanding circles[1] (Kachru, 1992). Sobering and thought-provoking questions challenging the hegemonic status of BANA-centric[2] norms were proffered by Inner Circle experts (e.g. Phillipson, 1992; Widdowson, 1993; Pennycook, 1994). Who owns English? Who are the native speakers of English? Is there 'Standard English'? Whose standards should be followed? These questions capture the hearts of many souls in the former colonies of Britain and America. The paradigm shift seems to have resulted in a more liberal attitude towards local varieties of English. Local usage not conforming to the British and American norms may not be regarded as errors as long as it is commonly adopted by the local community. As argued by Smith (1983: 39), who is one of the early advocates of world Englishes, 'a non-mother-tongue user does not need to become more like Americans, the British, the Australians, the Canadians or any other English speaker in order to lay claim on the language'.

The WE paradigm has boosted ESL/EFL users' confidence and heightens their awareness of their language rights. For example, Baxter (1991) boldly argues for the legitimate rights for Japanese to speak English in a manner appropriate to the local community because speaking English Japanese-ly 'does not threaten the speaker nor come into conflict with this person's identity' (p. 65).

At a more practical applied linguistic level, there have been various attempts to establish an international variety of English (EIL) (for example, Modiano, 1999) or a World Standard English (for example, McArthur, 1987; Crystal, 2003) which English users engaging in international communication should employ to facilitate mutual intelligibility. It is believed that this international variety of English could even supersede the British and American varieties (see Jenkins (2003) for a comprehensive review). In this sense, the paradigm seems to be moving from 'World Englishes' to an internationally accepted 'World English' (Brutt-Griffler, 2002). Jenkins' (2000; 2002) work on establishing a Lingua Franca Core (LFC) of English phonology for international communication is a representative and concrete endeavour to bring about a common understanding among World English users of what segmental and suprasegmental components ESL/EFL students and teachers should aim to master for mutual intelligibility in realistic interethnic communications. Her work was based on empirical and contrived studies that draw on data from natural interactions between EIL (English as an International Language) users from Japan, Switzerland, Germany, France, Taiwan, and Korea. Jenkins's (2000) work enhances mother-tongue and non-mother-tongue English users' awareness of pronunciation variants across varieties due largely to the inherent differences and practices of speech across different national phonological systems. Apart from adopting a teachability–learnability criterion, Jenkins (2000) selects phonological features to be included in a LFC core on two considerations: (1) whether empirical data have shown phonological features to be hampering speech intelligibility in real interethnic communications; and (2) whether the phonological features are commonly realized in most of the major phonological systems of world languages. For example, the voiced interdental fricative 'th' sound as in 'there' was found to be commonly substituted with the dental variant [d] by many L1 and L2 English users; or the dark [l] was found to be becoming vocalic in most other varieties of English and therefore it was quite unproblematic for words such as 'bill' to be pronounced as /bɪʊ/. The voiced interdental fricative 'th' and the dark /l/ are thus *not* to be included in the LFC core.

Jenkins's (2000) work seems to have pointed to a clear direction forward for a common understanding to be achieved about what a World variety of English used by people across all nations would be like. However, the everyday scenario may not really be that orderly and optimistic. As pointed out by Jenkins (2000), speakers substituting /t/ and /d/ for /θ/ and /ð/ respectively would still be stigmatized in the English L1 communities by speakers of RP, GA, and other more standard L1 varieties.

Brutt-Griffler (2002) also points out the resiliency of the tacitly assumed standpoint that the 'ownership of English' still rests with mother tongue users of English. The founding theorist of 'linguistic imperialism', Robert Phillipson, has on more than one occasion warned that ideology revealing 'linguistic ethnocentricity' and 'linguicism' largely goes unchallenged. He observes that there were still 'inequalities and asymmetry in "international communication" [which] places non-native users of English lower on a hierarchy of norms of communication than native English-speakers', and there were still tendencies to view 'Other' cultures and languages as 'deficits' (Phillipson, 2000b: 275).

So, what matters more seems not to be 'who owns English', but who owns the authority and control over value judgement of different norms of usage of English varieties. English as a commodity comes in many brands. Owning only the low-end English (i.e. English spoken with distinct non-standard characteristics) may not yield too much benefit to its owner. Brutt-Griffler (2002) mentions attempts to view the use of English as an international language (EIL) as reflecting features of an 'interlanguage' (IL) (Selinker, 1992) from a second language learning (SLA) perspective. Though these attempts have not been successful, they imply that users of English as an international language may be viewed by some mainstream second language educators as simply having deficient English proficiency.

The large body of work on World Englishes has recently been criticized by Pennycook (2003) who suggests that this represents only circular arguments because 'the WE paradigm focuses only on standardized norms of English in limited domains' (p. 517). Uncodified varieties in the expanding circle still hold the status of errors. It seems clear that hegemony continues to exist in the World English paradigm that is 'far too exclusionary to be able to account for many uses of English around the world' (p. 521). He offers support to Parakrama's (1995: 17) view that the WE paradigm 'cannot do justice to those Other Englishes as long as they remain within the over-arching structures that these Englishes bring to crisis. To take these new/Other Englishes seriously would require a fundamental revaluation of linguistic paradigms, and not merely a slight accommodation or adjustment.' Pennycook (2003) calls for actions to break away from the exclusionary constrictive circles that only incorporate codified national varieties and take seriously varieties arising from globalization, popular culture and Other Englishes.

The crux of the issue, perhaps, is *how* the new/Other Englishes should be taken seriously, by *whom*, and *who* would benefit from such an outcome. This chapter attempts to contribute to the discussion by revealing how English linguistic hegemony continues, perhaps with increased strength, to manifest itself through various social and political institutional apparatuses in the latest member of the post-colonial club, Hong Kong, with particular reference to accents and speaking proficiency. Through a critical analysis of the research literature, evidence from public discourses, and reflexive analysis of lived experiences of ESL/EFL speakers including the authors themselves, we will investigate how local people might have actually suffered, instead of benefited, from the WE paradigm. We will explore two forces at work that are pulling at different ends, one representing an applied linguistic theoretical view focusing on mutual intelligibility, and one representing an underlying sociopolitical ideology focusing on social stigmatization of accents in pronunciation. We will discuss how and why it would be difficult, and may not be desirable, to achieve 'a fundamental revaluation of linguistic paradigm', as advocated by Pennycook, in places such as Hong Kong.

Accent and World Englishes

We have chosen World Englishes accents to be our focus of analysis because of the intricate role speech accents play as a sociolinguistic phenomenon as well as, if not more than, a linguistic phenomenon. Accents are defined by Lippi-Green (1997) as 'loose bundles of prosodic and segmental features distributed over geographic and/or social space'. Accent is more than anything else a powerful linguistic marker of age generations, social identity, social class, education level, and ethnicity. The accent used by the flower girl in George Bernard Shaw's *Pygmalion* (*My Fair Lady*) immediately marked her off as belonging to a lower socio-economic class and a poor region. Stories about how L2 English users and their accented speech are negatively discriminated against in contexts ranging from the classroom to the workplace have been well documented (e.g. Eisenstein, 1983; Canagarajah, 1999; Lippi-Green, 1997). There were regular advertisements publicizing 'accent elimination' services and news broadcasting successful efforts.

Accent discrimination does not only happen to non-mother-tongue English speakers. As pointed out by Jenkins (2000), many teachers considered (which was felt to be wrong by Jenkins) Standard English to mean English spoken with a prestigious accent, RP, or a modified form of it. This implies that English spoken with non-RP accent will be perceived as sub-standard. Subjective and emotional adjectives such as 'stupid' were sometimes used to refer to regional accents. This negative mentality towards accents was also reflected in an early definition of the term 'accent' in a prestigious dictionary with a heavy judgemental tone by including 'mispronunciation of vowels or consonants, misplacing of stress, and misinflection of a sentence' (*Oxford English Dictionary*, 1989, quoted in Lippi-Green, 1997: 58) as features of accents. The authors of this chapter checked the 2003 version of the *Cambridge Advanced Learners' Dictionary* and found a much more neutral definition – 'the way in which people in a particular area, country or social group pronounce words'. However, one of the examples given ('She's French but she speaks with an impeccable English accent') still carries the myth behind accent and proficiency. First, there is an 'impeccable' English accent. Second, it is beyond most people's expectation that a non-native English speaker could speak with that impeccable English accent. Even recently, there were findings showing a general tendency to connect accent with teaching competence. Foreign teaching assistants speaking English with an accent perceived to be intelligible by the students were considered to have higher teaching competence than those who speak with a less intelligible accent (Bresnahan *et al.*, 2002).

Over the last two decades, there have been clear efforts to raise English users' awareness of the inequalities arising from such language ideology and attempts to counteract language subordination were proposed. Lippi-Green (1997) argues forcefully that language subordination based on accent discrimination is not about 'relative standards', but about 'taking away a basic human right: to speak freely in the mother tongue without intimidation, without standing in the shadow of other languages and peoples' (p. 243). To resist the process of language subordination, according to Lippi-Green, is to ask for 'recognition, and acknowledgement' of such linguistic human rights. However, the authors of this chapter would like to point out that to obtain recognition and acknowledgement of such human rights is one issue; to evaluate the gains and losses of social and cultural capital in highly sociopolitical situations arising from an overt display of such human rights is perhaps another.

Positioning postcolonial Hong Kong in the WE paradigm: speculations and realities

In the last few years running up to the handover of sovereignty from Britain to China on 1 July 1997, speculations about the language profile of the Hong Kong society permeated the public and academic discourses. Views were of course diverse, but one representative view tended to envisage a declining importance of English in Hong Kong.

For example, in his paper discussing societal accommodation to English and Putonghua in Hong Kong at the twentieth century's end, Pierson (1998) quotes several references (e.g. Harris, 1989; Purves, 1989; Lau, 1991; Godfrey, 1992; Surry, 1994) published a few years earlier predicting decreasing value of English as one of Hong Kong's greatest assets. It was reported that demand for English instruction had already experienced a noticeable slump, leading to the closing down of some commercially operated English tuition centres (Godfrey, 1992). It was even suggested by Surry (1994) that the ability to use English well is no longer of much concern to the business community. Lau (1991) speculated that Putonghua would replace English as the 'language of success'.

These views that forecast a decline in the status of English in preference for the national language of China, Putonghua, though speculative in nature, were by no means groundless as precedents could easily be found in other former colonies of Britain. In speculating the future of English as a global language, Crystal (2003) points out a common dilemma in several colonies-turned independent states such as Africa, India, the Philippines, Pakistan, and Singapore is that post-colonial subjects often display 'a strong reaction against continuity to use the language of the former colonial power, and in favor of promoting the indigenous languages' (Crystal, 2003: 124). However, Crystal (2003) was quick to add that it does not mean that these nations had totally rejected English. To fulfil the need to assert their national identity while making sure not to be left out from important world affairs, most of these postcolonial people continue to learn to master English, but tend to prefer using English in their 'own way' or a hybridized form of speech constituting several linguistic codes (Canagarajah, 2000). As suggested before, the feeling of identity and group solidarity has been found to be most palpable in the choice of accents in speaking the language of the former colonial masters. Kachru (1990 (1986)), for example, reports findings from a number of studies conducted in former colonies of Britain and America such as India, Singapore, Malaysia, Puerto Rico, the Phillipines, Nigeria, and Sri Lanka showing an almost unanimous attitude of the postcolonial subjects to demonstrate their preference for the localized varieties, and an overt unfavourable attitude towards accents bearing traits of the colonizers' speech.

As a new member of the post-colonial club, Hong Kong, however, does not seem to have displayed similar attitudes as described above.

In Kachru's (1992) concentric-circle model of World Englishes, India, Kenya, Pakistan, Sri Lanka, the Phillippines, and Singapore were all situated in the 'Outer Circle', which was described to be 'norm-developing' by Kachru. Hong Kong, as part of China, was situated under the 'Expanding Circle', which was said to be 'norm-dependent'. About a year before Hong Kong changed its sovereignty, a new colleague of the first author coming from the United States asked the first author after reading a book on common spoken errors in Hong Kong (Boyle and Boyle, 1991) why some of those examples mentioned in the book were considered errors, but not features of a local variety. The fact is, although a Hong Kong variety does exist with general public awareness in terms of a distinct accent (Bolton and Kwok, 1990; Luk, 1998; Hung, 2000) and a body of new vocabularies (*Macquarie Dictionary*, quoted in Bolton, 2000), it is not accepted as the variety to which Hong Kong English speakers aspire. Hong Kong English speakers, be they teachers or students, still look up to exonormative norms; that is, the norms provided by native-speaking countries, particularly Britain (for example, Luk, 1998; Tsui and Bunton, 2000) for correct and acceptable models of pronunciation and usage. The interesting thing is that this kind of mentality does not seem to be reflecting only linguicism or linguistic imperialism under colonial rule, but seems to be becoming increasingly deep-seated and naturalized in the minds of most Hong Kong citizens after Hong Kong has ceased to be a British colony for almost ten years. The following section reports some typical practices signifying a general tendency to move away from the WE paradigm in Hong Kong.

Moving away from the WE paradigm? Signifying practices in postcolonial Hong Kong

The following evidence has been collected through the lived experience of the two authors over the last few years, signifying a force that seems to be diverging from the WE paradigm.

Language proficiency assessments for English teachers

The most powerful mechanism to bring about standardization of norms conforming to the BANA-centric models in Hong Kong is by far the Language Proficiency Assessment for Teachers (LPAT for short). The LPAT started to be enforced in 2001 to ensure that teachers of English and Putonghua all reached a publicly recognized benchmark in terms of language proficiency. Pronunciation is an assessment item for the read aloud task of the speaking test and classroom language use. It was generally believed that only 'native' speakers or speakers with 'native-like' proficiency could attain level 5, which is the highest level in terms of pronunciation, stress and intonation, because the descriptors at this level require pronunciation to be 'completely error-free with no noticeable first language (L1) characteristics' (Government of Hong Kong Special Administrative Region, 2000: 110). These descriptors allude to a close connection between pronunciation errors and L1 characteristics, and also imply that *error-free* pronunciation is also *accent-free*.

Shohamy (2003) argues forcefully how powerful language tests can be in changing people's behaviour. The impact of LPAT tests on public attitude towards language proficiency has been tremendous. Glenwright (2002) reveals a growing tendency for Hong Kong schoolteachers to focus more than ever on accuracy in marking pupils' writing because one component in the LPAT writing tests requires candidates to identify and explain pupils' errors in compositions. This was found to be undermining pupils' creativity in writing. Similar self-disciplining has also been observed in the aspect of pronunciation.

Ms K (a pseudonym), a Cantonese-speaking local teacher educator who was by training a speech pathologist in the United States, has been actively involved in concrete application of the criteria in actual assessments of LPAT candidates' pronunciation, stress and intonation. In one of the standardization meetings Ms K conducted for a group of potential assessors which the first author attended, Ms K classified as errors pronunciation features such as replacing /ð/ with /d/ (e.g. 'there' pronounced as 'dare'); replacing the dark /l/ with /u/ (e.g. 'apple' pronounced as /'æpəʊ/) or dropping it altogether (e.g. 'mall' pronounced as 'more'); and placing equal stress on multisyllabic words (e.g. 'autumn' pronounced as /'ɔːˈtʌm/). In an interview with the first author, Ms K asserted that although these features did not normally create intelligibility problems, any features that do not conform to the British RP or American GA accents would be considered problematic by her. However, she went on to clarify that her judgements excluded accent features of other native English varieties such as Australian, New Zealand, or Canadian accents. Ms K admitted that this was discriminative but inevitable because of the existence of LPAT. In her job as a speech consultant at a teacher education institute in Hong Kong, she would advise local student teachers to try to reduce and/or eliminate any L1 characteristics because, in her understanding, these L1 characteristics would disadvantage them in their LPAT assessments.

An ever-high deferential attitude towards the NETs[3] (native English-speaking teachers)

The massive employment of NETs since 1998 was presented as a measure to raise English standards of both the students and the local English teachers 'with immediate effect' (Chief Executive, 1998). A questionnaire survey conducted by the first author in 1998 concerning secondary students' attitude towards the NETs reveals that most students favoured the recruitment of NETs in schools because they were felt to speak more 'accurate' and 'standard' English (Luk, 2001). A similar attitude has been found to prevail among tertiary level students. In a lecturer–student consultative meeting at the Institute of which the first author is a member, English major students who were all in-service English teachers commented negatively on the English accents used by some local lecturers teaching English and requested more expatriate lecturers.

Even school principals and education officials seem to be upholding the idea that native speaker models should be sought for English learning purposes. For example, at a focus group meeting organized by the Education and Manpower Bureau to develop Basic Competency Assessment tasks for primary pupils, a local English teacher pointed out the importance of clear and proper pronunciation in the audio-recordings. This point was immediately taken up by the chairperson and some other members as indicating the need to recruit native speakers to do the recording. Native English lecturers are also always the first choice many local school principals would consider inviting to give talks on English teaching and learning to staff and students.

Media and public discourses on 'proper' English pronunciation

The deferential attitude towards NETs has also been reinforced by the mass media. Recently, a Radio Hong Kong early morning infotainment programme began to air a 10-minute section on English idioms. At the beginning, the male host (who in the authors' opinion speaks good English) demonstrated the reading of the idioms. However, a few days later, a native speaker model was provided and the male host reiterated that this was the standard model and urged the public to follow the native speaker model.

There has also been a deluge of advertisements for learning packages and courses that flaunt the provision of standard native speaker models. A campaign was launched jointly by the Hong Kong Education City and Oxford University Press to teach teachers and students IPA in order to enhance their awareness of the differences between Cantonese and English phonology. According to the consultant of the project, who is a Chinese teaching comparative phonetics at the University of Hong Kong, 'Cantonese speakers are *particularly prone to* accent-laden spoken English' because 'more than 40 per cent of the English phonetic sounds are different from the Cantonese ones' (South China Morning Post, emphasis added). This seems to imply that only Cantonese-accented English is a kind of accent, and the phonological features of Cantonese, by being so different from those of the English phonetic system, have created 'obstacles' to speaking 'better' English (as suggested by the name of their website *www.speakbetterenglish. com.hk.*). This might have given the public the impression that 'good' English is spoken *without* an accent.

All of the above evidence seems to be suggesting that Hong Kong's linguistic ecology after 1997 is diverging from the WE paradigm. It seems to be a strong case illuminating Phillipson's (1992) configuration of 'English linguistic imperialism' and 'linguicism' (which means the inequitable allocation of language rights; see Skutnabb-Kangas, 1998) in which people engage themselves in a 'biased process of hierarchization of "legitimate and illegitimate offspring of English"' (Phillipson, 2000a: 88, quoting Mufwene, 1997) and the people who produce them. The question, however, is who are the agents effectuating the process of linguistic imperialism in post-colonial Hong Kong? Pennycook (2000) points out the importance of understanding the politics of global dominance of English through 'contextual sociologies rather than a priori assumptions about imperialistic effects' (p. 118). What have sustained the local hegemony of English may largely be the local forces. In the next section, we will attempt to explain such local hegemony in Hong Kong by drawing on theory from post-colonial and sociocultural studies.

Uncovering the sociopolitics in hegemonic privileging of BANA-centric accents in postcolonial Hong Kong

While the domination of English in Hong Kong is a clear case of colonialism and linguistic imperialism, the perpetuation of the local hegemony of English and, in particular, English spoken with the BANA-centric linguistic norms, seems to be an ideology of local production. Hegemony, in Gramsci's (1971: 28) sense, means 'domination by consent':

Fundamentally, hegemony is the power of the ruling class to convince other classes that their interests are the interests of all. Domination is thus exerted not by force, nor even necessarily by active persuasion, but by a more subtle and inclusive power over the economy, and over state apparatuses such as education and the media, by which the ruling class's interest is presented as the common interest and thus comes to be taken for granted. (Ashcroft *et al.*, 2000: 116)

In this sense, the privileging of the BANA-centric pronunciation norms is a clear case of hegemony in Hong Kong. The radio programme, the proliferation of the NET Scheme, the LPAT assessment, and the 'speakbetterEnglish' campaign are all examples of 'state apparatuses' to construct and effectuate an accent-based linguistic hierarchization, with Inner Circle norms being given privileged status while local features are suppressed to the lower end and presented as errors. Some readers might feel puzzled about the emergence of this mentality as the change of sovereignty has been in effect since 1 July 1997 and the ruling class is no longer the colonial master from Great Britain. Why would the ruling class, which is almost entirely composed of Hong Kong Chinese, still want to subscribe to the hegemonic domination of the former colonizers' language and their linguistic norms? Why is Hong Kong unlike other post-colonial places such as India, Pakistan, and Sri Lanka where citizens took pride in speaking the colonizers' language in their local manner?

A widely accepted explanation points to the utilitarian and practical minds of Hong Kong people. The Chief Executive of the Hong Kong Special Administrative Region, Tung Chee-wah, in his October 1999 Policy Address, highlighted his vision of Hong Kong as a 'world-class city', explaining that 'Hong Kong should not only be a major Chinese city, but could become the most cosmopolitan city in Asia, enjoying a status comparable to that of New York in North America and London in Europe' (Bolton, 2000: 283). To be a cosmopolitan city, a high English standard is indispensable. Actually, the hegemonic status of English all over the world has often been fortified by the notion of 'globalization'. In the face of a globalized economy and the need to conduct transnational communication, the ability to speak intelligible English as an international language is of crucial importance. Even in Singapore, where local people prefer using local varieties in order to sound like Singaporeans but not like Englishmen, Standard English is still generally viewed to be superior and the 'ideal' form of English to which highly educated people would aspire (Milroy and Milroy, 1999). Therefore, having a good English standard is believed to be able to bring about personal social advancement. Li (2002), for example, after making a comprehensive review of Hong Kong's colonial history and language attitude development, argues that perpetuating the status and demand for English in the postcolonial period (as evident in the parents' strong preference for English-medium education) reveals a pragmatic self-pursuit of English as a 'value-adding commodity' (p. 50) rather than a passive acceptance of social control through linguistic imperialism. Therefore, when the mastery of the former colonizers' accent proves to be value-adding social and cultural capital (Bourdieu, 1991), many people would strive hard to attain that goal. For example, obtaining level 4 in LPAT would qualify the candidate to obtain promotion to the English panel chair position. A pragmatic self-pursuit of English seems to be a personal choice on the surface, but may indeed be a self-naturalized uncritical acceptance of linguistic control under the coercive force of state apparatuses. This seems exactly the kind of 'domination by consent' to which Gramsci refers.

Apart from understanding the issue from Bourdieu's capital theory, we might be able to find some insights from a postcolonial mentality labelled as 'post-colonial re-membering' (Gandhi, 1998). According to Gandhi (1998), postcolonial remembering denotes an ambivalent stage during which the colonized (i.e. the Orientals) tend to long for a certain form of continuity with the colonizers (e.g. the US and UK) who have often portrayed themselves as 'the disinterested purveyor of cultural enlightenment and reform' (Gandhi, 1998: 14), or, in Phillipson's (2000a: 98) words, 'altruistic' in their foreign language policy. When the colonizers had left, people in the former colony may suffer a 'stigma of unauthenticity' because '[t]he Europe they [that is, the colonized] know and value so intimately is always elsewhere. Its reality is infinitely deferred, always withheld from them' (Gandhi, 1998: 12). It must be pointed out that the majority of the ruling party in post-colonial Hong Kong were government officials holding crucial posts in the colonial government. Most of them had children studying overseas, particularly in Britain. These government officials, who are still playing a part in devising Hong Kong's education and language policy, may still be affectively attached to the former colonizer. This mentality might have been further reinforced by a mixed feeling of apprehension and mistrust towards the Mainland China Communist ruling party, particularly after the 4 June incident in 1989.

It has been documented in works by local sociolinguists such as Chan (2002) and Lai (2003) that Hong Kong people before and after the 1997 sovereignty handover, particularly those born in Hong Kong, were very anxious to preserve and assert their Hong Kong identity. Accents, being powerful linguistic and identity markers, may have conveniently provided a form of social and cultural symbol for Hong Kong people to distinguish themselves from their fellow Mainlanders. Apart from speaking Cantonese with a 'pure' Hong Kong accent, it seems that a Hong Kong identity also consists of the ability to speak English with a 'standard' prestigious accent from the West.

Deconstructing the BANA-centric hegemony of English in Hong Kong: its likelihood of success

From a sociopolitical perspective, as long as high-stake English proficiency assessment mechanisms such as TOFEL, IELTS, and LPAT continue to be in the control of the Anglo- and US-centric hands, it is unlikely for World Englishes varieties to enjoy high status and wide acceptance as institutional varieties of English. To enable L2 English learners to score good grades in these tests so that they could have better advancements in their life opportunities, educationalists are often subject to demands that they should teach pupils to speak and write English 'properly' by conforming to the 'standard' models.

From an applied linguistics perspective, the term 'World Englishes' by its nature seems to be defeating its purpose of achieving globally intelligible communication by advocating 'pluricentricity' (Clyne, 1992) of standards. As Jenkins (1998) argues, when local norms diverge too far from each other, international unintelligibility will be the result. Informal sharing with fellow local colleagues in Hong Kong by the authors reveals that we often had difficulties understanding English spoken with strong national accents such as Japanese or Korean at international conferences. We conjecture that if we speak with a strong Hong Kong accent, some Japanese or Koreans might find our speech unintelligible too. Therefore, who is to suffer with the continued promotion of World Englishes? It could be the World Englishes speakers themselves. By speaking English in their own ways, they may feel gratified by being able to assert their national identity. However, at the same time, they may also be diverging from the 'points of reference and models for guidance' (Jenkins, 1998: 124) so far that what they speak is beyond recognition by other World Englishes users.

Are we then suggesting that the WE paradigm should be forgotten and we should let Inner Circle varieties of English continue to enjoy their hegemony? Not really. By revealing representative signifying practices epitomizing the hegemonic privileging of English varieties spoken with Anglo- and US-centric accents in postcolonial Hong Kong due to social and political considerations, the authors wish to make their voices heard by proposing three paradigmatic reforms in terms of *assessment*, *research*, and *curriculum* for the reflection of World Englishes users and activists.

Towards three reform paradigms: assessment, research, and curriculum

In the assessment paradigm, the authors feel that there is a need to review the concepts of accents and errors in high-stake proficiency assessment mechanisms such as LPAT in Hong Kong. As rightly argued by Davidson (1993), 'part of a test's standard is … the linguistic norm it promotes', and that '[i]t would be detrimental to believe that the linguistic standard promoted by a language test is somehow divorced from other considerations of testing ethics' and, therefore, it would be 'unwise to develop and promote EFL tests without attention to the linguistic norms to which those tests adhere' (p. 114). In the case of LPAT, the descriptors seem to imply that pronunciation free from L1 characteristics would be considered error-free. The general belief that only candidates with native speaker proficiency could attain the highest level for pronunciation, stress and intonation seems to be conveying the faulty view that native English speakers do not speak with an accent, and their linguistic features would be taken to be the norms for the standards of the test. This is problematic because it has been well documented that Inner Circle native English speakers speak English with a range of variations (see Bauer, 2003). However, the situation with LPAT is that although the 'L1 characteristics' of some of these 'native' English speakers may be noticeable, their 'L1' characteristics would not be considered errors by assessors such as Ms K, and probably the chief examiners and the assessors, the majority of whom are Inner Circle native English speakers who are relatively more familiar with most Inner Circle accents than those from the outer and expanding circles. It will therefore not be surprising that a native Australian who speaks English with a noticeable Australian English accent would be likely to score higher than a native Chinese who speaks with a noticeable Chinese accent even though both speak English with an accent.

Taking into consideration how high-stake assessment exercises such as LPAT affect people's life chances, something needs to be done to counteract this 'linguistic subordination' (Lippi-Green, 1997) and hegemonic practices.

However, we do understand that there is a need for any assessment mechanism to have an agreed standard. We acknowledge the need to distinguish between local accents and careless speech. Our contention is that if English is to enjoy the status of a world language, it should not be the sole privilege of the BANA-centric speakers to dictate the norms of usages for a more or less equal, or indeed growing, number of English L2 users[4] (Lowenberg, 2000). So, there is an urgent need for test designers and assessors in ESL/EFL settings to set standards based on a widely accepted local educated speaker variation. Such a variation should have its linguistic base established on a wider spectrum of educated professionals, not just a narrow circle of elitist language specialists. Reference could be made to representative literature (e.g. Bolton and Kwok, 1990; Hung, 2000) reporting the existence of a local variation of Hong Kong English with systematic features of its own used by educated people (for example, university graduates). However, as mentioned before, national/regional varieties that deviate too far from the standardized Inner Circle models may result from mutual unintelligibility among their users. Therefore, World Englishes variations would still need to undergo some sort of 'standardization' process, though not necessarily converging to the BANA-centric norms, to ensure that they serve the purpose of facilitating international communication, and this leads us to the research paradigm.

The research paradigm

The adoption of the singular form 'World English' by Brutt-Griffler (2002) seems to be a result of the realization that there needs to be some internationally acceptable norms for a World language. However, exactly what this 'World English' entails in terms of phonology, syntax, lexis and pragmatics remains uncertain. Jenkin's (2000) work to establish a core set of phonological features for an international variety of English is a laudable attempt. However, the selection of features based on the criteria of frequency of occurrence and teachability –learnability might not fully reflect phonological features of native languages in the outer and expanding circles, and might not fully address pronunciation-based communication problems. An international language for communication across the world must take into consideration the linguistic features of different families of languages across the world. The establishment of the common denominator of the World English phonologies, for example, should be a world project that solicits the joint efforts of phonologists from a variety of ethnic backgrounds well-versed in the major standard English varieties and their own L1 phonological systems. To begin with, a common regional system could be established first. For example, there could be an Asian Pacific variety of World English pronunciation based on representative authentic speech samples from educated speakers from the composite varieties. Some form of corpora could be established from which mutual identifications of unintelligible phonological features could be identified from regional informants. For every target phonological feature, there could be a range of variants, some of which could be incorporated as acceptable variants in the common regional variety after taking into consideration their systematicity in occurrence and degree of impact on cross-linguistic intelligibility.

The establishment of a regional variety of English with high mutual intelligibility does not aim to extinguish other forms of new Englishes suggested by Pennycook (2003) within a national boundary to cater for creativity and popular culture. However, we would like to see some sort of linguistic 'role differentiation' (as against hierarchization) in the different forms of Englishes within a nation or a region. We believe that a truly multilingual person should have at his/her command a repertoire of varieties to suit different communicative contexts and purposes.

The curriculum paradigm

Any attempt to establish non-BANA-based common regional varieties of English would be in vain however if the World Englishes users are not aware of their existence, or are not motivated to accept their variants as codified and institutionalized models of usage (Brown, 2001). It has now been widely recognized that the achievement of common understanding in cross-ethnic and cross-cultural communication is the 'mutual responsibility' and joint efforts of both interlocutors (Davis, 1991; Lippi-Green, 1997). As argued by Baxter (1991), Japanese English teachers could also speak English internationally if all speakers of English, including L1 speakers, could make an effort to cooperate to create an atmosphere of mutual acceptance. In this connection, we propose incorporating the more or less codified regional varieties of English into the English learning curriculum for all English users, with the intention of conducting international communication in English. These users should include those native English-speaking teachers, TESOL consultants, language proficiency assessors, TESOL curriculum, and materials designers from all sectors of the concentric circles. This curriculum paradigm would necessitate a kind of 'reverse training' on the part of the Inner Circle native English speakers of the diversity of acceptable linguistic variants emerging from World Englishes. A WE curriculum should also consist of an ideological critique against the entrenched and long-standing linguistic hegemony that naturalizes the status and privileges of speakers who happen to speak in the accents of the colonial masters.

Conclusion

In this chapter, we discuss how and why British–Australian–North American models of English accents continue to enjoy hegemonic status in postcolonial Hong Kong, despite the call for a liberal acceptance of multiple standards under the World Englishes paradigm. We approach the issue from a sociopolitical perspective, focusing on the connection between linguistic capital, and social and cultural capital. We also adopt an applied linguistic perspective, focusing on the need to establish international mutual intelligibility. To counteract an uncritical naturalization of the hegemonic ideology, we call for world efforts in reforming three paradigms – namely the assessment, the research, and the curriculum paradigms – with a view to reviewing test standards in EFL settings, achieving common understanding of mutually intelligible regional varieties of English beyond national boundaries, and establishing World Englishes linguistic systems as core components in TESOL curriculum.

Notes

1 The global spread and use of English is conceptualized by Kachru (1992) as forming three concentric circles; namely, the Inner Circle, Outer Circle, and Expanding Circle. The Inner Circle comprises countries where English is spoken as a native language. The Outer Circle consists of mainly former colonies of Britain and the United States, where English is used as a second language, whereas the Expanding Circle refers to countries where English is learned as a foreign language.
2 BANA is a term adopted by Halliday (1994, p.12) to refer to the British-Australasia-North American model of English.
3 In 1998, the first batch of more than 300 NETs was recruited to teach at secondary levels on a territory-wide basis. With the NETs, the government hopes that an authentic environment for using English will be created in local secondary schools, and the English standard of both the students and the local English teachers can be raised. Two years later, the NET Scheme was extended to primary level schools.
4 According to Crystal (1997), the figure for L2 English speakers could amount to 350 million as compared to 340 million of L1 speakers.

Bibliography

Ashcroft, B., Griffiths, G. and Tiffin, H. (2000) *Post-Colonial Studies: The Key Concepts* (London and NewYork: Routledge).

Bauer, L. (2003) *An Introduction to International Varieties of English* (Hong Kong: Hong Kong University Press).

Baxter, J. (1991) 'How should I speak English? American-ly, Japanese-ly, or internationally?', in A. Brown (ed.), *Teaching English Pronunciations: A Book of Readings* (London and New York: Routledge).

Bolton, K. (2000) 'The sociolinguistics of Hong Kong and the space for Hong Kong English', *World Englishes*, 19, 3: 265–85.

Bolton, K. and Kwok, H. (1990) 'The dynamics of the Hong Kong accent: social identity and sociolinguistic description', *Journal of Asian Pacific Communication*, 1, 1: 147–73.

Boyle, J. and Boyle, L. (1991) *Common Spoken English Errors in Hong Kong* (Hong Kong: Longman).

Bourdieu, P. (1991) *Language and Symbolic Power* (Cambridge, MA: Harvard University Press).

Bresnahan, M.J., Ohashi, R., Nebashi, R., Liu, W.Y., and Shearman, S.M. (2002) 'Attitude and affective response toward accented English', *Language & Communication*, 22: 171–85.

Brown, K. (2001) 'World Englishes in TESOL programs: An infusion model of curricular innovation', in A. Burns and C. Coffin (eds), *Analysing English in a Global Context: A Reader* (London and New York: Routledge).

Brutt-Griffler, J. (2002) *World English: A Study of its Development* (Clevedon: Multilingual Matters).

Canagarajah, A.S. (1999) 'Interrogating the "native speaker fallacy": non-linguistic roots, non-pedagogical results', in G. Braine (ed.), *Non-native Educators in English Language Teaching* (Mahwah: Lawrence Erlbaum) 77–92.

Canagarajah, A.S. (2000) 'Negotiating ideologies through English: Strategies from periphery', in T. Ricento (ed.), *Ideology, Politics and Language Policies* (Amsterdam/Philadelphia: John Benjamins).

Chan, E. (2002) 'Beyond pedagogy: language and identity in post-colonial Hong Kong', *British Journal of Sociology of Education*, 23, 2: 271–85.

Chief Executive, the Honourable Tung Chee Hwa (1997) *Building Hong Kong for a New Era*, Address at the Provisional Legislative Council Meeting (Hong Kong: The Hong Kong Special Administrative Region of the People's Republic of China).

Clyne, M. (1992) *Pluricentric Languages: Differing Norms in Different Nations* (Berlin: Mouton de Gruyter).

Crystal, D. (1997) *English as a Global Language* (Cambridge: Cambridge University Press).

Crystal, D. (2003) *English as a Global Language* (Cambridge: Cambridge University Press).

Davis, A. (1991) *The Native Speaker in Applied Linguistics* (Edinburgh: Edinburgh University Press).

Davidson, F. (1993) 'Testing English across cultures: summary and comments', *World Englishes*, 12, 1: 113–25.

Eisenstein, M. (1983) 'Native reactions to non-native speech: a review of empirical research', *Studies in Second Language Acquisition*, 5, 2: 160–76.

Gandhi, L. (1998) *Postcolonial Theory: A Critical Introduction* (New Delhi: Oxford University Press).

Glenwright, P. (2002) 'Language proficiency assessment for teachers: the effects of benchmarking on writing assessment in Hong Kong schools', *Assessing Writing*, 8: 84–109.

Godfrey, P. (1992) 'Josiah's school drops English', *Window*, 2, 19: 32–6.

Government of Hong Kong Special Administrative Region (2000) *Syllabus Specifications for the Language Proficiency Assessment for Teachers (English Language)* (Hong Kong).

Gramsci, A. (1971) *Selections from the Prison Notebooks of Antonio Gramsci* (Q. Hoare and N. Smith, comps and eds) (London: Lawrence & Wishart).

Halliday, A. (1994) *Appropriate Methodology and Social Context* (Glasgow: Cambridge University Press).

Harris, R. (1989) 'The Worst English in the World', Inaugural lecture by the chair of English language (University of Hong Kong).

Hung, T.T.H. (2000) 'Towards a phonology of Hong Kong English', *World Englishes*, 19, 3: 337–56.

Jenkins, J. (1998) 'Which pronunciation norms and models for English as an international language?', *ELT Journal*, 52, 2: 119–26.

Jenkins, J. (2000) *The Phonology of English as an International Language* (Oxford: Oxford University Press).

Jenkins, J. (2002) 'A sociolinguistically based, empirically researched pronunciation syllabus for English as an international language', *Applied Linguistics*, 23, 1: 83–103.

Jenkins, J. (2003) *World Englishes: A Resource Book for Students*, (London and New York: Routledge).

Kachru, B. (1990 (1986)) *The Alchemy of English: The Spread, Functions and Models of Non-native Englishes*, (Oxford: Pergamon Press, 1986, printed Urbana: University of Illinois Press, 1990).

Kachru, B. (1992) 'Teaching World Englishes', in B. Kachru (ed.), *The Other Tongue. English Across Cultures*, 2nd edn (Urbana, IL: University of Illinois Press).

Lai, M.L. (2003) 'Cultural Identity and Language Attitudes in Postcolonial Hong Kong', Paper presented at the International Conference in Language, Education, and Identity (LED).

Lau, E. (1991) 'The future tense', *Far Eastern Economic Review*, 151, 4: 18–19.

Li, D. (2002) 'Hong Kong parents' preference for English-medium education: passive victims of imperialism or active agents of pragmatism?', in A. Kirkpatrick (ed.), *Englishes in Asia: Communication, Identity, Power & Education* (Australia: Language Australia) 29–62.

Lippi-Green, R. (1997) *English With An Accent: Language, Ideology, and Discrimination in the United States* (London and New York: Routledge).

Lowenberg, P.H. (2000) 'Non-native varieties and the sociopolitics of English proficiency assessment', in J.K. Hall and W.G. Eggington (eds), *The Sociopolitics of English* (Clevedon: Multilingual Matters).

Luk, J.C.M. (1998) 'Hong Kong students' awareness of and reactions to accent differences', *Multilingua*, 17, 1: 93–106.

Luk, J.C.M. (2001) 'Exploring the sociocultural implications of the Native English-speaker Teacher Scheme in Hong Kong through the eyes of the students', *Asia-Pacific Journal of Language in Education*, 4, 2: 19–50.

McArther, T. (1987) 'The English Languages', *English Today*, 11: 9–13.

McArther, T. (1993) 'The English language or the English languages?', in W.F. Bolton and D. Crystal (eds), *The English Language* (London: Penguin Books).

Milroy, J., and Milroy, L. (1999) *Authority in Language: Investigating Standard English* (London and New York: Routledge).

Modiano, M. (1999) 'Standard English(es) and eductional practices for the world's lingua franca', *English Today*, 15, 4: 3–13.

Mufwene, S. (1997) 'The legitimate and illegitimate offspring of English', in L.Smith and M.L. Forman (eds), *World Englishes* (Hawaii: University of Hawaii and East-West Center) 182–203.

Parakrama, A. (1995) *De-hegemonizing Language Standards: Learning From (Post-) colonial Englishes About 'Englishes'* (Basingstoke, UK: MacMillan).

Pierson, H.D. (1998) 'Societal accommodation to English and Putonghua in Cantonese-speaking Hong Kong', in M.C. Pennington (ed.) *Language in Hong Kong at Century's End* (Hong Kong: Hong Kong University Press).

Pennycook, A. (1994) *The Cultural Politics of English as an International Language* (London and New York: Longman).

Pennycook, A. (2000) 'Language, ideology and hindsight: lessons from colonial language policies', in T. Ricento and T. Wiley (eds), *Ideology, Politics, and Language Policies: Focus on English* (Amsterdam/Philadelphia: John Benjamins) 49–65.

Pennycook, A. (2003) 'Global Englishes, rip slyme, and performativity', *Journal of Sociolinguistics*, 7, 4: 513–33.

Phillipson, R. (1992) *Linguistic Imperialism* (Oxford: Oxford University Press).

Phillipson, R. (2000a) 'English in the New World Order: variations on a theme of linguistic imperialism and "World" English', in T. Ricento (ed.), *Ideology, Politics and Language Policies: Focus on English* (Amsterdam/Philadelphia: John Benjamins).

Phillipson, R. (2000b) 'Integrative comment: living with vision and commitment', in R. Phillipson (ed.), *Rights to Language, Equity, Power, and Education: Celebrating the 60th Birthday of Tove Skutnabb-Kangas* (Mahwah, NJ: Lawrence Erlbaum) 264–79.

Purves, W. (1989) Statement to shareholders by W. Purves, Chairman, at the Annual General Meeting on 9 May 1989 (Hong Kong: Hong Kong Bank).

Selinker, L. (1992) *Rediscovering Interlanguage* (London: Longman).

Shohamy, E. (2003) 'The power of language tests in supressing language diversity in multilingual societies', Paper presented in the International Conference in Language, Education, and Identity (LED).

Skutnabb-Kangas, T. (1998) 'Human rights and language wrongs: a future for diversity?', *Language Sciences*, 20, 1: 5–28.

Smith, L. (ed.) (1983) *Readings in English as an International Language* (Oxford: Pergamon Press).

South China Morning Post (2003) 'ELT site provides teacher support', 15 November 2003.

Surry, M. (1994) 'English not spoken here', *Window*, 3, 12: 32–7.

Tsui, A.B.M. and Bunton, D. (2000) 'The discourse and attitudes of English language teachers in Hong Kong', *World Englishes*, 19, 3: 287–303.

Widdowson, H. (1993) 'The ownership of English', *TESOL Quarterly*, 28, 2: 377–89.

2
What the Other Half Gives: the Interlocutor's Role in Non-native Speaker Performance

Stephanie Lindemann

Introduction

Research on non-native speaker performance in the target language has, unsurprisingly, tended to focus on the non-native alone. Such a focus seems especially logical if we are investigating a speaker's basic language skills such as pronunciation, vocabulary, or grammar, which are relatively easy to assess in a rather artificial situation in which both the material to be tested and the amount of natural interaction are limited. Likewise, the behaviour of the 'interlocutor' is of lesser importance when we consider non-native writing, although it is not completely irrelevant, as for example Donald Rubin and Melanie Williams-James (1997) have shown that mainstream teachers' beliefs about writers' nationalities may influence their evaluation of the writing.

However, research on spoken language that has considered the higher-level processes involved in communicative competence, and especially research that has looked at communication difficulties between native and non-native speakers, has required more attention to the interlocutor. For example, examination of differences between native speakers of different languages in their use of discourse strategies (Scollon and Scollon, 1995; Tyler, 1995), including framing strategies (Watanabe, 1993) and contextualization cues (Gumperz, 1982), has been very fruitful in explaining dissatisfaction expressed by both native and non-native speakers in their interactions with each other. While such research has attended to both native and non-native speakers as having equally valid discourse strategies, it is worth noting that the communicative difficulties arising from the differences between various native-English speaking groups and various non-native speaker groups appear to be most easily addressed by training the non-native speakers in using more native-like discourse strategies.

In contrast to this non-native speaker focus, I will argue in this chapter that for oral communication in particular, it is important to consider that in some cases native–non-native communicative difficulties can clearly be seen as stemming from the native speaker, rather than from the non-native speaker or from discourse differences between the interlocutors. This is most obviously the case when native speakers have negative attitudes to their non-native interlocutors, in which case they may essentially refuse to listen. Less obviously, it is possible that assessments of L2 performance may also be influenced by more apparently benign expectations of a speaker. In the following sections, I will discuss how these attitudes and expectations about non-native speakers may play out in interactions and even non-interactive listening situations. I will conclude by considering possible ways to address the role of the native-speaking interlocutor and in some cases improve native–non-native communication, including approaches that go beyond further training of non-native speakers.

It takes (at least) two to converse

> Student 1: I took calculus in high school – it was really easy for me, and I got an A no problem. Now in college, we're covering the exact same material, but I've got this international TA, and I'm failing.
>
> Student 2: You know, I've had exactly the same experience. But my TA is American.

In cases of native–non-native communication, often the most obvious response to any difficulties is to blame them on the non-native speaker. In the context of the class discussion from which the above (reconstructed) exchange was taken, a student in my class on miscommunication was clearly implying that her poor performance in calculus was the result of insufficient language skills on the part of the ITA, although interestingly enough, she did not state this explicitly. With this 'obvious' justification for her difficulties, she might have felt no need to look further for an explanation. The second student, facing similar difficulties but without a non-native speaking instructor to hold responsible, was compelled to consider alternative explanations, including, as several other students pointed out, the fact that college is simply much more difficult than high school. (In further discussion, some students also suggested that even a native-speaking instructor may have poor communication or teaching skills.)

In the scenario above, Student 1 appears to go so far as to hold her non-native-speaking TA responsible for her failing grade which, as other students point out, may have nothing to do with communication at all. However, in most cases, complaints about non-native speakers' proficiency in the L2 are front and centre. Of course, it may sometimes be the case that non-native speakers have insufficient communicative competence in the L2, making anything beyond rudimentary interaction difficult or impossible. Nevertheless, speakers' communicative competence is not the only requirement for successful communication, as Rosina Lippi-Green (1994; 1997) has pointed out; listeners must also make some effort to understand. This is particularly clear for conversation, which is always a collaborative achievement (Schegloff, 1982), with the listener as well as the speaker playing a major role (Clark and Schaefer, 1987; 1989). Herbert Clark and Deanna Wilkes-Gibbs (1986) call this the principle of mutual responsibility: 'The participants in a conversation try to establish, roughly by the initiation of each new contribution, the mutual belief that the listeners have understood what the speaker meant in the last utterance...'. This model, then, makes explicit the necessity for the listener as well as the speaker to work to ensure that the listener understands what the speaker means; instead of clear communication as the speaker's responsibility alone, both speaker and listener must work together. Clark and Wilkes-Gibbs further note that 'the heavier burden usually falls on the listener, since she is in the best position to assess her own comprehension'.

This suggests that the listener's role is a key factor in the success or failure of communication. In fact, an interlocutor's high degree of willingness to carry a greater share of the 'communicative burden' (Perkins and Milroy, 1997) can even make up for relatively poor communicative competence on the part of their co-participant in the interaction. Lisa Perkins and Lesley Milroy (1997) provide examples of interactions in which willing interlocutors were able to communicate with aphasics with severe linguistic impairments, for example by asking questions, suggesting possible interpretations of the aphasic's speech, and making inspired guesses that the aphasic could then confirm or disconfirm. In the case of non-native speakers, however, Lippi-Green (1994; 1997) argues that many listeners may reject the communicative burden entirely, making successful communication much less likely even when the non-native speaker has sufficient communicative competence.

In a study designed to test the relationship between attitude to and comprehension of Korean-accented English, I found that the native speakers' (attitude-linked) choice of communication strategies appeared to determine the overall accuracy of communication (Lindemann, 2000; 2002). In the study, native speakers of English who had been assessed as having either relatively positive or relatively negative attitudes to native speakers of Korean were paired with native speakers of Korean to complete an interactive map task based on that developed by Anne Anderson and her colleagues (Anderson *et al.*, 1984). In each pairing, the Korean had a map with a route drawn on it, while the native English speaker had a similar map with some differing landmarks and no route. The native Korean partners were asked to describe the route so that their partners could replicate it on their maps; participants were told that the maps differed, that they could not look at each other's maps, and that partners could communicate with each other freely (other than using gestures to pantomime the route), including asking each other questions. Because of the differences in maps, successful completion of the task required both participants to accept the communicative burden. All interactions resulted in relatively accurate communication except where the native speaker used 'avoidance' strategies, partially rejecting the communicative burden; such strategies were only used by interlocutors who had independently been assessed as having negative attitudes to Koreans. These interlocutors failed to provide feedback to their non-native English speaking partners in several instances of important differences between their partners' descriptions and their own maps. One of the most dramatic examples of this is shown in (1) below, in which Sean appears to accept his partner Kyunghan's description of the route in spite of the fact that it is quite different from what he has drawn on his own map. (See Appendix, p. 45, for transcription conventions.)

(1)   Kyunghan/Sean factory–castle (Lindemann, 2002: 427–8)
   → 133 **K**   okay, (.8) once you: reach the factory, go- (.4) go: to
                   the: .hh right side straight? then there is a castle.
       134 **S**   alright. =yip, =I'm at the castle.
       135 **K**   that's it.
           (.5)
   → 136 **S**   (d')you go straight down from the factory then,
           (1)
       137 **K**   [(excuse me,)]
   → 138 **S**   [like-] from: like where the factory be: just go straight
                  down from there?
       139 **K**   straight, to the right.

→ 140 **S**   straight to the right, alright.
 141 **K**   which is (.7) at the: (.6) right down end of the map.
      (.6)
 142 **S**   alright,

In this excerpt, Sean does not comment on or appear to take note of the fact that Kyunghan refers to 'reach[ing] the factory' in turn 133 although the route he has drawn on his own map does not go anywhere near the factory. In fact, his follow-up question in turn 136 asks if he is to go 'straight down from the factory', implying that his route *does* go to the factory. Kyunghan's answer in turn 139 should have suggested that there was a problem, as he does not confirm the 'down' direction, but rather says it is 'to the right'. However, Sean simply repeats Kyunghan's utterance and adds 'alright', although on his map the line neither goes 'from the factory' nor 'to the right'; instead, it goes straight down from the landmark before the factory to the castle. Unsurprisingly, Sean's finished map is substantially different from his partner's. In contrast, another native English speaker with a more positive attitude to Korean-accented English was successful in completing an equivalent map task with the same partner.

In some cases, study participants who had been assessed as having a negative attitude to Koreans carried more of the communicative burden, but used 'problematizing' strategies, which involved withholding acknowledgement when they understood their partners' instructions. In example (2), Tara uses a series of questions and repetitions of her partners' words using marked, sharp rising intonation. What is interesting about this strategy is that while it is ultimately successful in the sense that Tara produces a map that very closely matches Hyo Young's, it also has the effect of minimizing Hyo Young's contributions, making her appear less competent than she actually is.

(2) Hyo Young/Tara McDonalds–hospital
       178 **HY**   and then- . going straight no- i mean south
         (1)
→ 179 **T**   straight south?
    180 **HY** uh-huh,
→ 181 **T**   where do i go
    182 **HY** uh:: like two inch
→ 183 **T**   two inches?
    184 **HY** yeah
→ 185 **T**   =what's there

186 **HY**   nothing.
→   187 **T**   i just stop,
188 **HY**   yeah.
189 **T**   okay.

It should be noted that while Tara also had a tendency to repeat her partner when she completed a similar map task with a native speaker, she was much more likely to follow up these repetitions with explicit acceptance (such as 'okay') of what her partner said. The fact that she seldom did so with her non-native-speaking partner is consistent with her general tendency to pose her own questions to that partner, ignoring the partner's attempts to explain the route in her own words.

In these two examples, we see that the attitude-linked strategy choice of the native-speaking interlocutor affects the actual performance of the non-native speaker. In neither example is the non-native speaker able fully to explain the route; in the first case because the interlocutor provides misleading feedback on what he has understood, and in the second because the interlocutor takes control of the interaction and does not validate her partner's attempts to explain.

All study participants were also asked to rate the success of their interactions. These ratings showed the most compelling relationship between attitude and communicative outcome, as native-speaker attitudes to Korean-accented English proved to be directly related to the native speakers' perception of the success of the interaction. No participants with negative attitudes to Koreans rated their interactions with Korean partners as successful, while all participants with positive attitudes rated their interactions with Korean partners as successful (which they largely were). In other words, the accuracy of communication could be roughly predicted by the native speaker's choice of communication strategies, and the native speaker's perception of the success of the interaction could be predicted by the native speaker's own attitude. Interestingly, the proficiency of the non-native speakers (which varied, although all were undergraduates at a large US university) played very little role in actual or perceived success at all.

'Hearing with an accent' may not require interaction with the speaker

Failure to collaborate with a non-native speaker in conversation is one possible consequence of negative attitudes that may affect interlocutors' understanding of non-native speech. However, listeners' negative attitudes may play a role even if there is no true interaction. In the case of lectures where listeners are physically present or otherwise visible (or audible) to the lecturer, the speaker still may adapt her speech to her listeners as they ask questions, nod enthusiastically, look puzzled, shuffle papers and books, or fall asleep. As in conversation, listeners with different attitudes to the lecturers may react more or less helpfully, facilitating different degrees of success in communication. Since it is possible to have a lecture in the absence of collaborative listeners – for example in the case of a recorded lecture – whereas this is not possible for conversation, the behaviour of the listener is not likely to play as great a role in lectures or other non-interactive speech genres as in conversations. However, in this section I argue that attitudes may be related to perception of speech aside from issues of collaboration.

To see how attitude could have this kind of effect on non-interactive speech perception, it is helpful to consider research on stereotype maintenance. In their literature review, von Hippel *et al.* (1995) point out that expectations and stereotypes guide our understanding of the world. They further argue that these expectations and stereotypes play a role at the most basic level of perceptual encoding of information. Thus, to take one of their examples, those who hold certain stereotypes about African-Americans may *see* an African-American's auto alarm remote control as a gun, or in terms particularly of concern here, those who are prejudiced against groups of non-native speakers may *hear* a non-native speaker who is competent in English as unintelligible.

Although most of the evidence presented by von Hippel *et al.* deals with visual rather than auditory perception, there are a number of phenomena showing the susceptibility of speech perception to influence by information from non-auditory channels, of which the most well-known is probably 'the McGurk Effect' (McGurk and MacDonald, 1976). In the McGurk effect, listeners who are presented with the auditory stimulus 'na-na' while watching a (silent) video of a speaker saying 'ba-ba' report hearing 'ma-ma', thus integrating nasal information from the auditory channel with bilabial information from the visual channel. Other studies show an apparent influence of top-down processing on perception. To take one example, Arthur Samuel (1981) found that listeners presented with a word with one phoneme replaced by white noise tended to hear (or 'restore') the missing phoneme along with the white noise. In this case, the listeners' identification of the word being presented results in their 'hearing' the whole word, despite the fact that one phoneme is actually missing. In other words, expectations about what is being heard (an entire word) influence what is actually heard. Likewise, it is possible that attitude-influenced expectations about a non-native speaker's speech (for example, that the speech will be unintelligible) could have an effect on a listener's perception of it.

Although in an additional component of my study discussed above (Lindemann, 2000) I did not find a correlation between attitude to Korean-accented English and non-interactive perception of it, the test was limited to identification of individual whole words. Other studies (discussed in the section below) have found a relationship between other social factors and the perception of individual sounds, suggesting that it is possible that attitude could likewise play a role in listeners' perception of individual sounds. For example, there may be a greater tendency for those with more negative attitudes to perceive a phoneme the speaker has produced correctly as some incorrect phoneme.

A study by Janet Anderson-Hsieh and Kenneth Koehler (1988) suggests that there is a relationship between listener attitude and non-interactive *comprehension* of connected speech. They recorded three male native speakers of Chinese at different levels of speaking proficiency reading brief passages on fairly obscure (but not very difficult) academic topics. Each speaker read two passages at a slow speed, a medium speed, and a fast speed. Native-speaking undergraduates listened to a subset of the recordings. They heard all speakers, all speeds, and all passages, but only heard one version of each passage. They then completed six multiple-choice comprehension questions based on each passage. They also completed a questionnaire on their language background and on reactions to 'foreigners' and 'foreign English'. The researchers found small but significant correlations of attitude to foreigners or non-native English and comprehension of the fastest and most heavily accented English. This suggests that future studies looking for a relationship between attitude and comprehension (or perception) may need to look specifically at comprehension of speech that puts a greater burden on the listener (such as faster and more heavily accented speech), as well as looking for an overall relationship between attitude and comprehension of any non-native speech.

In addition to possible mishearing or poorer comprehension of a non-native speaker, another possible effect of attitude on perception is suggested by a study that investigates the relationship between perceived accent and intelligibility. Murray Munro and Tracey Derwing (1995) asked native speakers of English to listen to utterances in English produced by Mandarin native speakers, to rate the speakers' degrees of accent and comprehensibility, and to write down the utterances as produced by the speakers (used as a measure of speaker intelligibility). They found that while most listeners showed a significant correlation between their ratings of the speakers' comprehensibility and the accuracy of their transcriptions, there was a wide range of significant correlations. Furthermore, most of the listeners did not show a significant correlation between their rating of the speakers' degree of accent and transcription accuracy. While ratings of accent varied widely, most transcriptions were very accurate: 53 per cent of the transcriptions had no errors, and more than one third of the errors were regularizations or omissions of function words.

Munro and Derwing's findings suggest that listeners' perception of what a non-native speaker has said is quite separate from their evaluations of the speaker's accent. It is possible, then, for either of these two factors to correlate with listener's attitude toward non-native speech. Of the two, perceived degree of accent may be more susceptible to attitudinal influence than perception of the speech itself. The fact that considerable inter-listener differences have been found in listeners' evaluations of the degree of a non-native speaker's 'foreign' accent in another study (Southwood and Flege, 1999) gives further support to this hypothesis. So, a possible alternative to the example discussed previously would be that those who are prejudiced against groups of non-native speakers may hear a non-native speaker with accurate English pronunciation as having a heavy accent – even if they comprehend that speaker perfectly. Such a finding, yet to be directly investigated, would parallel my (2000; 2002) finding discussed above that those with negative attitudes to Korean-accented English rated an interaction with a Korean as unsuccessful even when the communication showed a high degree of accuracy.

'Hearing with an accent' may not require negative attitudes to the speaker

Whether or not attitude in particular influences non-interactive perception or evaluations of non-native English, there is clearly evidence that there is a relationship between speech perception and other social factors, including beliefs about the speaker's social groups. Importantly, beliefs about the speaker have been demonstrated to influence speech perception at a very low level, which would make this influence difficult to detect outside of an experimental setting. For example, Elizabeth Strand (1999) showed that gender stereotyping was related to listeners' perception at the level of the phoneme, specifically in their perception of /s/ versus /ʃ/. Since male speakers typically use a less fronted, more grooved variant of /s/ (Naslund, 1993, cited in Strand, 1999), which results in a lower-frequency (and therefore more /ʃ/-like) variant, we would expect listeners to accept more tokens of an /s/-/ʃ/ continuum as /s/ if they believe the voice to be that of a male speaker. What is particularly striking about Strand's findings is that this shift occurs gradiently, depending on whether the voice is a prototypical or non-prototypical male or female voice. Further, the perceived boundary between /s/ and /ʃ/ shifts depending on the sex of a 'speaker' the listener watches on video – who may or may not be the same sex as the voice they are hearing. Strand argues that listener expectations about what the speaker *should* sound like based on gender stereotypes are affecting how they actually process the speech.

Similarly, Nancy Niedzielski (1999) found that Detroit-area listeners' beliefs as to whether a speaker was a Canadian or a Detroiter made a difference in their perception of that speaker's vowels. Two different groups heard utterances by the same Detroit speaker and were asked to choose from sets of resynthesized vowels to match the speaker's vowels. The sets of resynthesized vowels from which listeners had to choose always included the vowel actually produced as well as more 'standard' versions of the same vowel. The group that was told that the speaker was a Canadian tended to choose raised variants of a diphthong as matching the speaker's production – which in fact was the correct match – whereas the group that was told the speaker was a Detroiter was much more likely to choose a less raised token. In general, when listeners believed the speaker was from Michigan, they chose vowels that were different from the Northern-Cities-shifted vowels the speaker actually produced. This shows perception consistent with their beliefs; Preston (1993; 1996b) has found that Michiganders believe their English is more 'correct' than that of other US English speakers. Again, social information – in this case, the speaker's perceived nationality – appears to have been taken into account in the perception of speech at a very basic level. In this case, the perceived nationality in question (Canadian) is not a particularly stigmatized one; we might expect even stronger results where the speaker is believed to be a non-native speaker, especially a non-White one.

An important study by Donald Rubin (1992) specifically investigated perceived non-native accent at a higher level of perception, showing that listener expectations based on speaker ethnicity can have an effect both on recall of what was said and on evaluation of speech as native or non-native. In his study, participants listened to a few minutes of a tape-recorded lecture produced by a native speaker of a non-stigmatized variety of US English. Listeners who were shown a picture of an Asian apparently delivering the lecture perceived more of a foreign accent and scored lower on a cloze recall test than those who were shown a photo of a Caucasian, even though what they heard was in fact identical. Similarly, Kimberly Brown (1992) found that listener beliefs about a non-native speaker's country of origin (Sudan as opposed to Iran or Italy) affected judgements of the speaker's language competence.

In a pilot study that followed up on Rubin's research, Eriko Atagi (2003) found that undergraduates perceived different levels of accent based on the speaker's supposed nationality and first-language background. Listeners were asked to listen to and rank accents of three recorded native speakers of US English who were identified as French Canadian, Korean, and Mexican. Although listeners were given the option to say the speakers had no accent or had equal levels of accent, only three of the twenty took this option, while more than half of respondents ranked the 'French Canadian' as having the most native-like English.

Although Rubin found no relationship between attitude and accuracy in recalling the speaker's words and the other researchers did not try to assess attitude, we may question whether less prejudiced listeners would perceive speakers in the biased ways described above. Rubin's test of attitude consisted of a relatively straightforward questionnaire (for example, 'strongly agree … strongly disagree: I would be willing to have a nonnative English speaker as my roommate' (p. 520)), which is so direct that it is likely to tap whatever attitude respondents want to project, rather than underlying (but still ideologized) attitudes and values. Aware that their attitudes are being tested, respondents are likely to answer more favourably than they might otherwise (Potter and Wetherell, 1987). Thus, it is possible that a more sensitive measure of attitude would have discovered a link between attitude and recall of the speaker. In Atagi's study, attitude was not measured at all, but the highly negative reaction of one participant to a speaker ('does he even know how to talk?') suggests that attitude is likely to have been a factor. (Interestingly, Atagi mentions this particular comment in the context of her discussion of why the familiarity some listeners had with some speakers' voices turned out to be irrelevant. In the case quoted here, the listener had in fact had multiple conversations with the speaker.)

The possibility that native-speaker interlocutor difficulties chiefly arise from negative attitudes to the non-native speaker may suggest that such difficulties only become relevant in cases where native-speaker interlocutors are obviously prejudiced. In this case, we might expect that identifying the relevant cases may be comparatively easy and that we as TESOL practitioners (presumably with more-positive-than-average attitudes to non-native speakers) are largely immune. However, it is certainly clear that biased evaluations do not require obviously negative attitudes (Rubin, 1992). In any case, no listener will be completely devoid of some sort of bias, much less of more apparently benign expectations that nevertheless affect perception (for example Niedzielski, 1999; Strand, 1999).

Expectations may influence reactions to non-native speakers in conflicting ways

Investigating attitudes to and expectations about different groups and how they may influence collaboration with non-native speakers and evaluations of those speakers' English can be difficult because these are likely to depend on the greater context and vary over time from group to group. Even if we believe we have discovered typical attitudes to and expectations about a particular group, allowing us to predict when some 'non-native speaker difficulties' may be due to the native listener, reactions to particular speakers are sometimes very difficult to predict.

Numerous studies looking at reactions to different language varieties have suggested that listeners typically evaluate the language of historically more (socially, politically, and/or economically) powerful groups more highly than the language of less powerful ones, especially on status qualities of its speakers such as intelligence and education. More generally, we have seen that attitudes to language can really be seen as attitudes to the speakers of that language. For example, Rosina Lippi-Green (1997) and others have pointed out that negative attitudes to African-American English in the US are a manifestation of racist attitudes that are no longer more openly expressible.

In terms of non-native accents, Lippi-Green has similarly argued that 'not *all* foreign accents, but only accent linked to skin that isn't white, or which signals a third-world homeland ... evokes such negative reactions' (pp. 238–9, italics in original). My own findings (2005) suggest that, at least for many US undergraduates, all non-native English except perhaps for that of Western Europeans may be negatively evaluated, and even the English of Western Europeans is on average rated as less correct, friendly, and pleasant than that of speakers from the US, UK, or Australia. These findings are based on US undergraduates' ratings of numerous non-native varieties when presented with country names rather than actual voice samples. Other studies that have presented US English speakers with voice samples have likewise found negative evaluations (at least under some study conditions) of native speakers of Chinese (Cargile, 1997), Japanese (Cargile and Giles, 1998), Korean (Lindemann, 2003), Malay (Gill, 1994), Spanish (Ryan *et al.*, 1977; Ryan and Sebastian, 1980), German (Ryan and Bulik, 1982), and Italian, Norwegian, Czech, Polish, and Russian (Mulac *et al.*, 1974). In these studies, the speakers themselves were rated negatively, for example on status and solidarity traits, with obvious implications for native–non-native interaction. Studies based on country names or voice samples have both found varying degrees of negative evaluation depending on country of origin. For example, Ryan and Bulik (1982) found that German-accented English was not rated as negatively as Spanish-accented English. This suggests that some non-native speakers are more likely to be affected by native-speaker attitudes and expectations than others.

A complicating factor in determining which non-native speakers are most likely to be affected by listener attitudes and expectations is that native US speakers often do not recognize various non-native accents, making it more difficult to determine to what degree they will evaluate these accents in stereotypical ways. The above studies have found that speakers evaluate native speakers of various languages negatively, but the question remains as to whom listeners believe themselves to be evaluating. Although studies that looked at evaluation of native varieties (of British English (Milroy and McClenaghan, 1977) and of German (Dailey-O'Cain, 1999)) found that listeners evaluated the varieties in the same stereotyped ways even if they did not identify them accurately, it is unclear as to whether the same applies to evaluation of less familiar non-native varieties in the US.

A second complicating factor is that when listeners do have information about what groups a speaker belongs to, in some cases lower expectations of certain groups may lead to more positive evaluations of speakers who exceed those expectations. A relevant finding by Bartek Plichta (2001) concerned perceptions of non-stigmatized English apparently spoken by African-Americans or European-Americans. Respondents viewed video-recordings of two European-Americans and two African-Americans reading a passage with non-stigmatized speech dubbed in for each speaker; all speakers actually heard were European-

American, and all had similar voices and accents. Although listeners who were presented with audio tracks and no video showed no significant differences in their ratings of the four speakers, European-American listeners presented with the video judged African-American speakers as significantly more standard and educated than the European-American speakers. (Interestingly, this pattern did not hold for African-American listeners, who showed no difference in their ratings of the two pairs of speakers.)

Kimberly Brown's (1992) study showed what may be comparable results for non-native speakers, although it is less obvious what constitutes expected evaluations of various non-native-speaking groups. Her results included the finding that a speaker was rated as having higher language competence if he was believed to be from Sudan than if he was believed to be from Italy or Iran. One explanation Brown suggested was that the speaker may have been perceived as particularly fluent or 'correct' for a Sudanese speaker but disfluent or 'incorrect' for an Italian speaker. Perhaps more importantly for the general point of this section, she found that a speaker's country, status as a bilingual or ESL speaker, and status as a TA or professor interacted to yield a complex pattern of influences on listeners' perceptions of the speaker's personal aesthetic qualities and language competence.

Implications

We have seen that attitudes and beliefs about non-native speakers can influence evaluation and even actual performance of the non-native speaker. In the following sections, I discuss the implications of this interlocutor influence for language teaching, including the necessity for:

1 carefully controlled investigation (beyond self-report) on what listeners react to negatively – not just what is likely to impede intelligibility directly – in order to decide whether and what pronunciation issues to focus on in the classroom;
2 assessing performance of non-native speakers in the context of the interlocutor/listener;
3 acknowledging that not all native–non-native difficulties are due to the non-native speaker, nor even to simple native–non-native differences, so not all are solvable by further or better language teaching; and

4 perhaps most importantly, raising awareness of this issue beyond
   the ESL classroom in order to combat language prejudice, 'the last
   widely open backdoor to discrimination' (Lippi-Green, 1994: 171).

**Find out what particular non-native features listeners react to
negatively**

Although this chapter is focusing on the native speaker, it is worth
noting that a closer look at native-speaking interlocutors can also
inform us about what may be most useful in teaching the non-native
speaker. Often the assumption in teaching pronunciation is that any
pronunciation that is not native-like is to be 'improved'; for example,
in Griffen's (1991) identification of the goal of pronunciation instruction as 'speak[ing] the language as naturally as possible, free of any
indication that the speaker is not a clinically normal native' (p. 182,
cited in Munro, 2003: 40). In fact, an underlying assumption for many
practitioners is that even native-like speech may not be sufficient.
Instead, the language learner should strive toward pronunciation that
matches that of native speakers of non-stigmatized dialects; in some
cases non-native pronunciation that is similar to a native but stigmatized pronunciation is also seen as problematic and in need of 'improvement'. For example, the pronunciation of interdental fricatives as stops
is often seen as an area for pronunciation work, although it is not
uncommon in native accents of English and is unlikely to significantly
impair intelligibility.

The goal of pronunciation instruction has been refined in observations that it is most important to address those features of pronunciation that are likely to impede intelligibility; as discussed above,
Munro and Derwing (1995) point out that intelligibility does not
require a native-like accent. This suggests that research on what non-
native features most interfere with intelligibility (for example Tajima
et al., 1997) or comprehensibility[1] (for example Anderson-Hsieh and
Koehler, 1988) are of greatest relevance for learners' pronunciation
goals. However, the research discussed above suggests that listeners
may react negatively to certain accents (and thus claim to find them
unintelligible) even when we would expect that the features of those
accents themselves do not directly impede intelligibility.

While it is important to keep in mind that the non-native speaker
cannot fairly be held accountable for native-speaking interlocutors'
negative reactions, non-native speakers may in some cases wish to gain
control over features of their pronunciation that may be seen as

leading to these reactions. Of course, this may have a limited effect on how native speakers perceive them in most circumstances, as ultimately it is not the features but the speaker that is judged negatively, as discussed above. However, as listeners may react even more negatively to certain stereotyped features of a given accent (for example, for African-American English, negative reactions to pronunciation are more likely to focus on an item such as 'ask' rather than postvocalic r-deletion), it may nevertheless be helpful to investigate which such features are most relevant for non-native speech. Thus, in order to support non-native speakers who wish to change their pronunciation to try to minimize listeners' negative reactions to their speech, research is needed in at least two areas. One is an investigation of how and to what degree attitudes to non-native speakers may be mitigated by the speakers' more native-like pronunciation of particular features. The second arena for investigation, assuming that avoidance of at least some negatively stereotyped features in some situations may be helpful, would be to look at exactly what features are most saliently negative for listeners. Especially needed are carefully controlled experimental studies that can detect relevant features of which listeners may not be consciously aware. As Dennis Preston (1996a) has pointed out, linguistic awareness of 'foreign accents' typically does not include awareness of specific linguistic features.

One set of features of which listeners are typically aware at least in a global sense is prosody, although listeners are likely to interpret prosodic differences not as linguistic at all, but as directly revealing personality traits or at least emotional or attitudinal states (Tannen, 1981; Gumperz, 1982). Kyril Holden and John Hogan's (1993) study of English and Russian speakers' reactions to intonation typical of their own and the other's language provide an example of how certain intonation patterns may be interpreted negatively by listeners. They found that typical Russian intonation used in English yes–no questions, wh-questions, and exclamations were rated by native English speakers as sounding as more angry and critical than typical English intonation on the same sentences. They suggest that Russian learners of English need to be 'cautioned against retaining their Russian intonation' (p. 85).

Another study that specifically related particular features of pronunciation to evaluations of speakers (Ray and Zahn, 1999) found speaking rate and pitch range to be more predictive of how listeners evaluated speakers than speakers' accents, although they were looking at native accents ('standard American' versus New Zealand English) evaluated by

New Zealanders. Citing a number of studies, the authors pointed out that speaking rate and pitch range have been found to correlate with evaluations of speakers' competence and social attractiveness. Specifically, faster speaking rates and wider pitch ranges have tended to be evaluated as more competent, and moderately fast rates and medium and high levels of pitch variation have tended to be evaluated as more socially attractive. It is not obvious how these findings may apply to evaluations of non-native varieties, which may also use different intonation patterns (as in Holden and Hogan's study discussed above) in addition to whatever differences may exist in rate and pitch; this bears further investigation.

Other research has looked more generally at what features of non-native speech are particularly noticed by native listeners aside from issues of evaluation. Such research suggests possibly useful directions for attitudes research to take, as salient features are likely to be more available to listeners for evaluation, whether positive or negative. In general it has been found that greater accentedness is evaluated more negatively (Ryan *et al.*, 1977; Cargile and Giles, 1998), suggesting that any salient non-native feature may contribute to listeners' negative reactions. However, it is possible that some salient non-native features are evaluated more positively, as it has been suggested that some non-native accents may be more prestigious, or at least less stigmatized (Lippi-Green, 1997; Lindemann, 2001, 2005). It would therefore be worthwhile to systematically investigate salient features of non-native accents to determine which are most likely to be evaluated negatively and which neutrally or even positively.

Studies that have investigated these patterns of salience (as opposed to evaluation) of various non-native features have in some cases looked at the features in a more detailed and controlled way, giving a better idea of where future studies of feature evaluation might look. For example, Murray Munro's (1995) study examined perception of native versus non-native prosody, considering what specific aspects of prosody were likely to be relevant to listeners. By presenting untrained listeners with recordings in which segmental information had been filtered out leaving utterances unintelligible, he found that untrained listeners could reliably distinguish Canadian English from Mandarin-accented English on the basis of prosody alone. He went on to hypothesize that relevant prosodic cues may have included slower speaking rates of Mandarin speakers (although there was considerable overlap between the native and non-native speakers in speaking rate), some non-native pitch patterns, and lack of reduction (specifically of the /t/

in *sitting* and the /d/ in *and*). However, he argues that there is little evidence to support the common view that prosodic features should be a focus of pronunciation teaching, especially as nonsegmental information did not appear to be used in accentedness judgements of unfiltered speech; he found no relationship between listeners' ratings of filtered and unfiltered speech. He also pointed out that clues to accentedness may differ from talker to talker and utterance to utterance, which certainly would complicate the picture of what features are most important for pronunciation practice.

Harriet Magen's (1998) study of Spanish-accented English explored the salience of both segmental and nonsegmental features by asking listeners to rate phrases that had been acoustically manipulated on how native-like they were. Listeners were particularly sensitive to epenthetic vowels, final /s/, and the distinction between /tʃ/ and /ʃ/. On the other hand, they were not particularly sensitive to voicing effects or vowel reduction (although this may have been due more to interference from orthography, as listeners were less likely to notice non-native pronunciations if they corresponded to spelling).

Finally, the literature on mispronunciation detection (considering mispronunciations by native as well as non-native speakers) may also be brought to bear on the question of what issues are most important in the pronunciation classroom. For example, the findings that mispronunciations are more likely to be detected at word beginnings rather than word endings (Cole *et al.*, 1978) and in stressed rather than unstressed syllables (Cole and Jakimik, 1980) suggest that word beginnings and stressed syllables would be more fruitful areas of focus in pronunciation teaching. As in Magen's study, Peggy Schmid and Grace Yeni-Komshian (1999) found that changes in voicing in word-initial stops were not particularly easy to detect. They also found that place changes and stops mispronounced as nasals were more detectable than either voicing differences or stops mispronounced as fricatives.

Assess performance of non-native speakers in the context of the listener

It has been suggested (for example by Levis, this volume) that more relevant assessments of international teaching assistants' English would be those by undergraduates who are their potential students, rather than those by English-teaching specialists who are much more likely to be familiar with features of non-native speech and therefore much more likely to understand it. Although there is clearly a pragmatic logic to this approach, the findings above suggest that great care is needed to avoid further institutionalizing the bias against speakers from less positively-viewed backgrounds. Such a bias may already be apparent in who is tested in the first place, as at least some universities have the policy that 'international' students, rather than 'non-native-speaking' students must be tested for English proficiency. When the suggestion is made that this implies that British and English Canadian students should be tested for language proficiency, the suggestion may be met with laughter and an assurance that such obvious exceptions will be made, yet students from India who are also native speakers of English frequently find themselves in the position of needing to prove their proficiency. Of course, as there is no simple definition of what constitutes a non-native speaker, a satisfactory way of determining who should be tested remains to be found.

Other possible biases in testing suggested by the research discussed here include biases in the perception of the degree of accent, which may be influenced by knowledge or beliefs about where the speaker is from. Unfortunately, it is not always clear what direction this influence will be in, as discussed above, making it more difficult to determine how to account for this possibility. This kind of bias may well be present even in those with relatively positive attitudes to non-native speaking groups, as even relatively benign expectations of how a person is likely to speak have been shown to affect perception at the level of the phoneme (as in the Niedzielski (1999) and Strand (1999) studies discussed above). Further research is needed to discover how such processes may be affecting pronunciation assessment. (Not discussed here, but also open for research, is how similar expectations may influence perceptions of grammatical accuracy. Preston (1996a) has pointed out that even careful transcriptions of native speech done by native-speaking linguists-in-training often diverge in subtle ways from the grammar actually used; it is possible that listening to a non-native speaker who may be expected to make some grammatical errors may result in mishearings that differ in grammaticality from what was actually produced.)

Similarly, the role of interlocutor collaboration in speaker performance brings up questions about possible biases in oral proficiency interviews. Clearly, what the interviewer says and does will influence the non-native speaker's performance (Young and He, 1998), yet attempts to control for different interviewer responses in different interviews may lead to very unnatural linguistic behaviour, making the interview a less accurate measure of how the interviewee is likely to function in a more normal situation.

Acknowledge that not all problems can be solved by better language teaching

As discussed above, those who are outside the disciplines of linguistics, applied linguistics, and language teaching often take it as self-evident that communication problems between native and non-native speakers are largely due to the non-native speakers' lack of proficiency in the language. This sort of 'deficit' theory often carries over into the thinking of language practitioners as well. Of course, this may be at least in part because it is the non-native speakers whom we have the opportunity and responsibility to teach; difficulties arising from the native speaker are not something we are in a position to address so directly. A result is that in some cases the standards for non-native speakers may end up being higher than those for native speakers. For example, non-native speakers are often given much more training as teaching assistants, not only in language issues *per se* but sometimes also in 'Western' teaching methods which may not be used by native-speaking teaching assistants. They may also learn about culture differences and ways of dealing with various communication difficulties that arise, whereas there is no obvious venue for teaching native speakers of English such things. Here, in instruction as well as in day-to-day interactions, we see the 'communicative burden' placed disproportionately on the non-native speaker. To some extent, this focus in instruction may be seen as a way of dealing with the reality that native speakers will not always carry their share of the communicative burden and that non-native speakers will have to pick up the slack; additional training simply gives them the tools to do so. On the other hand, training that focuses on non-native speakers so that they will not have too many communication difficulties with native speakers may also be seen as reinforcing the status quo.

For example, above I discussed how we might improve pronunciation instruction by discovering more about which aspects of pronunciation are likely to trigger negative reactions. However, working on pronunciation only goes so far; not all language learners will be able or willing to acquire pronunciation that will be more positively viewed by native-speaking listeners. Nor should they be required to. When we continually address communication problems between native and non-native speakers by looking only at how to 'improve' the non-native speaker, we may convey the message that the complaints we are responding to are valid, even though in some cases they may stem from native-speaker prejudice rather than from non-native speaker proficiency.

Furthermore, there is a limit to what could be accomplished even if we were able to help learners become completely native-like: if native speakers have negative attitudes to certain groups, they are likely to discriminate against those groups even if they cannot logically do so on the basis of language. This is in part because, as discussed above, speakers may be perceived as having a non-native accent (Rubin 1992) or as being less than fully competent communicators (Lindemann 2002), even if these perceptions have no basis in linguistic reality. In addition, if, as numerous researchers have pointed out, negative attitudes to language varieties are really negative attitudes to speakers, changing the variety will not change the attitudes to the speakers. In other words, while it is possible that we will lessen the amount of discrimination by addressing the language, it is also possible that native speakers will find other criteria by which to discriminate.

Although I do not wish to say that the evaluation of stigmatized native varieties and the evaluation of non-native varieties are necessarily equivalent, the situation faced by some non-native speakers of English may in some ways parallel the situation faced by African-American English speakers in the US. Although individual speakers can escape some discrimination by learning a non-stigmatized variety of English, they will still be discriminated against because they are African Americans. Additionally, the fact that some are able to learn a second variety may be held against speakers who are not able to learn a second variety; they must be 'ignorant' or 'uneducated' if they continue speaking that way, since other educated speakers apparently do not speak that way. Simply acknowledging this state of affairs to ESL students in the classroom can be beneficial; they are often relieved that someone recognizes that some of the difficulties they are having are not the fault of their language proficiency (much less 'their fault'). A few have found the discussion depressing because they had not observed evidence of any prejudice against them. However, in general, bringing native-speaker issues up for discussion can be helpful on a number of levels. On one level, the validation of students' experiences and recognition of the skills they have already achieved may help alleviate some of the anxiety they may feel stemming from such experiences and life in a foreign country more generally. On a more concrete level, such a topic can spur lively discussion among students, who may share ways they have dealt with interlocutors who use avoidance or problematizing strategies. Finally, such consciousness-raising makes it less likely that they will discriminate against other non-native speakers.

Raise awareness beyond the ESL classroom

Of course, if some communication problems between native and non-native speakers arise from native-speaker issues, then in order to solve these problems we ultimately need to work with native speakers. Although this is probably the most difficult aspect of the problem to address, it is also the most important. Unless we also work toward greater understanding and acceptance of different varieties of English, solutions we find to attitude-related problems of native–non-native communication will be limited to stopgap measures that may help individual non-native speakers but do not address the larger problem.

A logical place to start for those of us working in university settings is with the graduate students we are training to be ESL/EFL teachers, as well as with undergraduates in linguistics, applied linguistics, and language studies classes. Many introductory linguistics classes already challenge commonly-held notions of language, including issues of language prejudice. A first step towards general awareness-raising would be to ensure that confronting language prejudice is a major component of multiple courses and that discussion of language prejudice addresses attitudes to non-native speakers as well as to stigmatized native speakers. However, comparatively few students take linguistics courses, so ideally these issues would be addressed in other courses as well, such as psychology, sociology, anthropology, education, communication, English, and foreign language courses.

Another possibility for work in a university setting (and perhaps more achievable than finding colleagues in some of the departments listed above who would be likely to discuss language prejudice) would be creating some sort of required workshop for all undergraduates, perhaps as part of new student orientation. A workshop of this nature would be especially beneficial at large universities with many non-native-speaking teaching assistants; as Lippi-Green (1997) has pointed out at the University of Michigan, the administration has acknowledged that communication problems between students and non-native-speaking instructors may stem from students' bias as well as from insufficient language proficiency of instructors, but only language proficiency issues are officially addressed by university policy.

One possible limitation of a required workshop is that short-term or shallow interventions are less likely to have much effect (Rubin, 1992). However, an intense workshop coming at the beginning of the college experience may set the tone for continuing discussion of prejudice and discrimination. It may also contribute to better relationships among native and non-native speakers if the workshop involves native and non-native speakers working collaboratively, where the native speakers are not in the position of helping the non-native speakers (Coleman and De Paulo, 1991; Rubin, 1992).

Ideally these issues would be brought up earlier in the educational system, perhaps in foreign language, language arts, or English courses. Not everyone goes to college, and deep-seated prejudices are much more likely to be diminished if they are addressed early and over a long period of time. A first step toward achieving such long-term interventions in pre-university schooling is in requiring those studying to be primary and secondary school language teachers to take suitable courses in linguistics or applied linguistics (or other disciplines that specifically address language prejudice), itself an uphill battle but not an impossible one.

Finally, language practitioners can engage the community beyond the educational system in a number of ways. For example, we can write newspaper columns or letters to the editor responding to articles that exhibit or report on language prejudice (and we can encourage our students to do likewise!). We (or our students) may have opportunities to hold workplace workshops, especially if the workshops are geared toward communicating with non-native speakers more generally; for example, presenting strategies that facilitate communication. Perhaps readers may have other ideas on how to address this issue, ideas that could be shared and further developed in a continuing discussion. As in dealing with any prejudice, it is essential to challenge language prejudice in constructive ways at every opportunity; as language practitioners, we have both the opportunity and the responsibility to do so.

Appendix

Transcription symbols

[ ]	overlapping speech
( )	uncertain transcription
(4.5)	length of pause, in seconds
.	(immediately preceded by a space) micropause, less than half a second
=	'latched' speech, i.e. no pause between speech preceding and following
:	elongated sound (greater number of semicolons denotes more elongation)
-	audibly cut off sound
,	low rise intonation
?	rising intonation
.	(no space immediately preceding) falling intonation
.h	inhaling audibly (.hhh = extended inbreath)

Note

1 Intelligibility refers to identification of the speaker's words, whereas comprehensibility refers to identification of the speaker's meaning.

Bibliography

Anderson, A., Brown, G., Shillcock, R. and Yule, G. (eds) (1984) *Teaching Talk: Strategies for Production and Assessment* (Cambridge: Cambridge University Press).

Anderson-Hsieh, J. and Koehler, K. (1988) 'The effect of foreign accent and speaking rate on native speaker comprehension', *Language Learning*, 38: 561–613.

Atagi, E. (2003) 'Are you a native speaker? The role of ethnic background in the hallucination of foreign accents on native speakers', Paper presented at NWAV-32, Philadelphia, Pennsylvania.

Brown, K. (1992) 'American college student attitudes toward non-native instructors', *Multilingua*, 11: 249–65.

Cargile, A.C. (1997) 'Attitudes toward Chinese-accented speech: an investigation in two contexts', *Journal of Language and Social Psychology*, 16: 434–44.

Cargile, A.C. and Giles, H. (1998) 'Language attitudes toward varieties of English: an American-Japanese context', *Journal of Applied Communication Research*, 26: 338–56.

Clark, H.H. and Schaefer, E.F. (1987) 'Collaborating on contributions to conversations', *Language and Cognitive Processes*, 2: 19–41.

Clark, H.H. and Schaefer, E.F. (1989) 'Contributing to discourse', *Cognitive Science*, 13: 259–94.

Clark, H.H. and Wilkes-Gibbs, D. (1986) 'Referring as a collaborative process', *Cognition*, 22: 1–39.

Cole, R.A. and Jakimik, J. (1980) 'How are syllables used to recognize words?', *Journal of the Acoustical Society of America*, 67: 965–70.

Cole, R.A., Jakimik, J. and Cooper, W.E. (1978) 'Perceptibility of phonetic features in fluent speech', *Journal of the Acoustical Society of America*, 64: 44–56.

Coleman, L.M. and De Paulo, B.M. (1991) 'Uncovering the human spirit: moving beyond disability and "missed" communication', in N. Coupland, H. Giles and J.M. Wiemann (eds), *Miscommunication and Problematic Talk* (Newbury Park: Sage Publications) 61–84.

Dailey-O'Cain, J. (1999) 'Misidentification of where speakers are from and the effect on the use of the matched-guise technique', Paper presented at NWAV-28 (Toronto, Canada).

Gill, M.M. (1994) 'Accent and stereotypes: their effect on perceptions of teachers and lecture comprehension', *Journal of Applied Communication Research*, 22: 349–61.

Griffen, T.D. (1991) 'A nonsegmental approach to the teaching of pronunciation', in A. Brown (ed.), *Teaching English Pronunciation: A Book of Readings* (London: Routledge) 178–90.

Gumperz, J.J. (1982) *Discourse strategies: Studies in Interactional Sociolinguistics* (Cambridge: Cambridge University Press).

Holden, K.T. and Hogan, J.T. (1993) 'The emotive impact of foreign intonation: an experiment in switching English and Russian intonation', *Language and Speech*, 36: 67–88.

Lindemann, S. (2000) 'Non-native speaker "incompetence" as a construction of the native listener: Attitudes and their relationship to perception and comprehension of Korean-accented English', Unpublished PhD dissertation (Ann Arbor, Michigan: University of Michigan).

Lindemann, S. (2001) '"Non-standard" or non-native? Ideologies about non-native speakers of US English', Paper presented at NWAV-30, Raleigh, North Carolina.

Lindemann, S. (2002) 'Listening with an attitude: a model of native-speaker comprehension of non-native speakers in the United States', *Language in Society*, 31: 419–41.

Lindemann, S. (2003) 'Koreans, Chinese, or Indians? Attitudes and ideologies about non-native English speakers in the United States', *Journal of Sociolinguistics*, 7: 348–64.

Lindemann, S. (2005) 'Who speaks "broken English"? US undergraduates' perceptions of non-native English', *International Journal of Applied Linguistics*, 15: 187–212.

Lippi-Green, R. (1994) 'Accent, standard language ideology, and discriminatory pretext in the courts', *Language in Society*, 23: 163–98.

Lippi-Green, R. (1997) *English with an Accent: Language, Ideology, and Discrimination in the United States* (New York: Routledge).

Magen, H.-S. (1998) 'The Perception of Foreign-Accented Speech', *Journal of Phonetics*, 26: 381–400.

McGurk, H. and MacDonald, J. (1976) 'Hearing lips and seeing voices', *Nature*, 264: 746–8.

Milroy, L. and McClenaghan, P. (1977) 'Stereotyped reactions to four educated accents in Ulster', *Belfast Working Papers in Language and Linguistics*, 2: 1–11.

Mulac, A., Hanley, T.D. and Prigge, D.Y. (1974) 'Effects of phonological speech foreignness upon three dimensions of attitude of selected American listeners', *Quarterly Journal of Speech*, 60: 411–20.

Munro, M.J. (1995) 'Nonsegmental factors in foreign accent', *Studies in Second Acquisition*, 17: 17–34.

Munro, M.J. (2003) 'A primer on accent discrimination in the Canadian context', *TESL Canada Journal*, 20: 38–51.

Munro, M.J. and Derwing, T.M. (1995) 'Foreign accent, comprehensibility, and intelligibility in the speech of second language learners', *Language Learning*, 45: 73–97.

Naslund, D.T. (1993) 'The /s/ phoneme: A gender issue', Unpublished manuscript (University of Minnesota, Duluth).

Niedzielski, N. (1999) 'The effect of social information on the perception of sociolinguistic variables', *Journal of Language and Social Psychology*, 18: 62–84.

Perkins, L. and Milroy, L. (1997) 'Sharing the communicative burden: a conversation-analytic account of aphasic/non-aphasic interaction', *Multilingua*, 16: 199–215.

Plichta, B. (2001) 'Hearing faces: the effects of ethnicity on speech perception', Paper presented at NWAV-30, Raleigh, North Carolina.

Potter, J. and Wetherell, M. (1987) *Discourse and Social Psychology: Beyond Attitudes and Behavior* (London: Sage).

Preston, D.R. (1993) 'Two heartland perceptions of language variety', in T.C. Frazer (ed.), *'Heartland' English: Variation and Transition in the American Midwest* (Tuscaloosa: University of Alabama Press) 23–47.

Preston, D.R. (1996a) 'Whaddayaknow?: the modes of folk linguistic awareness', *Language Awareness*, 5: 40–74.

Preston, D.R. (1996b) 'Where the worst English is spoken', in E.W. Schneider (ed.), *Focus on the USA* (Amsterdam/Philadelphia: John Benjamins) 297–361.

Ray, G.B. and Zahn, C.J. (1999) 'Language attitudes and speech behavior: New Zealand English and Standard American English', *Journal of Language and Social Psychology*, 18: 310–9.

Rubin, D.L. (1992) 'Nonlanguage factors affecting undergraduates' judgments of nonnative English-speaking teaching assistants', *Research in Higher Education*, 33: 511–31.

Rubin, D.L. and Williams-James, M. (1997) 'The impact of writer nationality on mainstream teachers' judgments of composition quality', *Journal of Second Language Writing*, 6: 139–53.

Ryan, E.B. and Bulik, C.M. (1982) 'Evaluations of middle class and lower class speakers of standard American and German-accented English', *Journal of Language and Social Psychology*, 1: 51–61.

Ryan, E.B., Carranza, M.A. and Moffie, R.W. (1997) 'Reactions toward varying degrees of accentedness in the speech of Spanish-English bilinguals', *Language and Speech*, 20: 267–73.

Ryan, E.B. and Sebastian, R.J. (1980) 'The effects of speech style and social class background on social judgements of speakers, *British Journal of Social and Clinical Psychology*, 19: 229–33.

Samuel, A.G. (1981) 'Phonemic restoration: insights from a new methodology', *Journal of Experimental Psychology: General*, 110: 474–94.

Schegloff, E.A. (1982) 'Discourse as an interactional achievement: Some uses of "uh huh" and other things that come between sentences', in D. Tannen (ed.), *Analyzing Discourse: Text and Talk. 32nd Georgetown University Roundtable on Languages and Linguistics 1981* (Washington, DC: Georgetown University Press) 3.

Schmid, P.M. and Yeni-Komshian, G.H. (1999) 'The effects of speaker accent and target predictability on perception of mispronunciations', *Journal of Speech, Language, and Hearing Research*, 42: 56–64.

Scollon, R. and Scollon, S.W. (1995) *Intercultural Communication: A Discourse Approach: Language in Society* (Oxford: Blackwell).

Southwood, M.H. and Flege, J.E. (1999) 'Scaling foreign accent: direct magnitude estimation versus interval scaling, *Clinical Linguistics & Phonetics*, 13: 335–49.

Strand, E.A. (1999) 'Uncovering the role of gender stereotypes in speech perception', *Journal of Language and Social Psychology*, 18: 86–100.

Tajima, K., Port, R. and Dalby, J. (1997) 'Effects of temporal correction on intelligibility of foreign-accented English', *Journal of Phonetics*, 25: 1–24.

Tannen, D. (1981) 'New York Jewish conversational style', *International Journal of the Sociology of Language*, 30: 133–49.

Tyler, A. (1995) 'The coconstruction of cross-cultural miscommunication', *Studies in Second Language Acquisition*, 17: 129–52.

von Hippel, W., Sekaquaptewa, D. and Vargas, P. (1995) 'On the role of encoding processes in stereotype maintenance', in M.P. Zanna (ed.) *Advances in Experimental Social Psychology, Vol. 27* (San Diego: Academic Press) 177–254.
Watanabe, S. (1993) 'Cultural differences in framing: American and Japanese group discussions', in D. Tannen (ed.) *Framing in Discourse* (New York: Oxford University Press) 176–209.
Young, R. and He, A.W. (eds) (1998) *Talking and Testing: Discourse Approaches to the Assessment of Oral Proficiency* (Amsterdam: John Benjamins).

Part II

Prosody: New Models for Meaning

3
Reading Aloud

Wallace Chafe

Introduction

Those of us who live in a world of literacy have two quite different ways of producing and receiving language. Most often we use our mouths to make sounds and our ears to listen to sounds made by others. At other times, however, we use our hands to make visible marks on paper or a computer screen, and then we use our eyes to look at those marks. These two uses of language are of course called, on the one hand, speaking and listening, on the other hand, writing and reading.

In the course of human history the evolution of these two uses has been very different and has had different consequences. Spoken language evolved as a fundamental aspect of the evolution of the human species itself. People have been speaking and listening for as long as they have been people. Written language, very differently, arose only during the last few millennia and it is only within very recent times that literacy has been widespread. Writing has also lent itself to uses that are very different from the typical uses of speaking. It should not be surprising, then, that the ways in which writing has been used have affected the nature of written language itself. Differences between written and spoken language have been seriously and widely studied for only the last few decades, but it has become clear that language adapts itself in various ways to the uses people make of it. For a survey of earlier work, see Chafe and Tannen (1987); for a comparison of the two uses see Chafe (1994: 41–50).

The topic of this chapter, however, is neither speaking nor writing in their natural forms, but a third way of using language, a way that shares some features of speaking and some of writing but differs from both. Reading aloud consists of language that was first produced as writing and then, at some later time, delivered as speaking. In spite of its origin as writing, its audience does not read it but hears it. It is written at the beginning, spoken at the end. Its special properties have been little studied, and especially not within the perspectives developed below. A different, more statistical approach can be found in works by Esser and Polomski (1987; 1988).

The nature of reading aloud

As with the other uses of language, reading aloud itself has various purposes and shows different varieties. Sometimes the language is written for the express purpose of being read aloud. Sometimes it is written to be read silently but then, for one reason or another, someone reads it aloud nevertheless. Sometimes the producer of the language and the person who reads it aloud are the same, sometimes they are not. When they are not, there are of course three parties involved in the process rather than the usual two: the creator of the language, the person who reads it aloud, and the audience. A special situation arises in the case of acting, where the creator is a playwright whose written language is memorized by someone else, who may then make an effort to produce it as if it had been spoken language from the start. The playwright may or may not try to create language that will mimic ordinary speaking. People do not ordinarily speak in iambic pentameter, but it can be an effective dramatic resource.

Why do people read aloud? One can imagine various scenarios. There are, for example, situations in which listeners are simply incapable of reading to themselves, either because they have not yet learned to read, as with young children or illiterate adults, or because of a physical deficit, as with the blind. But, in other cases, people may want to share a piece of writing with someone, not by loaning that person a book but to foster the social intimacy of ordinary speaking, as when husbands and wives read to each other. Probably either spouse would be able to read the written text silently at a faster speed, but that would circumvent the experience of sharing. An oral reader may feel satisfaction in performing as a secondary creator of the language, not as the person who put the words together in the first place, but as someone who is able to deliver them effectively. That kind of satisfaction reaches its height in orators and actors, but others can enjoy it too. In other cases, the writer and oral reader are the same person. Some authors read their own works aloud professionally, a common practice in the nineteenth century but one that continues to this day. Quite different in motivation and effect is the presentation of so-called papers at academic conferences, an example of which will be presented below.

Why should reading aloud be a topic of scholarly interest? Can it teach us anything about the nature of language in general? I believe it can, in several ways. For one thing, it can highlight properties of language production and reception that might otherwise escape our attention. It can also provide ways of manipulating and testing hypotheses concerning the nature of language and language use. Understanding the nature of reading aloud can have practical results as well, results that might, for example, influence the delivery of political speeches and academic papers.

Table 3.1 Properties of speaking, writing, and reading aloud

	Speaking	**Writing**	**Reading aloud**
Production	*Making sounds* Fast Interactive Natural	*Making marks* Slow Isolated Unnatural	→
Product	↓	*Lasting marks* Special lexicon Special syntax Covert prosody	→
Delivery	↓	↓	*Making sounds* Special prosody
Reception	*Listening* Easy	*Reading* Harder	*Listening* Hardest

Table 3.1 contains three columns that represent, from left to right, speaking, writing, and reading aloud. In the left-hand column, there is a simple two-way distinction between the production of the language and its reception. As suggested at the top, it is typical of spoken language production that it is relatively fast, that it is interactive (the producer at one moment becoming the receiver at the next), and that it is natural (every normal person learning to speak without special training). As suggested at the bottom of this column, listening to speaking is easy. Humans have been equipped by evolution to process ordinary spoken language without making a special effort.

In the middle column, the production process is separated from the product. Producing written language involves making marks of some kind, normally a slower process than speaking. Writing is typically performed in isolation, lacking the possibilities for interaction that are typical of speaking. And writing is unnatural in the sense that it must be deliberately taught and learned. The product of writing consists of marks whose relative permanence contrasts with the evanescence of speaking. This permanence has made it possible to create language in one place and time and have it received at a totally different place and time, an ability that has had an enormous impact on recent human history. The written product is likely to exhibit its own special lexicon and syntax, which may differ significantly from those typical of speaking. Writing is relatively impoverished with respect to the prosodic qualities that contribute importantly to speaking: the variations in pitch, loudness, tempo, and voice quality that are only covertly present (Chafe, 1988). At the bottom of this second column is a suggestion that the reception of written language, in other words reading, is more difficult than listening to ordinary speech.

The right-hand column shows properties of reading aloud. The production and product are those of written language, but reading aloud is special in that the language is ultimately delivered by making sounds, as with ordinary speaking. The result, however, is not equivalent to ordinary speaking, in part because of the special lexicon and syntax intrinsic to written language, in part because reading-aloud prosody is likely to have its own properties that diverge from those of ordinary speaking. At the bottom of this third column is a suggestion that the reception of language read aloud may be the most difficult of all three varieties. Because of its special lexicon, syntax, and prosody, listening to such language may require a mental effort exceeding that which is necessary for silent reading, and far exceeding that which is necessary for listening to conversation.

My own interest in this topic developed above all from attending academic conferences. When I first began to give papers at such conferences, sometimes I read them and sometimes I spoke them more or less extemporaneously, guided by notes. In general, I spoke long papers and read short ones, because I wanted to make sure that the short ones fitted within the allotted time. I gradually shifted to speaking more and reading less, believing that I could communicate better in that way. In the opposite role, listening to others, I noticed a difference in my ability to assimilate what others were saying that was correlated with its spokenness or writtenness. I often experienced a sinking feeling when someone began to read. But that was not always the case. I noticed that some oral readers were especially good at producing language in that way, that their papers were just as easy to follow as those that were spoken. They seemed to be making a special effort to read *as if* they were speaking. I noticed also, in spite of the above, that the majority of people at the conferences I attended read their papers instead of speaking them. In the meantime I have come to realize that these practices differ from one discipline to another. In general, scholars in the humanities tend to read their papers while those in the sciences tend to speak them, although of course there are always exceptions. It seemed to me in any case paradoxical that, even though spoken language was easier to assimilate, so many people chose to present what they had to say by reading it aloud.

Conference practices

To examine this phenomenon a little more systematically, some years ago I distributed a questionnaire to one hundred linguists chosen from the membership list of the Linguistic Society of America. I received 89 replies. The first question I asked was whether the respondent was in the habit of reading aloud or speaking when he or she presented a conference paper. From their answers, 56 per cent turned out to be readers and 37 per cent speakers, while 7 per cent said they did both equally.

I then asked why they did what they did. Their answers are summarized in Table 3.2. Among the readers, 81 per cent said they read in

Table 3.2 Readers versus speakers

	Readers (56%)		Speakers (37%)	
		%		%
Why	Time constraints	81	Listenability	90
	Security	72	Written unfinished	33
	Elegance	68	Out of habit	18
	Out of habit	11		
Preference	None/depends	44	Speaking	94
	Reading	36	Reading	3
	Speaking	20	None/depends	3
Reasons to prefer reading	Organization	48		
	Listenability	20		
Reasons to prefer speaking	Listenability	25	Listenability	91
	Memorability	4	Memorability	30

order to stay within the allotted time, 72 per cent said it made them feel more secure, and 68 per cent found the practice more elegant (they were allowed to give more than one answer). A smaller number, 11 per cent, said they did it out of habit. Among those who spoke their presentations, the answers as to why they did it were quite different. Almost all of them, 90 per cent, said they spoke because they believed they were easier to listen to when they did that; 33 per cent said they did it, at least sometimes, because they had not yet finished their written version; and 18 per cent said they did it out of habit.

The most interesting differences between the two groups, however, had to do with what they themselves preferred to listen to, and the reasons for those preferences. Almost half of the oral readers, 44 per cent, said they had no preference or that it depended on the circumstances. No more than 36 per cent had a clear preference for listening to read papers, but fewer still, only 20 per cent, had a clear preference for spoken papers. In striking contrast, almost all the speakers, 94 per cent, said they preferred listening to papers that were spoken. When the readers who preferred listening to read papers were asked why, approximately half of them, 48 per cent, said it was because read papers were better organized. Only 20 per cent of this group said read papers were easier to listen to. But when those who spoke their papers were asked why they preferred listening to spoken papers, 91 per cent of them attributed it to listenability; 30 per cent said spoken papers were easier to remember. In short, speakers were strikingly more consistent than readers in their preference for hearing others do what they themselves did, and in agreeing on the main reason for their preference, greater listenability.

Listenability

What, then, is listenability, and why might it be greater for language that is produced spontaneously than for language read aloud? Listenability is not a topic that has been well studied, but its companion process, readability, has been studied a great deal because of its obvious practical applications. A long tradition of readability research, dating at least from the 1920s, was usefully surveyed in Klare (1974). The goal of much of that research was to discover a readability formula that could be applied to written works in order to determine their suitability for school children at different grade levels. These mechanical formulas never touched the heart of what makes something more or less readable, and other, more recent attempts have tried to identify cognitive factors that affect the ease or difficulty of written selections (for example, Hirsch, 1977; Holland, 1981; Chafe, 1991).

One needs to recognize at the outset that both readability and listenability are influenced by external factors, such as the extent to which a reader or listener has prior knowledge of or interest in the subject matter. Obviously, prior knowledge and interest can have important effects on reading or listening ease. Our concern here, however, is the extent to which the language itself, apart from its subject matter, can affect the ease with which it is processed.

With reference again to Table 3.1, problems with listenability may arise at either the production or the delivery stage. On the one hand, the producer of the language may create something that will be more or less easy or difficult to process when it is subsequently read aloud. On the other hand, the person who delivers the language, as he or she reads it aloud, may also influence the ease or difficulty of processing. What happens at the two stages is different.

An example

The excerpt that follows was transcribed from the beginning of an academic talk. Part of it was spoken, part read aloud. I have divided it into four sentences, and even a casual perusal should suggest the spokenness of the first two sentences and the writtenness of the third and fourth, although all were delivered orally. I will mention first some differences in situatedness and spontaneity, and then different uses of prosody. (The sequences of two, three, or four dots indicate pauses of increasing length, while the commas and periods show, respectively, continuing and final pitch contours.)

(1)   ... I'm standing over here to talk to you, because, (laugh) I'm too short to be seen, you know over the podium. ... (laugh)

(2)   ... You-most people have, .. uh, ... an image of me, .. mainly cowlick and eyebrows, .. and, ... so this, .. this is a .. good compromise.

(3)   .... Most students, .. of human development, .. seek to discover. .. what is universal, ... in the developmental process. ... no matter what aspect of human development, .. they happen to be investigating.

(4)   ... They assume that the course of development, ... to one extent or another, ... is largely shaped. ... by biological dispredispositions.

(1) and (2) were situated and interactive, (3) and (4) abstract and detached. There are several kinds of evidence that sentences (1) and (2) were situated in the immediate time and place of the presentation, as contrasted with the detachment of sentences (3) and (4), and that the first two sentences exhibited an involvement with the audience that was lacking in the second two. Although this was not an interactive conversation, in (1) and (2) the audience was invited to join in the predicament created by the speaker's short stature. There were references to *I*, *me*, and *you*, to *here* and *this*, and to immediately visible features like the podium and the speaker's hair and eyebrows. There was the interactive phrase *you know*. Much of sentence (1) was accompanied by laughter, inviting the audience to share the speaker's feeling of non-seriousness with regard to the situation. These manifestations of situatedness vanished in (3) and (4), where the speaker introduced generic participants in generic situations detached from the time and place of the delivery.

(1) and (2) were spontaneous, (3) and (4) preplanned. The speaker had not written out what she said in sentences (1) and (2); the language was produced, so to speak, on the run. In (2) there were several false starts, including the *you* at the beginning and the word *and* that was replaced by *so*, not to mention the pause filler *uh*. These features, typical of spontaneous production, were absent from the read-aloud sentences (3) and (4), although at the very end the speaker stumbled briefly in reading the word *predispositions*.

(1) and (2) adhered to a colloquial style, (3) and (4) an academic style. There were two occurrences of the contraction *I'm* in sentence (1), contrasting with the uncontracted sequence *what is* (rather than *what's*) in sentence (3). Contractions are ubiquitous in spontaneous speaking, but there is a tendency to avoid them in academic writing, and that avoidance can lead to their absence in academic language that is read aloud.

(1) and (2) used more common words than (3) and (4). In spontaneous speaking, it is necessary to choose words and phrases that come quickly to mind. Writers have more time for lexical choice, the leisure to consider words and phrases that will match what they are thinking in more nuanced ways. It follows that writing will show a larger proportion of less commonly used words, and listeners may need longer processing times for items that are not in frequent use. The tendency of written language to exploit less common vocabulary can contribute

to its diminished listenability. In (3) and (4) the speaker introduced items with an academic flavour, saying *seek to discover* instead of *try to find*, and *largely shaped* instead of *mostly shaped*, not to mention specialized words like *predispositions*.

(1) and (2) were syntactically simpler, (3) and (4) more complex. The ability of writers to plan and rework their clauses, sentences, and paragraphs at a leisurely pace can lead to greater syntactic complexity than is found in spontaneous speaking (Chafe and Danielewicz, 1987). Writers have the time and editing ability to construct sentences that lie beyond the range of those who are speaking off the cuff. Here, for example, we can notice the heavy grammatical subject of (3), *most students of human development*, in contrast to the simple pronoun *I* that was the subject of (1). Sentence (4) contained a passive construction, *is largely shaped*, in which the agent was the abstract idea expressed as *biological predispositions*. Although (1) also contained a passive in *I'm too short to be seen*, the structure *too X to be Yed* is a familiar collocation. The agent of this passive, furthermore, was the immediately present audience itself.

Writing also favours a more exuberant use of prepositional phrases. In sentences (3) and (4) there were six of them:

> *of human development* [twice]
> *in the developmental process*
> *of development*
> *to one extent or another*
> *by biological predispositions*

There were also four attributive adjectives, another feature that tends to occur more often in writing than in spontaneous speaking:

> *human development* [twice]
> *developmental process*
> *biological predispositions*

All things considered, then, the interactive situatedness, spontaneity, colloquial style, and relatively simple vocabulary and syntax of sentences (1) and (2) contrasted with the displaced abstractness, preplanning, academic style, and more complex syntax of sentences (3) and (4), yielding a clear distinction between what was spontaneous and what was read aloud.

The role of prosody

It is of some interest to consider also the prosody of these two segments: the variations in pitch, loudness, timing, and voice quality that accompany spoken language of any kind, whether it is spontaneous or read aloud. One of the functions of prosody is to segment speech into larger coherences, and the boundary between sentences (2) and (3) in this example – between the spontaneous and read-aloud portions – was especially clear. There was, for one thing, a five-second pause, a long time in the ordinary flow of speech, occupied in part by shifting to a written manuscript but also signalling the change in style. The read-aloud portion, furthermore, began with a noticeably higher pitch. Figure 3.1 shows in the middle the long pause between the end of (2) and the beginning of (3), as well as the heightened pitch at the beginning of (3), which reached 408 hertz, well above this speaker's normal range (see Wichmann, 2000, regarding such boundary phenomena).

Figure 3.1   Fundamental frequency at the boundary between sentences (2) and (3) (academic talk)

Prosody segments speech into smaller units as well. Oral language, whether it is spontaneous or read aloud, is produced in prosodic phrases, or intonation units. In the transcription above, these intonation units were separated by commas or periods. It is interesting to find that the intonation units in both the spoken and read-aloud portions were almost identical in length, in each case averaging 1.9 seconds, a figure that is typical of spoken English in general, regardless of how it is produced. This consistency of intonation unit length in both speaking and reading aloud is by no means confined to this example. In Chafe (1988), I described a broader sample of read-aloud materials whose intonation units were comparable in length to those of ordinary speech. Evidently, our language production abilities constrain us to produce spoken language in brief units of this kind, regardless of the nature of that spoken language.

Paradoxically, that constraint leads to another difference between spontaneous and read-aloud language. The following repeats the first two sentences of this example with each line representing a separate intonation unit. In Chafe (1993), I suggested that intonation units could be profitably divided into those that are substantive (expressing ideas), regulatory (linkages, interactive expressions, and so on), and fragmentary (incomplete), as indicated to the right of each line.

(a)	. . . I'm standing over here to talk to you,	(substantive)
(b)	because,	(regulatory)
(c)	(laugh) I'm too short to be seen,	(substantive)
(d)	(laugh) you know over the podium.	(substantive)
(e)	. . . (laugh)	(regulatory)
(f)	. . . You-	(fragmentary)
(g)	most people have,	(substantive)
(h)	. . uh,	(regulatory)
(i)	. . . an image of me,	(substantive)
(j)	. . mainly cowlick and eyebrows,	(substantive)
(k)	. . and,	(regulatory)
(l)	. . . so this,	(fragmentary)
(m)	. . this is a . . good compromise.	(substantive)

The mean intonation unit length of 1.9 seconds that was mentioned above was calculated with respect to the substantive units only. Spontaneous speech, however, is typically characterized by the frequent occurrence of regulatory and fragmentary units as well, as this example illustrates.

The same is not true of read-aloud speech, where online production is replaced by language already tailored through writing. This preplanning is evident in the restriction of sentences (3) and (4) to substantive intonation units only.

(n)	. . . . . most students,
(o)	. . of human development,
(p)	. . seek to discover.
(q)	. . what is universal,
(r)	. . . in the developmental process.
(s)	. . . no matter what aspect of human development,

    (t)   . . they happen to be investigating.
    (u)   . . . They assume that the course of development,
    (v)   . . . to one extent or another,
    (w)   . . . is largely shaped.
    (x)   . . . by biological dis-predispositions.

As already noted, however, constraints on speaking lead to intonation units of the same or similar lengths for both styles. In the process of reading aloud, this restriction can easily lead to mismatches between the prosody and the syntax of the language involved. Syntactically, for example, one might expect the noun phrase subject consisting of (n) and (o), *most students of human development*, to be produced as a single unit, and the same to be true of the predicate consisting of (p) through to (r), *seek to discover what is universal in the developmental process*. Throughout this excerpt, what was actually produced was prosodically choppier, and led even to the introduction of sentence-final falling pitches at non-final points, as at the ends of lines (p), (r), and (w). Prosody and syntax were at odds.

In spontaneous production, a speaker's consciousness is focused on the flow of thought, not on the sounds. When that is the case, the prosody flows naturally and unconsciously out of the thoughts. When a speaker, reading aloud, focuses more on producing the sounds and less on the thoughts that lie behind those sounds, as happens frequently in the reading-aloud environment, the prosody no longer emerges unconsciously and naturally, often sounding artificial or inappropriate.

Another example

Different people read aloud in quite different ways. For an example, very different from that just described, we can turn to a press conference. Press conferences yield good examples of the same person first reading aloud with a prepared statement and then speaking more or less spontaneously. I say 'more or less' because the answers to reporters' questions may consist in part of practiced material that has already been used in both private and public discussions. Nevertheless, differences between the initial reading aloud and the more spontaneous answers to questions can be noteworthy.

In the example that follows, the American President, George W. Bush, opened a press conference on 26 January 2004 with some read-aloud material in which he employed a flat prosody, conveying minimal involvement with his audience or with his subject matter.

The usual segmentation into relatively brief intonation units was absent. The following intonation unit, in which an entire syntactic sentence was uttered as a single prosodic phrase, occupied a full five seconds, far above the mean length of 1.9 mentioned above.

> The House and the Senate are now considering my supplemental request for operations in Iraq and Afghanistan.

Figure 3.2 shows the fundamental frequency of this long intonation unit, with minimal pitch variation and a final falling contour. The same prosodic pattern was repeated throughout the President's prepared remarks.

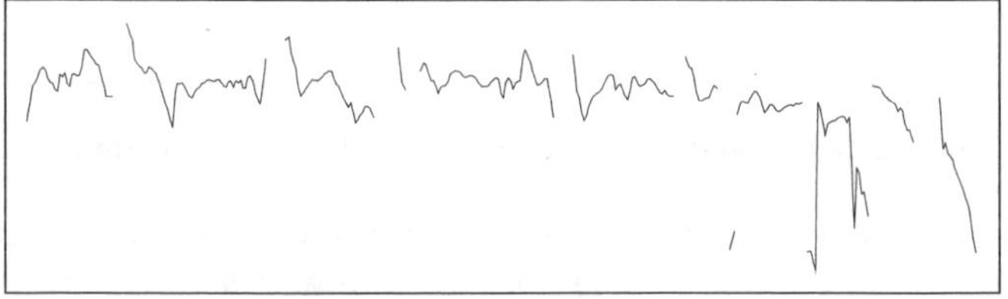

Figure 3.2　Fundamental frequency of President Bush reading aloud

In contrast, at one point during the question period that followed the President spoke as follows:

(a)　Yeah.
(b)　I think it's-
(c)　I think it's a very interesting point you make in your question.
(d)　They're trying to send a warning.
(e)　.. Basically what they're trying to do is-
(f)　.... is uh,
(g)　.... cause people to run.
(h)　.. You know?

The difference in style is obvious. The initial colloquial response in (a) was followed by a fragmentary intonation unit in (b) that was repeated at the beginning of the successful but less spontaneous answers in (c) and (d), whose wordings are employed by the President on other occasions. The more spontaneous explanation in (e) through to (g) exhibited disfluencies that included a repetition and two unusually long

pauses. The sequence ended with a very softly spoken colloquial interactive phrase, *you know*. The considerable pitch variation that is visible
in Figure 3.3 is in marked contrast to the flat prosody in Figure 3.2.

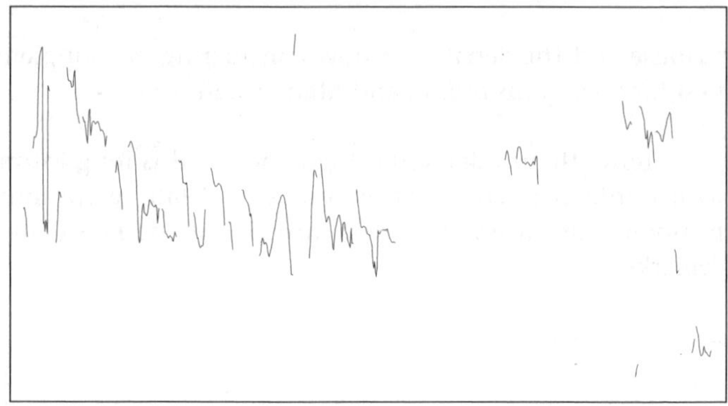

Figure 3.3   Fundamental frequency of President Bush speaking spontaneously

In short, the read-aloud portion was prosodically less diverse than in
the previous example, whose speaker followed a more spoken-like
pattern in spite of its disconnect from the syntax. Here, there was no
attempt to mimic the prosody of ordinary speaking. The spontaneous
portion was distinguished by its disfluencies, apart from two memorized phrases.

Silent reading

Although it was not always true in the past, today most writing is
meant to be read silently. It is thus of some interest to compare those
who read aloud with silent readers. Writing itself may show prosody to
some extent with punctuation, but it does so only partially and incon-
sistently. Nevertheless, it seems that many people at least, when they
read silently to themselves, do assign prosodic boundaries, accents,
intonation contours, and perhaps even voice qualities to the language
they are reading. In Chafe (1988), I included several quotes to show
that I was not alone in experiencing such prosody. The following are
from a textbook on linguistics by Dwight Bolinger and an autobiogra-
phical book by Eudora Welty. Statements like these reinforce a belief
that writers when they write, and readers when they read, experience
auditory imagery of specific intonations, accents, pauses, rhythms, and
voice qualities, even though the writing itself may show such features
poorly, if at all.

> We monitor our writing sub-vocally, reading in an intonation, and the fact that the intonation is not actually shown and our reader is going to have to guess at it is as likely as not to escape our attention (Bolinger, 1975: 602).
>
> Ever since I was first read to, then started reading to myself, there has never been a line read that I didn't hear. As my eyes followed the sentence, a voice was saying it silently to me ... My own words, when I am at work on a story, I hear too as they go, in the same voice that I hear when I read in books (Welty, 1983: 12–13).

In Chafe (1988), I was concerned with showing how and to what extent punctuation was used by various writers to capture the prosody of their writing, both as they experienced it and as a silent reader might experience it. How a silent reader experiences the prosody of writing is of course a private experience to which no outside observer has direct access. I attempted, nevertheless, to tap into that experience in two ways, first by having people read aloud and then by having others insert punctuation into samples of writing from which all punctuation had been removed. I called the latter *repunctuators*. Both the prosody of the oral readers and the punctuation supplied by the repunctuators can be compared with the punctuation of the original authors. In general, the repunctuators came closer than the oral readers to matching the ways in which the writing had originally been punctuated. The situation was complicated by the fact that written English has favoured different styles of punctuating at different times. The nineteenth century favoured more punctuation marks, the so-called closed style, while the current open style favours fewer such marks. Practices have varied a great deal, however, and different authors have had their own punctuation styles. In any case, it appeared that what may be called *punctuation units* (stretches of language bounded by punctuation marks), whether produced by the repunctuators or by the original authors, were generally longer than the intonation units created those who read aloud. That finding may suggest that both writers and silent readers surpass both ordinary speakers and people who read aloud in their ability to process larger stretches of language at a time. Written language, in other words, can be processed in somewhat larger chunks, so long as one is reading it silently and not aloud.

One of the passages used in that study came from Henry James's *The Turn of the Screw*. James's punctuation units had a mean length of 9.6 words, and the repunctuators created punctuation units of an almost identical length, 9.7 words. When people read the same passage aloud, the mean number of words per intonation unit dropped to 6.5. The second sentence in the following excerpt provides a subtle example of what was happening.

> we were of a common mind about the duty of resistance to extravagant fancies. We were to keep our heads if we should keep nothing else – (James, 1966: 34)

A majority of the repunctuators agreed with James in preserving the second sentence with no punctuation in the middle. But most who read the passage aloud inserted a prosodic boundary with a rising intonation contour after the word *heads*. The oral readers, in other words, interpreted the second sentence in terms of two intonation units, each of which came closer to the norm for spoken language.

Is it possible to relate this difference between a written interpretation of this sentence and a spoken interpretation to anything functional in the language? In ordinary speaking there is a constraint that usually limits the amount of information in a single intonation unit to one new idea – one idea that is being activated in a conversation for the first time (Chafe, 1994: 108–19). New information contrasts with given, already active information. There exists a grey area, however, consisting of information that might at first appear to be new, but that can be inferred from the context. It is contextually *accessible*. The first clause in the second sentence, *we were to keep our heads*, conveys information that is in fact accessible from what immediately preceded: *we were of a common mind about the duty of resistance to extravagant fancies*. The expression *keeping our heads* is essentially a paraphrase of *resisting extravagant fancies*. From that point of view *we were to keep our heads if we should keep nothing else* does not express two new ideas. Beginning with the accessible idea expressed as *we were to keep our heads*, it adds only the second clause, *if we should keep nothing else*. Even that idea, in fact, failed to carry the narrative forward, serving only to reinforce the idea of *keeping our heads*.

All this is to say that, although the second sentence may appear to contain two clauses expressing new information, in fact there is little that is new. Thus, a silent reader's cognitive capacities are not severely taxed by treating this segment as a single prosodic unit, as was demonstrated by the repunctuators. By failing to insert a comma after the word *heads*, James, who used commas very liberally otherwise, showed an intuitive understanding of the small cognitive price exacted by this sequence in its context. But although a punctuation unit of twelve words was no problem for a silent reader, someone who read this passage aloud was constrained by the size of spoken intonation units to break it into two parts at the obvious place. Silent readers, that is, are able to tolerate longer prosodic units than those who read aloud.

If it is true that silent readers interpret written language prosodically, those who read it aloud are constrained by the basic nature of speaking to do it differently. Sometimes they insert more prosodic boundaries, as we have just seen, but sometimes they may insert boundaries in the wrong places and thus create inappropriate intonation contours. Oral readers are often prone to disconnect themselves from the flow of thought as it is reflected in a natural flow of prosody. To the extent that they devote their attention to producing sounds, they can fall into the trap of assigning prosody in nonfunctional ways.

Esser and Polomski (1987: 73–4) discuss an equally subtle example in which the following sentence was interpreted differently by different oral readers:

The debate is more important than the division.

Two out of ten readers followed a pattern in which they gave the most prosodic prominence to the word *division*, less to *debate*, and least to *is more important*. The authors mention that the word *debate* was introduced three sentences earlier; thus that idea was contextually accessible. Furthermore, the idea of greater importance was 'implied in the preceding sentence through the phrase *what lies at the heart of the system*'. They remark that 'such points of reference are too difficult for most of our readers', some of whom, for example, gave maximum prominence to *debate* in spite of the accessibility of that idea, thus showing a disconnection from the flow of thought, or from what Esser and Polomski called a text orientation.

Conclusion

I began by characterizing reading aloud as a rather special use of language that is produced as writing but delivered, often by another person, as speaking. It can be, although it need not be, the most difficult kind of language for an audience to process. In a survey of scholars who presented papers at academic conferences, the majority said they read them aloud instead of speaking them directly. Those who read aloud, however, were less unanimous in their preferences as listeners than those who spoke, almost all of whom preferred to listen to spoken presentations because they believed them to be easier to process.

I discussed an example in which the speaker began by speaking off the cuff and then switched to reading aloud. The differences, even in this small sample, appeared in vocabulary, syntax, and prosody. I then discussed a second example in which a press conference began with prepared, read-aloud remarks that were followed by a more spontaneous sequence of questions and answers. The read-aloud portion was syntactically more elegant, but its prosody might be characterized as monotonous. The spontaneous portion was less fluent and, at the same time, prosodically more varied.

Finally, I mentioned a study of the covert prosody of written language, a private experience that can be investigated in part by asking people to punctuate passages from which all punctuation has been removed, in part by asking people to read the passages aloud. In general, although authors differ in their punctuation habits, there was fairly close agreement between the repunctuators and the punctuation of the original. Those who read the same passages aloud, however, introduced more prosodic breaks than either the authors or the repunctuators, apparently under the constraints of universal speaking habits. Problems for listeners can arise when oral readers introduce prosodic boundaries in the wrong places and inappropriate prosodic contours.

Examining the various ways people read aloud has the potential to teach us more about language in general, in both its written and spoken varieties, and at the same time to make better oral readers of all of us whose professions call for performing language in this way.

Bibliography

Bolinger, D. (1975) *Aspects of Language*, 2nd edn (New York: Harcourt Brace Jovanovich).

Chafe, W. (1988) 'Punctuation and the prosody of written language', *Written Communication*, 5: 395–426.

Chafe, W. (1991) 'Sources of difficulty in the processing of written language', in A.C. Purves (ed.), *The Idea of Difficulty in Literature* (Albany: State University of New York Press) 7–22.

Chafe, W. (1993) 'Prosodic and functional units of language', in J.A. Edwards and M.D. Lampert (eds), *Talking Data: Transcription and Coding in Discourse Research* (Hillsdale, NJ: Lawrence Erlbaum) 33–43.

Chafe, W. (1994) *Discourse, Consciousness, and Time: The Flow and Displacement of Conscious Experience in Speaking and Writing* (Chicago: University of Chicago Press).

Chafe, W. and Danielewicz, J. (1987) 'Properties of spoken and written language', in R. Horowitz and S.J. Samuels (eds), *Comprehending Oral and Written Language* (San Diego: Academic Press) 83–113.

Chafe, W. and Tannen, D. (1987) 'The relation between written and spoken language', *Annual Review of Anthropology*, 16: 383–407.
Esser, J. and Polomski, A. (1987) 'Reading intonation', *Language and Communication*, 7: 59–75.
Esser, J. and Polomski, A. (1988) *Comparing Reading and Speaking Intonation* (Amsterdam: Rodopi).
Hirsch, E.D., Jr. (1977) *The Philosophy of Composition* (Chicago: University of Chicago Press).
Holland, V.M. (1981) 'Psycholinguistic Alternatives to Readability Formulas', Technical Report, 12 (Washington, DC: American Institutes for Research).
James, H. (1966) *The Turn of the Screw: An Authoritative Text, Backgrounds and Sources, Essays in Criticism*, Robert Kimbrough (ed.), (New York: W.W. Norton).
Klare, G.B. (1974) 'Assessing readability', *Reading Research Quarterly*, 10: 62–102.
Welty, E. (1983) *One Writer's Beginnings* (New York: Warner).
Wichmann, A. (2000) *Intonation in Text and Discourse: Beginnings, Middles and Ends* (Harlow: Longman).

4
Intonational Meaning Starting from Talk

Ann Wennerstrom

Introduction

In recent years it has become widely acknowledged that intonational meaning is an essential component of spoken English. The pitch during speech – both its association with text, and the direction and extent of its movement up and down – conveys a great deal of meaning beyond the words themselves. Intonational meaning plays its role at the discourse level, involving the cohesion of a text as information is presented as new, given, or contrastive, and as one phrase is linked to the next. In interactive genres, intonation is central to turn-taking as each participant indicates the intention to retain or relinquish the floor. Topic shifts are also indicated intonationally as are many matters of attitude and self-expression. Thus, in any speech event, participants are continuously providing meaningful cues about the discourse through their own intonation while attending to those cues in others' speech.

In the field of TESOL, the increase in pronunciation textbooks and teacher resource books that include intonation among their topics indicates an interest in this area, as it pertains to language teaching. The development of more sophisticated software for analyzing intonation has contributed to our understanding as well, opening up new possibilities for both materials development and research. This interest goes well beyond an enthusiasm for 'helping learners sound native-like'. Intonation is, instead, becoming accepted as necessary to a full description of English, central to both comprehension and comprehensibility of spoken discourse.

Nevertheless, the field still has a long way to go in fully incorporating intonational meaning into its research and pedagogy. As Chun (2002) laments, intonation has been underrepresented in research journals and books that cover other aspects of language learning. Given the broad acceptance of communicative competence (Canale and Swain, 1980) as a reasonable goal for language learners, it is curious that intonational meaning, which is central to spoken communication, has not kept pace as a focus of research and pedagogy (see Chun, 2002: 99–118 for a review). Questions about intonation are often discussed in isolation rather than integrated with other topics under investigation in the field. Likewise, textbooks have traditionally taught intonation separately from other skills as a part of pronunciation. In fact, relatively little is known about intonation in language learning processes. Language theorists do not even agree upon a complete description of the English intonation system, let alone understand how it is acquired by adult learners. What might it mean to 'have acquired' an intonation pattern? Nor is it understood which aspects of intonation are universal and what the role of transfer is during the acquisition process. Further, little is understood about how intonational meaning is perceived by learners as they listen to spoken English. Does the intonation they hear as input contribute to their language acquisition? There remain many open questions on these topics.

In this chapter I will investigate several issues of intonational meaning in language learning. As a starting point, I will discuss certain formal models of intonation that describe general categories of meaning in English. Drawing from these models, I will provide a brief overview of the major discourse functions of intonational meaning. However, it should also be recognized that language learner discourse may have intonation patterns of its own that do not always coincide neatly with categories available in models developed for standard varieties of English. Because matters of intonation and language learning are so little understood at this stage, I advocate discourse-analytic approaches with a focus on the details of actual learner talk as a promising direction of study. To illustrate this, I will present three short sample analyses of intonation in naturally occurring speech. These show how microanalysis can broaden our understanding of the role played by intonation in learner discourse in the context of the communication as a whole. In addition, I argue that such methods offer possible insights into more general research questions on language learning processes.

Theoretical models of intonational meaning

One arm of past theoretical work on intonational meaning has involved model building; that is, developing systematic inventories of meaningful intonation units for standard varieties of English. From the outset, there have been different schools of thought on what the basic unit of intonational meaning should be. Scholars in the so-called British tradition have focused on the contour as the basic intonational unit, finding a core set of interpretations for an inventory of intonation contours (O'Connor and Arnold, 1961; Halliday, 1967a; Crystal, 1969; Ladd, 1980; Gussenhoven, 1984; Bolinger, 1986; 1989; Cruttendon, 1997; and others). An example of a contour approach is Halliday's (1967a) system of five intonation contours, developed for British English. For each contour, the meaning is mainly conveyed in the tail of the intonation contour, from its 'information focus' or 'tonic syllable' to its end.

In contrast, others in the American tradition have recognized components below the level of the contour (Pike, 1945; Trager and Smith, 1951; Pierrehumbert, 1980). In terms of interpretation, Pierrehumbert and Hirschberg's model (1990) has probably gone the farthest in attempting to assign meaning to small tonal units. In their model, a binary system of meaningful high and low tones defines a skeletal structure of intonation in discourse. The surface intonation contour that we hear is the result of phonetic processes that link the pitch of these basic meaningful tones together.

Other models differ in the type of intonational meaning on which they focus. Brazil's interactional model (1985; 1997) takes Halliday's contours as a starting point but, in fact, identifies several meaningful components within the contour. Specifically, his model emphasizes how speakers continually react to each other in spoken discourse, aligning their pitch at the onsets and terminations of utterances. Theorists have also made various proposals about the sources of intonational meaning. Bolinger (1986; 1989), for example, argues for an emotional basis for intonational high points. Chafe (1994) presents a psycholinguistic model of intonational meaning in which each intonation unit reflects what is currently active in the speaker's consciousness.

This array of theoretical intonation models, each of which is fairly complex, can make it frustrating for classroom teachers, textbook writers, and language researchers from other areas of Applied Linguistics to incorporate intonation into their work. It seems as if whichever book one reads requires one to learn yet another intonation system with its corresponding set of terminology. However, despite the differences among theoretical perspectives, I believe it is possible to draw together some common themes about intonational meaning, especially since theorists are in consensus on its discourse basis. What follows is an outline of four very general areas of discourse meaning for which intonation has been said to make a contribution. This synthesis draws from several of the models mentioned above and is presented in more detail in Wennerstrom (2001a).

Intonation segments the discourse

Virtually all scholars agree that intonation is divided into short units, which I will call *intonational phrases*. These have been variously labelled the 'intermediate phrase' (Pierrehumbert, 1980), the 'tone group' (Halliday, 1967a), the 'intonation-group' (Cruttenden, 1997), the 'tone unit' (Brazil, 1985) and other terms. Intonational phrasing serves to segment the speech into 'information units' (Halliday, 1967a) or 'sense groups' (O'Connor and Arnold, 1961). Chafe (1994) has claimed that each intonational phrase is the optimal length to be held in short-term 'echoic' memory so that listeners can process language in manageable increments as the speaker moves from one intonational phrase to the next.

Intonation also plays a role in segmentation at the topic level of spoken discourse: the initial pitch range is expanded to mark a topic shift in what has been called an 'intonational paragraph' (Lehiste, 1975), or 'paratone' (Brown, 1977; Yule, 1980; Brown and Yule, 1983; Couper-Kuhlen, 1986. See Tench, 1990; Wichmann, 2000 for overviews). Correspondingly, utterances that are meant as asides, when the speaker is 'going off on a tangent', are often presented in a lower pitch range, as a kind of intonational parentheses (Kutik *et al.*, 1983; Bing, 1985; Bolinger, 1989; Wennerstrom, 2001a). These prosodic shifts provide an organizational framework for the discourse much as the formatting conventions of subtitles and paragraph indentations do in written discourse genres.

Intonation provides interactional meaning

Most models of interpretation give a special status to the ends of intonational phrases, which I will call *intonation boundaries*. Although there is disagreement about where 'the end' starts, most would agree that intonation contours undergo 'final lengthening' (Klatt, 1975) so that they are slightly elongated in the last syllables. They also have a direction, such as falling, low-rising, or high-rising. In spoken discourse, these intonation boundaries help to perform a linking function from utterance to utterance to convey a speaker's intentions about how each phrase coheres with the next (Pierrehumbert and Hirschberg, 1990). Thus, in interactive genres of discourse, participants continually attend to intonation boundaries, along with syntactic, lexical, and pragmatic cues in their turn-taking (see Ford and Thompson, 1996; Wennerstrom and Siegel, 2003). Others can anticipate the end of another speaker's turn slightly before its arrival, in part, because of the elongated syllables. Certain typical meanings have come to be associated with particular intonation boundary shapes in conversation. For example, a flat, extended intonation boundary is often used in listing, or in hesitating during a word search, and is therefore frequently a floor-keeping signal. A high-rising boundary is typical in yes–no questions and echo questions, and tends to be a signal of turn relinquishment. Low-rising boundaries usually indicate that the same speaker will continue, but both low- and high-rising boundaries can be used to solicit backchannels, indications that the listener is following the thread of the conversation (see Wennerstrom and Siegel, 2003, for a detailed model).

Another meaningful part of an intonational phrase in interaction comes at the beginning: the term *key* (Brazil, 1985; 1997) refers to the level of pitch, relative to a speaker's overall pitch range, on the first stressed syllable of an intonational phrase. The key indicates the current speaker's stance toward what has come before. *Tone concord* (Brazil, 1985: 86) occurs when the key used at the onset of one speaker's utterance (high, mid, or low in the speaker's pitch range) matches that of the relative pitch level at the termination of the last speaker's utterance. When the second speaker is taking a similar stance to the first, these pitch range choices can be matched, whereas *concord breaking*, a mismatch of pitch ranges from one utterance to the next, may be present in disagreement, or in Brazil's words, 'at moments when there is a discrepancy between the ways the two parties assess the context of interaction' (ibid.). In interactive genres of discourse, these subtle intonational cues are continuously attended to as participants respond to each other.

Intonation is part of discourse cohesion

Another area of agreement among intonation theorists is that in discourse, intonation is important in carrying the thread of the main ideas because it reflects the information value of lexical items. Generally speaking, the stressed syllables of content words (nouns, verbs, adjectives, and adverbs) are slightly more prominent – higher pitched, louder in volume, and longer in duration – than are the surrounding unstressed syllables and the function words (such as prepositions, articles, auxiliaries, and so on). At a higher level, the information structure of the discourse also plays a role in pitch choices – ideas that are newly introduced or otherwise the 'information focus' (Halliday, 1967b) are usually associated with higher pitch – Brazil's 'tonic syllable' or Pierrehumbert's (1980) 'high pitch accent', while information assumed to be accessible is usually uttered with a lower pitch, or 'deaccent' (Ladd, 1980). Contrasts in discourse are especially marked intonationally with a high pitch peak relative to the rest of the intonational phrase.

Intonation provides expressive and pragmatic meaning

Whatever the basic structure of an intonational sequence may be, it can also be exaggerated or minimized due to emotional delivery or other pragmatic factors, as in shouting to be heard at a distance or murmuring a snide remark under one's breath. In such cases, speakers can exploit pitch range so that an entire sequence is uttered in an expanded or compressed range, or in an extremely high or low pitch range. Speakers can also delineate each individual word intonationally instead of the more common intonational phrasing with a main focus for every several words.

These pragmatic functions of intonation are little studied and apparently quite vast. Clearly, the genre is important in how they are used. Tench (1991) identified distinctive intonational patterns that characterize particular genres, such as anecdote, prayer, news reading, and informal conversation. Thus, each genre can be said to have its own 'intonational signature'. Social identity is also a factor in these paralinguistic aspects of intonation. Chun (2002) points out that intonation is one of the features that affect hearers' perceptions of age, sex, regional background, and occupation. She also emphasizes the role of intonation in perceptions of foreign accent (pp. 66–7), which can be quite important since, as Lippi-Green (1997) documents, discrimination against those with nonstandard accents is prevalent in many social realms.

Intonation and the discourse of language learners

So far, we have seen an overview of some of the major aspects of intonational meaning that have been attributed to English by model builders. By describing a basic set of meaningful categories for the intonation of native speakers of standard varieties of English, such work provides an important starting point for researchers and teachers in ESOL. Models such as these can provide pedagogical targets, as in Bradford (1988), who uses Brazil's model to develop pronunciation materials. Theoretical models can also provide bases of comparison in research on interlanguage speech. For example, Wennerstrom (1994) focused on simply demonstrating that learners' intonation did not match the native-speaker model of Pierrehumbert and Hirschberg (1990). Finally, theoretical models can be used to estimate native-speaker interpretations of learners' intonation. Pickering (1999; 2001; 2004) makes effective use of Brazil's model to investigate the interaction between foreign graduate teaching assistants in the United States and their native-speaking American undergraduate students. In a 1999 study of chemistry lab sessions, Pickering concluded that the American students interpreted a frequent use of high key at utterance onsets as a criticism or distancing on the part of their Chinese-born teaching assistants.

However, there are also some limitations to what these formal models have to offer regarding matters of language learning. I will suggest that additionally, a bottom-up analysis of the details of intonation in talk can compliment top-down, model-based work. At issue is the fact that the main models of intonational meaning that exist at the time of this writing were all developed for standard varieties of English. Furthermore, the methodology of formal model building itself must necessarily rely on abstract categories, since the goal is to identify an inventory of linguistic forms that correspond to distinctive meanings. Therefore, the categories of meaning one finds in theoretical models tend to be idealized and may fail to capture local details of nonnative speech. It may be that the intonation found in learner discourse cannot be precisely described in terms of a native speaker model because of patterns transferred from the learner's native language, or because the learning process itself leads to intermediate interlanguage patterns. Perhaps the communication strategies entailed in negotiating cross-cultural discourse situations may also lead to certain intonational patterns, not only in learners themselves, but also in native speaker interlocutors. Studies of the minute details of intonation in learner discourse can lead us to a better understanding of the contribution of these patterns to the interaction, their psychological or social sources, and their effects on participants' comprehension of the discourse.

A discourse-first approach

In order to go 'below' the abstract categories presented in theoretical models, I suggest a 'discourse-first' methodology to understand language learners' intonation. By identifying a discourse phenomenon as a starting point and then looking for accompanying linguistic patterns, we can enrich our understanding of intonational meaning in action and eventually refine our theoretical models. Such analyses also provide natural contexts in which to integrate intonation analysis with other applied linguistic research.

Examples of this type of microanalysis can be found in the work of Gumperz, who has long taken a social action approach to understanding cross-cultural communication. His studies of interactions between British and Indian speakers of English start with cross-cultural misunderstandings, which he traces to mismatches in 'contextualization cues' (Gumperz, 1982; 1992). He defines contextualization cues to include various linguistic mechanisms, among which is intonation. Gumperz (1982) discusses cross-cultural miscommunications between British and Indian speakers of English. In one conversation, for example, an Indian speaker used a prosodic pattern of slowed rhythm and an exaggerated intonation contour to cue the listener that what was to come was of particular importance. The British listener instead dismissed what followed as unimportant, apparently missing or ignoring this contextualization cue (p. 178). According to Gumperz, most Indian speakers would have recognized this cue but cross-culturally the prosodic discourse features differed.

In another example, Davies and Tyler (1994) analyzed the discourse of international graduate students who were employed as teaching assistants at American universities. Their study looked at sequences in which the teaching assistants and their native-speaker undergraduate students misunderstood each other. One of their examples focused on a Chinese teaching assistant who was interrupted by a native speaker. Davies and Tyler noticed a mismatch between the lexicogrammatical structure and the intonation, which dropped to the bottom of the nonnative speaker's pitch range. This was followed by overlapping speech between the two – the teaching assistant had not finished speaking, yet the falling pitch was apparently interpreted as a turn closure by the native speaker.

Another microanalytic study by Edmondson *et al.* (1984) investigated spontaneous role plays between German learners of English and native speakers. They found that the German speakers gave contradictory signals due to a prevalence of rising intonation at syntactic boundaries where the native speakers used falling intonation. This contrasts with Davies and Tyler's (1994) finding, where it was the falling intonation that was confusing to the native speaker. In both cases, it seems to be the mismatch between the intonation and the lexicogrammatical structure that was problematic from a native speaker perspective.

This type of exploratory, microanalytic work on intonation can lead to an understanding of a greater variety of its discourse functions. By starting with the talk itself and by keeping an open mind about what the appropriate intonational categories might be, theorists can gain new insights into interlanguage intonation in various discourse contexts and eventually develop more sophisticated models. More generally, because intonation is central to oral communication – we have seen how it relates to discourse segmentation, turn-taking, information structure, discourse coherence, and self-expression – questions about the intonation of learners in talk can be naturally integrated with broader questions in the fields of TESOL and Applied Linguistics.

Sample analyses

In this section, three short sample analyses are presented to demonstrate how research on intonation through the microanalysis of talk might proceed. By zeroing in on seemingly eclectic details, we can consider patterns of intonation not necessarily predicted by the native-speaker intonation models. Moreover, such analyses can help us revisit more general questions about language learning that have traditionally been asked about syntax, segmental phonology, and other aspects of learner discourse. All of the analyses here are taken from discourse contexts of Japanese ESOL students in an intensive English programme in the United States. In the first two samples, the students are conversing with American native speakers in a 'conversation partners' programme of volunteers. In the last one, the speaker is telling an informal anecdote as part of a classroom assignment.

Taking a 'discourse-first' approach, I have chosen three topics to highlight in the sample analyses. The first centres on the heavily monitored, word-by-word speech of a learner who was frequently interrupted. This raises the question of how intonational phrasing interacts with the information structure of the discourse in less fluent speech. If high points are associated with new ideas, then what do short intonational phrases, with as few as one word per intonational phrase, tell us about the psycholinguistic processes of this and other similar learners? The second topic involves the intonation of the 'foreigner talk' of a native speaker in conversation with an ESOL student. Although the importance of foreigner talk as simplified input has been the focus of much research, its intonational patterns have hardly been discussed in the literature. Because intonation conveys discourse meaning, and because it has been claimed as important in processing (Chafe, 1994), the intonation of foreigner talk could be important in broader questions about listening comprehension and the role of input in acquisition. The third topic involves the use of quoted speech in story telling, where a speaker was found to use especially high pitch. This fact connects to research on the pragmatics of self-expression and on the utility of invoking a variety of discourse genres for teaching and research purposes. In this case, the genre of story telling provided an opportunity for the student to use language more expressively than other genres might have.

The brief sample analyses that follow are not meant to be fully fledged studies, but rather suggestions for how others might proceed with the added dimension of intonational meaning as part of future discourse analyses. These topics represent mere possibilities among a range of other options in this little-studied area.

Analysis 1: intonational phrasing and fluency

Many pronunciation textbooks devote page space to linking and phrasing (see, for example, Gilbert, 1993; Grant, 2001; Meyers and Holt, 2001), the goal being to help students connect words together within phrases instead of pausing between each word. Often the final consonant of one word can be resyllabified with the onset of the next. As these textbook writers recognize, many language learners tend to produce an interlanguage pattern of word-by-word speech rather than more fluent phrasing.

The following short dialogue between a Japanese woman studying English (Keiko)[1] and an American man (Jack) illustrates word-by-word speech.[2] The woman is explaining her plan to speak to a group of American elementary school students ('they' in line (1)), who don't know very much about modern Japanese lifestyle. In this transcript, the numbers in parentheses indicate the approximate pause length between each word, the upward arrow (↗) represents a low-rising intonation boundary, and the accent mark (á) indicates an accented syllable (see Appendix, p. 94 for a full set of transcription symbols):

(1) Keiko: ... but (.2) théy dón't knów thé (.3) ah (.6) uh (.5) áctual↗

(2)   Jápanese↗ lífe (.9).

(3)   So (.3) Í wánt- (.6) -téd to sáy thé (1.5) ah (.4)

(4)   Jápanese lífe↗ ís símilar to yóurs. (1.0)

(5) Jack: the whát↗

(6)   Keiko: Jápanese↗ (.2) lífe↗ (.6)   /stýle↗
(7)   Jack: \lífestyle lífestyle   /yéah
(8)   Keiko: \yeah
(9)   wé dón't (.3) wéar↗ (.6) kimóno↗ (.2) wé wéar↗ (.3)
             súits↗ (.6)
(10) Jack: y /és↗
(11) Keiko: \ór (.6) jéans↗ (.5)
(12) Jack: yés↗

Figures 4.1 and 4.2 zero in on the intonation of a small portion of the utterance in line 9.[3] The amplitude (roughly speaking, the volume) is shown in the upper half of the diagram and the pitch is shown in the lower half:

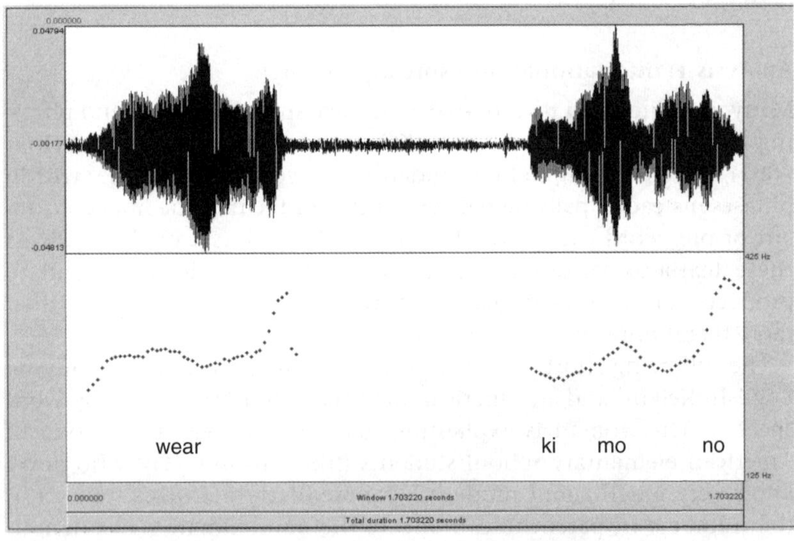

Figure 4.1   Word-by-word speech (in this Japanese speaker's carefully monitored English, each word occupies a single intonational phrase)

In these figures, we can see that Keiko gives a high pitch accent to every word and inserts a low-rising intonation boundary after many words. This pattern is representative of her intonation throughout the passage: function words are accented, intonational phrases are short, and there are frequent pauses between words. In part, the pattern may be the result of transfer from Japanese intonation, which does not have unstressed function words as English does (Thompson, 2001: 299).

However, transfer does not explain the short phrases, since Japanese has been described as having longer intonational contours to coincide with syntactic phrases and sentences (Abe, 1998: 362).

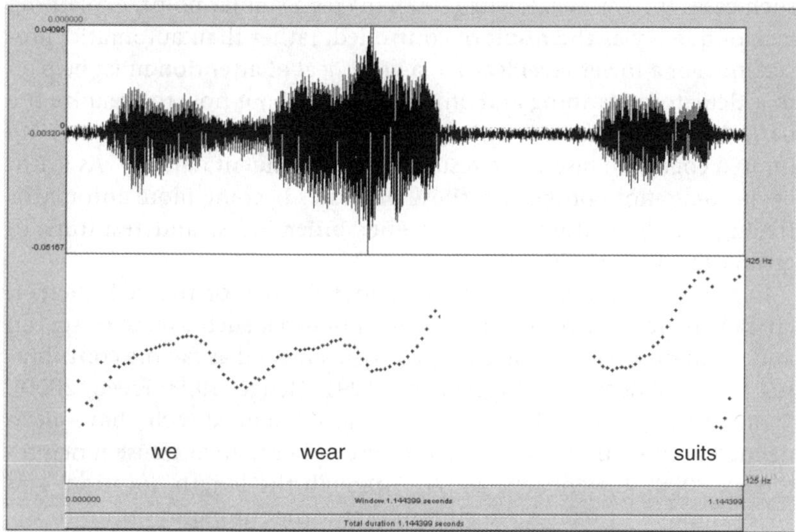

Figure 4.2 Continuing from Figure 4.1 (each word is intonationally distinct)

As discussed in Wennerstrom (2000), this speaker and nine others were rated in fluency by two ESOL teachers, and factors in the speech that might have led to these ratings were compared. In the study, Keiko was rated the lowest in fluency of the ten speakers (p. 109). Her speech segment also seemed to present processing difficulties to the American participant, Jack, who misinterpreted Keiko's point through-out several turn exchanges (pp. 122–3). Although there may have been a combination of reasons for his lack of comprehension, I suggested that Jack was attuned to hearing longer intonational phrases with a single main focus per phrase. The main points may not have been as apparent when almost every content word was singled out as a main idea with its own intonational high point. Moreover, it may have been difficult to judge when Keiko was signalling a turn completion because the frequent low-rising intonation boundaries could be interpreted as requests for confirmation that Jack was following. In fact, Keiko was frequently interrupted during this conversation as Jack attempted to reassure her that he understood her at each stage (ibid.).

It has been proposed that the reason for short intonational phrases in the speech of language learners is the high cognitive load involved in speaking an unfamiliar language. As Hewings (1995) notes, the amount of linguistic material that can be pre-planned is restricted in such cases (p. 37). Segalowitz (2000) makes a similar point, explaining lack of fluency as the result of controlled, rather than automatic, processing. For a lower-level learner, a great deal of attention must be paid to articulatory planning and other decisions about how to organize the basic linguistic elements of speech. Controlled processing uses up limited cognitive resources, resulting in a less fluent delivery. As learners become more proficient, these processes become more automatic, freeing up their attention for higher order ideas, and resulting in greater fluency (pp. 209–10).

In studies of raters' judgements about fluency or the lack thereof, characteristics related to intonational phrasing, such as rate of speech and nonnative pauses, have frequently been cited as factors contributing to raters' decisions (Riggenbach, 1991; Hedge, 1993; Freed, 2000). 'Nonnative' pauses, characteristic of less fluent speech, have been defined as those that occur in mid-clause rather than at clause junctures (Freed, 2000; Riggenbach, 2001). Although the length, location, and sheer number of pauses are all important, the intonation prior to the pauses may also enter into raters' judgements of fluency. In the study of Keiko's speech mentioned above (Wennerstrom, 2000), I found that some of the more fluent speakers used long 'plateau' intonation boundaries on the words prior to the pauses, in contrast to Keiko's frequent rising intonation. The plateaus seemed to imply a careful consideration of the subject matter rather than an overmonitoring of the speech itself and raters thus judged the speech as more fluent (pp. 119–20).

Another related topic raised by this analysis is the relationship between learners' intonation and individual differences in learning style. It has been shown that some learners approach a new language more holistically while others take a more analytical approach (for discussions see Larsen-Freeman and Long, 1991: 65–9; Mitchell and Myles, 1998: 89–94; Skehan, 1998: 237–57). Word-by-word speech, such as Keiko's, may represent the analytical end of the spectrum of learning styles, in which the speaker pre-plans and monitors each word very carefully. In contrast, a more holistic style with less self-monitoring and a greater reliance on routinized language chunks would be characterized by longer intonational phrases. Such speech may sound more fluent even if the grammar is less accurate (Lennon, 2000). As

Wong-Fillmore (1995), has pointed out, the holistic style may create a social advantage, affording the language learner greater access to target-language social networks and thus an increased opportunity for the meaningful interaction necessary for language acquisition.

A more practical question stemming from this analysis concerns pedagogical practices. Derwing and Rossiter (2003) conducted a controlled study of ESOL students in three different instructional settings: one with pronunciation instruction that emphasized segments; a second with pronunciation instruction that emphasized prosody; and a third, control setting with no special pronunciation instruction. They found that instruction in pronunciation with a focus on prosody led over time to higher ratings in comprehensibility and fluency than did the segmental instruction. These authors suggest that an overemphasis on segmental pronunciation can distract a learner's attention and actually lead to a loss of fluency in speech (pp. 12–13). This may well be a factor in Keiko's word-by-word speech. In the excerpt we saw in Figures 4.1 and 4.2, where the word *wear* is repeated twice and the word *kimono* is Japanese, it is unlikely that an extended lexical search is responsible for the short phrases associated with these particular items. Instead, a concentration on careful articulation of the segments seems a more likely explanation.

Although the Derwing and Rossiter study indicates that instruction that focuses on prosody is helpful, it is not clear what sort of instruction will be most effective. If it is true that word-by-word speech can stem from the expenditure of cognitive resources on monitoring one's linguistic choices overall, then perhaps general language instruction that includes lexical and grammatical development is necessary before longer intonational phrases can be produced naturally. Many researchers have also emphasized the importance of routinized lexical patterns in language development and fluency (Nattinger and DeCarrico, 1992; Lewis, 1993; Oppenheim, 2000). Perhaps explicit instruction in producing useful lexical chunks with appropriate intonational phrasing could encourage a more holistic speech style for those learners who over-monitor their speech.

To summarize, this analysis of a very short segment of speech has shown a pattern of interlanguage intonation with interesting characteristics. Keiko's short phrases can be discussed in terms of the cognitive mechanisms that underlie them, the learning style involved, and the resulting native-speaker judgements of a lack of fluency. I hope to have provided some insight into an interlanguage intonation pattern that differs from the native-language model, while showing how a careful look at intonation can be relevant to other areas of applied linguistic research.

Analysis 2: the intonation of foreigner talk

One question that has appeared on the agenda of second language researchers over the years is how to characterize 'foreigner talk', the discourse used by native speakers to address language learners, which is noted to be more simplified than speech directed to other native speakers. Early on, research questions about foreigner talk included how to characterize it in terms of syntax and lexicon (Ferguson, 1975; Freed, 1978; Arthur *et al.*, 1980), what its higher order discourse features were (Hatch, Shapira and Wagner-Gough, 1978; Long 1980; 1983; Tarone, 1980); how it compared to 'parentese' – the talk of parents to their infants (Freed, 1980); and whether it was beneficial to the language acquisition process. On the last question, opinions varied as to whether foreigner talk, being sometimes ungrammatical, was a poor source of input for second language acquisition (Ferguson, 1975), or whether it occurred as a natural result of a desire to negotiate meaning and achieve understanding, and was thus an aid in comprehension and thereby acquisition (Long, 1980; 1996). As to its intonation, although it has been claimed that foreigner talk includes 'wider pitch range/exaggerated intonation' (see Larsen-Freeman and Long, 1991: 125), to my knowledge there have been no systematic attempts to characterize what exactly this 'exaggerated intonation' is like.

Let us turn then to a sample of foreigner talk with an eye for intonational meaning. The following dialogue occurred between a female speaker of Standard American English (Janet) and a Japanese female ESOL student at an intermediate level (Miyako). They are discussing whether Miyako and her parents might move in together when the parents get older:

```
(1)  Janet:      Would your parents move in with you
(2)              when they get    /old?
(3)  Miyako:                      \nnn yes
(4)              they wants me to take care of them.
(5)  Janet:      But would it be more easy for you
(6)              even if you were married
(7)              to move back into the family house
(8)              even     /if it is bigger?
(9)  Miyako:              \no::::::::::
```

(10)		I don't hh
(11)		I don't want to live them.
(12)		But I ha-
(13)		maybe I have to do.
(14)	Janet:	To do that?

From this text, one can read a lexico-syntactic simplification typical of foreigner talk from the native speaker, Janet, in line 5 (*would it be more easy* instead of *would it be easier*). Janet also recasts Miyako's grammar in line 14 (the addition of *that* to Miyako's *maybe I have to do*). A quick look with computerized speech technology at Janet's intonation also reveals some interesting facts. Figure 4.3 shows a small section of her speech from line 5, *more easy for you.*

As we might expect from past research on foreigner talk, Janet has a rather slow rate of speech – about two seconds for the entire phrase. The reader is invited to do the experiment of reading this phrase aloud while timing two seconds to get a sense of the slow speed. In addition, we can see in the lower part of the figure that the speaker is elongating and flattening each syllable, with *more* and *you* being almost com-

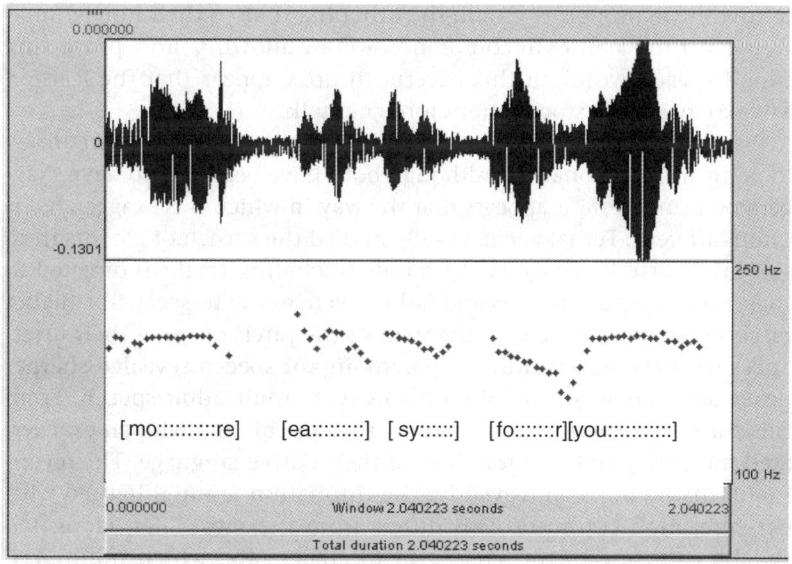

Figure 4.3   Foreigner talk (this segment of foreigner talk is characterized by flat, elongated syllables and a lack of reduction on *for* and the second syllable of *easy*)

pletely flat and *ea-*, *-sy*, and *for* falling slightly in pitch during the extension. These flattened syllables contrast with the usual sharper peaks of English spoken at a faster speed. Of particular interest is the function word *for* and the second syllable of *easy*. Although these would be unstressed in standard speech, their pitch and duration are on par with those of the other syllables of the phrase. We also observe a separation between words within the phrase, most marked after *more* and *easy*. In some ways, this resembles the situation in Sample Analysis 1 where we saw the word-by-word speech of a learner. There, I hypothesized that this pattern tended to obscure the thread of the discourse because the distinctions between content words and function words were not emphasized and each word was presented as a new idea.

With this in mind, we can now return to past literature on foreigner talk and frame new questions about whether it enhances acquisition: If it is true that high pitch is a signal to call attention to a new or contrastive idea, then do these elongated, flat pitch patterns on every syllable allow learners to make distinctions in the information structure? Do they even allow for a distinction between content and function words? Are they thus 'deviant input' intonationally, providing a bad model of intonation for learners to emulate while making it difficult to follow the main point? Or, on the other hand, does their longer duration assist the learner in comprehension by allowing more processing time for each word? In this excerpt, it does appear that the learner, Miyako, has understood Janet's foreigner talk.

We can also revisit the comparison of foreigner talk to 'parentese', looking at this intonation. Although both have been said to have exaggerated intonation, it appears that the way in which it is exaggerated is quite different. Fernald *et al.* (1989) studied the speech of parents from several diverse language backgrounds (including English) directed to their infants. Both mothers and fathers were found to speak in a higher pitch range and to increase the span of the pitch range of their utterances (p. 491). As a result, the parent–infant speech revealed sharper peaks and valleys in the pitch tracks than adult–adult speech. From this study, it appears that parentese provides children with an exaggerated modelling of the intonation of their native language. The meaningful distinctions conveyed by the intonation are highlighted with extreme pitch contrasts. This differs from the rather flat, elongated syllables we saw in the sample of foreigner talk, which minimized the intonational distinctions between content and function words. Although this brief analysis of foreigner talk probably raises more questions than it answers, the point is simply to suggest that foreigner talk might be an interesting area to reconsider by including an intonation analysis because studies in the past have not addressed this meaningful aspect of discourse in detail. Such an analysis could reopen broader topics such as the learner's processing of information structure in foreigner talk and its role in acquisition.

Analysis 3: high pitch, quoted speech, and the pragmatics of self-expression

The focus of the final sample analysis is on how, regardless of their language background, speakers exploit their pitch range for expressive and pragmatic functions. One area where this is clearly the case is in quoted speech, which is often set off by prosodic boundaries (Bauman, 1986; Wennerstrom, 2001a; b). As Labov (1972) noted, quoted speech in personal narratives is evaluative; that is, it is used when speakers wish to express their personal attitude toward the events they are describing. Bauman (1986) also found that quoted speech could be used to deliver the punch line of funny anecdotes told by rural West Texan males. In a study of German conversations, Selting (1994) described a higher pitched 'emphatic speech style' used at points of high emotional involvement. Based on these prior findings, it is not unexpected that speakers who use quoted speech for evaluative purposes will alter their pitch range, exploiting the paralinguistic, expressive function of intonation

The following excerpt is drawn from a personal anecdote, told in English by a Japanese woman (Yoko). It concerns a three-hour car trip to a beach during which the teller, helpfully trying to keep the driver's brand new car clean, took off her shoes and left them on the curb at the start of the trip. We find quoted speech used in line (4):

(1)   And so two cars are heading for the beach.
(2)   It wa- took about three hours to go to the beach,
(3)   but when we arrived at the beach,
(4)   'Okay, we are here. Let's swim',
(5)   one- one of my friends said.
(6)   And they got out of the car and waited.
(7)   They're waiting for me.
(8)   But I couldn't find my shoes.

This is a highly evaluative sequence as Yoko is recounting the main tension of the story: her friends expect that she will join in the fun at the beach, but she cannot participate because she is uncomfortable leaving the car without shoes. Figure 4.4 shows the transition from the narrated portion of the story to the quoted portion, where the pitch jumps to a higher range. This intonation pattern is not unexpected from a Japanese speaker. According to Abe (1998), heightened pitch to show 'psychological involvement' or to give special emphasis is a feature in Japanese (p. 362) just as it is in English. Thompson (2001) makes a similar claim, suggesting that the broadening of pitch range in Japanese 'to show interest and involvement' may be a 'near-universal' (p. 299).

This sample analysis of high-pitched quoted speech ties into the literature on pragmatics and language learning. The use of expressive intonation may be universal, but decisions about how and when to express emotion or enthusiasm appropriately have a cultural basis. We have just seen an appropriate use of exaggerated pitch to introduce a quotation in Yoko's story, where transfer from Japanese of a similar, pragmatic story telling device may be at work. However, there may be other pragmatic uses of expressive pitch that do not transfer as positively and may involve subtle issues of politeness. Brown and Levinson (1987) claim that exaggerated prosody can either mitigate or augment the degree of politeness (or lack thereof) conveyed in the words themselves. While expanded pitch range can be used to show enthusiasm and emotional affiliation (p. 104), it can also make an utterance sound more challenging (p. 133).

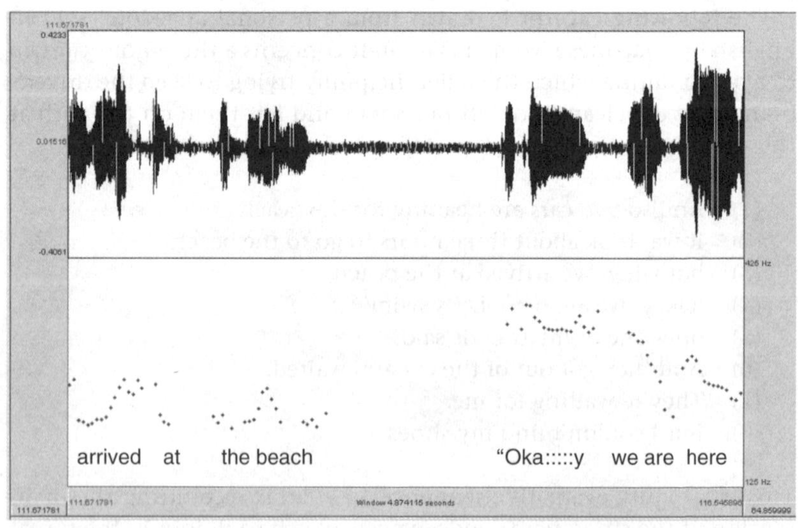

Figure 4.4 Quoted speech (a Japanese speaker of English quotes another's words in a higher pitch)

In a cross-cultural study of pitch and politeness, Loveday (1981) investigated the intonation of Japanese learners of English reading dialogues containing polite phrases. These were compared to the same dialogues read by native speakers of American English. Among the Americans, both males and females used a higher, expressive pitch on the polite phrases. However, among the Japanese, in whose native language pitch is used to distinguish genders, the females raised their pitch on the polite phrases but the males' pitch remained very flat. One Japanese man said that he felt 'feminine' (and thereby uncomfortable) when intoning politely in English (p. 71). As Chun (2002) points out, the males' flat pitch range could indicate 'boredom and detachment', rather than politeness, to native speakers (p. 107). In sum, there may be a range of uses for expressive pitch whose pragmatic effects vary from language to language.

Bardovi-Harlig (1992) and Kaspar and Rose (2001) argue that such matters of cross-cultural pragmatics can to some extent be taught in the ESOL classroom. Explicit teaching can heighten language learners' awareness of the pragmatic conventions of the target culture and provide linguistic means to express the pragmatic functions. According to Kaspar and Rose, learners of a new language usually have a good deal of pragmatic knowledge already, either from universal pragmatic principles, or from similar conventions in their own culture, but they tend to underuse their knowledge. Since expanded pitch range to express emotion is common to many languages, this intonation could offer an entry point to discussions in the classroom of the pragmatics of emotional expression. Perhaps as a consciousness-raising activity, students could role-play and videotape their discourse and later observe their own uses of heightened pitch along with other expressive language. This could lead to further discussion of the pragmatic effects of different forms of expressive language as they vary from one culture to another.

Another connection between this sample analysis of quoted speech and broader areas of Applied Linguistics has to do with the role of genre in language use (see Swales, 1990; Bhatia, 1993; Johns, 1997; Paltridge, 2001; Wennerstrom, 2003). Genres can be understood as conventionalized forms of discourse that accomplish repeated social actions within particular discourse communities. As Biber (1995) has shown through the analysis of large corpora of texts in several languages, certain lexical and grammatical patterns are more apt to occur in some genres of discourse than in others. This body of work (see also Biber, 1988; 1992; Biber, Conrad and Reppen, 1998) has vast implications for language teaching, assessment, and research because it shows that the genres to which learners are exposed will influence the linguistic structures to which they have access and thus have the opportunity to acquire. This means that by studying a variety of discourse genres, students can become more versatile language users. Hughes (1989) has made the same point for testing, urging that multiple genres be included in assessment measures in order to understand the full range of a language learner's proficiency.

Intonational patterns, I have argued (Wennerstrom, 1997), also cluster according to the genre of spoken discourse in which speakers engage. For example, we are obviously more likely to find the turn-taking functions of intonation in conversation than in monologic genres such as lecturing. Conversely, the lecture genre is a more likely site for the higher order topic-marking functions of intonation – the 'paratones' (Brown, 1977; Brown and Yule, 1983; Couper-Kuhlen, 1986). This leads to the conclusion that a pedagogy that exposes students to a variety of genres will give learners more versatility, not only in lexicon and grammar, but also in using intonation patterns in discourse. Our sample analysis provided an example of how the story telling genre naturally led to the inclusion of expressive elements, such as the high-pitched quoted speech. These expressive functions might be less frequent in pedagogical materials that were restricted to, for example, the more academic genres.

In sum, the point of this short analysis is to show that by studying a small detail of expressive intonation, we were able to link research on prosody to broader topics such as cross-cultural pragmatics, the role of genre, and language universals.

Conclusion

I have argued that because intonational meaning is central to a full understanding of spoken English, it deserves more attention in TESOL and Applied Linguistics. If researchers are to better understand language acquisition, language production, listening comprehension, and discourse strategies in the context of communication as a whole, intonational meaning should be a central part of the programme. Likewise, if language teachers are to foster communicative competence in their students, it is essential that intonational meaning be integrated with other skills in the classroom. I have recommended that the discourse of language learners could provide a good starting point for both teaching and researching intonational meaning in context. As we saw in the first two sample analyses, there are patterns of interlanguage intonation that cannot be precisely classified using categories from theoretical models developed for native speakers. In Sample Analysis 1, a language learner's intonational phrasing was constrained by the cognitive demands of overmonitoring in conversation. In Sample Analysis 2, a native speaker's 'foreigner talk' was slowed down and the syllables elongated in an attempt to be more comprehensible. Both of these intonation patterns seem to be artifacts of discourse construction in cross-cultural talk rather than the result of a native-language pattern. In Sample Analysis 3, intonation was used in quoted speech in story telling, which may tap into a universal tendency to associate high pitch with expressive language.

Implications are apparent for the instruction of spoken English. There is a need for pedagogical materials that integrate consciousness raising about intonational meaning within the context of communication as a whole. In the classroom, language learning activities can focus on tapes and transcripts of actual speech as learners themselves explore their own interactions (see Riggenbach, 1999 for a discourse-analysis approach to classroom practice). With teacher guidance, learners can discuss and analyze a variety of language patterns in context, including those of intonation. By varying the genre, additional special functions of intonation might be discovered.

These sample analyses have also shown how intonation research is immediately connected to broader questions in the field of Applied Linguistics, concerning an array of topics: fluency, psycholinguistic processing, language monitoring, cross-cultural pragmatics, the role of input in acquisition and comprehension, and the role of genre in language use are only a few of the possibilities. Research on intonation need not be isolated from other areas, but can actually serve as a starting point to reconsider issues of language learning and cross-cultural communication that have previously been addressed from different perspectives and with other research methodologies.

In the future, more studies are needed of intonational meaning in the discourse of language learners. There is a particular need for longitudinal studies of how the intonation of individuals changes over time. Taking a discourse first approach, researchers might ask, for example, how a learner's strategy for making a contrast changes over time, or how the ability to keep the floor in conversation develops over time. Such studies have the potential to enrich our theoretical understanding of intonational meaning while providing insights about other aspects of language acquisition and use. As we move forward in our research on spoken genres of discourse, intonational meaning must become more and more integrated with other aspects of language. The analysis of intonation in naturally occurring talk offers theorists, educators, and language students a bottom-up methodology to better understand spoken communication as a whole.

Appendix

Transcription symbols

The following transcription symbols are used:

sa:::::y	extended syllable
á	stressed syllable
↗	low-rising intonation boundary
ca-	cut-off speech
(.4)	pause duration in seconds
/word \word	overlapping speech
hh	syllables of laughter

Notes

1 Pseudonyms are used throughout these analyses.
2 This transcript and Figures 4.1 and 4.2 are adapted with kind permission from the University of Michigan Press from Wennerstrom (2000), 'The role of intonation in second language fluency', in H. Riggenbach (ed.), *Perspectives on Fluency* (Ann Arbor, MI: University of Michigan Press, 102–27.
3 The software used to generate this figure was PRAAT.

Bibliography

Abe, I. (1998) 'Intonation in Japanese', in D. Hirst and A. Di Christo (eds), *Intonation Systems: A Survey of Twenty Languages* (Cambridge: Cambridge University Press) 360–75.

Arthur, B., Weiner, M., Culver, J., Young, L. and Thomas, D. (1980) 'The register of impersonal discourse to foreigners: verbal adjustments to foreign accent', in D. Larsen-Freeman (ed.), *Discourse Analysis in Second Language Research* (Rowley, MA: Newbury House) 111–24.

Bardovi-Harlig, K. (1992) 'Pragmatics as a part of teacher education', *TESOL Journal*, 1: 28–32.

Bauman, R. (1986) *Story, Performance, and Event* (Cambridge: Cambridge University Press).

Bhatia, V. (1993) *Analyzing Genre: Language in Professional Settings* (London: Longman).

Biber, D. (1988) *Variation Across Speech and Writing* (Cambridge: Cambridge University Press).

Biber, D. (1992) 'On the complexity of discourse complexity: a multidimensional analysis', *Discourse Processes*, 15: 133–63.

Biber, D. (1995) *Dimensions of Register Variation: A Cross-Linguistic Comparison* (Cambridge: Cambridge University Press).

Biber, D., Conrad, S. and Reppen, R. (1998) *Corpus Linguistics: Investigating Language Structure and Use* (Cambridge: Cambridge University Press).

Bing, J. (1985) *Aspects of English Prosody* (New York: Garland).

Bolinger, D. (1986) *Intonation and Its Parts* (Stanford: Stanford University Press).

Bolinger, D. (1989) *Intonation and Its Uses* (Stanford: Stanford University Press).

Bradford, B. (1988) *Intonation in Context: Intonation Practice for Upper-Intermediate and Advanced Learners of English* (New York: Cambridge University Press).

Brazil, D. (1985) 'The communicative value of intonation', Discourse Analysis Monograph 8, (Birmingham: University of Birmingham English Language Research).

Brazil, D. (1997) *The Communicative Value of Intonation in English* (London: Cambridge University Press).

Brown, G. (1977) *Listening to Spoken English* (London: Longman).

Brown, G. and Yule, G. (1983) *Discourse Analysis* (Cambridge: Cambridge University Press).

Brown, P. and Levinson, S. (1987) *Politeness: Some Universals in Language Usage* (Cambridge: Cambridge University Press).

Canale, M. and Swain, M. (1980) 'Theoretical bases of communicative approaches to second language teaching and testing', *Applied Linguistics*, 1: 1–47.

Chafe, W. (1994) *Discourse, Consciousness, and Time: The Flow and Displacement of Conscious Experience in Speaking and Writing* (Chicago: University of Chicago Press).

Chun, D. (2002) *Discourse Intonation in L2: From Theory and Research to Practice* (Amsterdam: John Benjamins).

Couper-Kuhlen, E. (1986) *An Introduction to English Prosody* (Baltimore: Edward Arnold).

Cruttendon, A. (1997) *Intonation*, 2nd edn (Cambridge: Cambridge University Press).

Crystal, D. (1969) *Prosodic Systems and Intonation in English* (Cambridge: Cambridge University Press).

Davies, C. and Tyler, A. (1994) 'Demystifying Cross-cultural (mis)communication: improving performance through balanced feedback in a situated context', in C. Madden and C. Myers (eds), *Discourse and Performance of International Teaching Assistants* (Alexandria, VA: TESOL) 201–20.

Derwing, T. and Rossiter, M. (2003) 'The effects of pronunciation instruction on accuracy, fluency and complexity of L2 accented speech', *Applied Language Learning*, 13, 1: 1–17.

Edmondson, W., House, J., Kasper, G. and Stemmer, B. (1984) 'Learning the pragmatics of discourse: a project report', *Applied Linguistics*, 5, 2: 113–27.

Ferguson, C. (1975) 'Towards a characterization of English foreigner talk', *Anthropological Linguistics*, 17: 1–14.

Fernald, A., Taeschner, T., Dunn, J., Paponsek, M., DeBoysson-Bardies, B. and Fukui, I. (1989) 'A cross language study of prosodic modification in mothers' and fathers' speech to preverbal infants', *Child Language*, 16: 477–501.

Ford, C. and Thompson, S. (1996) 'Interactional units in conversation: syntactic, intonational, and pragmatic resources for the management of turns', in E. Ochs, E. Schegloff, and S. Thompson (eds), *Interaction and Grammar* (Cambridge: Cambridge University Press) 134–84.

Freed, B. (1978) 'Foreigner talk: a study of speech adjustments made by native speakers of English in conversation with non-native speakers' (Unpublished doctoral dissertation, University of Pennsylvania, Philadelphia, P.A.).

Freed, B. (1980) 'Talking to foreigners versus talking to children: similarities and differences', in R. Scarcella and S. Krashen, (eds), *Research in Second Language Acquisition* (Rowley, MA: Newbury House) 19–27.

Freed, B. (2000) 'Is fluency, like beauty, in the eyes (and ears) of the beholder?', in H. Riggenbach (ed.), *Perspectives on Fluency* (Ann Arbor, MI: University of Michigan Press) 243–65.

Gilbert, J. (1993) *Clear Speech: Pronunciation and Listening Comprehension in North American English*, 2nd edn [Student's book] (New York: Cambridge University Press).

Grant, L. (2001) *Well Said: Pronunciation for Clear Communication*, 2nd edn (Boston: Heinle & Heinle).

Gumperz, J. (1982) *Discourse Strategies* (Cambridge: Cambridge University Press).

Gumperz, J. (1992) 'Contextualization and understanding', in A. Duranti and C. Goodwin (eds), *Rethinking Context* (New York: Cambridge University Press) 229–52.

Gussenhoven, C. (1984) *On the Grammar and Semantics of Sentence Accents* (Dordrecht: Foris).

Halliday, M.A.K. (1967a) *Intonation and Grammar in British English* (The Hague: Mouton).

Halliday, M.A.K. (1967b) 'Notes on transitivity and theme in English' (Parts 1–3), *Journal of Linguistics*, 3, 1: 37–81; 3, 2: 199–244; 4, 2: 179–215.

Hatch, E. Shapira, R. and Wagner-Gough, J. (1978) 'Foreigner talk discourse', *International Review of Applied Linguistics*, 39/40: 39–60.

Hedge, T. (1993) 'Key Concepts in ELT (fluency)', *English Language Teaching Journal*, 47, 3: 275–6.

Hewings, M. (1995) 'The English intonation of native speakers and Indonesian learners: a comparative study', *Regional English Language Conference Journal*, 26, 1: 27–46.

Hughes, A. (1989) *Testing for Language Teachers* (Cambridge: Cambridge University Press).

Johns, A. (1997) *Text, Role, and Context: Developing Academic Literacies* (Cambridge: Cambridge University Press).

Kasper, G. and Rose, K. (2001) 'Pragmatics in language teaching', in K. Rose and G. Kasper (eds) *Pragmatics in Language Teaching* (Cambridge: Cambridge University Press) 1–9.

Klatt, D. (1975) 'Vowel lengthening is syntactically determined in a connected discourse', *Journal of Phonetics*, 3: 129–40.

Kutik, E., Cooper, W. and Boyce, S. (1983) 'Declination of fundamental frequency in speakers' production of parenthetical and main clauses', *Journal of the Acoustical Society of America*, 73, 5: 1731–8.

Labov, W. (1972) *Language in the Inner City* (Philadelphia: University of Pennsylvania Press).

Ladd, R. (1980) *The Structure of Intonational Meaning* (Bloomington: Indiana University Press).

Larsen-Freeman, D. and Long, M. (1991) *An Introduction to Second Language Acquisition Research* (London: Longman).

Lehiste, I. (1975) 'The phonetic structure of paragraphs', in A. Cohen and S. Nooteboom (eds), *Structure and Process in Speech Perception* (Berlin: Springer) 195–203.

Lennon, P. (2000) 'The lexical element in spoken second language fluency', in H. Riggenbach (ed.), *Perspectives on Fluency* (Ann Arbor, MI: University of Michigan Press) 25–42.

Lewis, M. (1993) *The Lexical Approach: The State of ESL and a Way Forward* (Hove, England: Language Teaching Publications).

Lippi-Green, R. (1997) *English with an Accent* (London: Routledge).

Long, M. (1980) 'Input, interaction, and second language acquisition' (Unpublished doctoral dissertation, University of California at Los Angeles).

Long, M. (1983) 'Linguistic and conversational adjustments to non-native speakers', *Studies in Second Language Acquisition*, 5: 177–93.

Long, M. (1996) 'The role of the linguistic environment in second language acquisition' in W. Ritchie and T. Bhatia, (eds), *Handbook of Second Language Acquisition* (San Diego: Academic Press) 413–68.

Loveday, L. (1981) 'Pitch, politeness and sexual role: an exploratory investigation into the pitch correlates of English and Japanese politeness formulae', *Language and Speech*, 24, 1: 71–89.

Meyers C. and Holt, S. (2001) *Pronunciation for Success*, 2nd edn (Burnsville, MN: Aspen Productions).

Mitchell R. and Myles, F. (1998) *Second Language Learning Theories* (London: Arnold).

Nattinger, J. and DeCarrico, J. (1992) *Lexical Phrases and Language Teaching* (Oxford: Oxford University Press).

O'Connor, J. and Arnold, G. (1961) *Intonation of Colloquial English* (London: Longman).

Oppenheim, N. (2000) 'The importance of recurrent sequences for nonnative-speaker fluency', in H. Riggenbach (ed.), *Perspectives on Fluency* (Ann Arbor, MI: University of Michigan Press) 220–40.

Paltridge, B. (2001) *Genre and the Language Learning Classroom* (Ann Arbor: University of Michigan Press).

Pickering, L. (1999) 'The analysis of prosodic systems in the classroom discourse of NS and NNS teaching assistants' (Unpublished doctoral dissertation, University of Florida, Gainesville, FL).

Pickering, L. (2001) 'The role of tone choice in improving ITA communication in the classroom', *TESOL Quarterly*, 35, 2: 233–55.

Pickering, L. (2004) 'The structure of intonational paragraphs in native and non-native speaker instructional discourse', *English for Specific Purposes*, 23: 19–43.

Pierrehumbert, J. (1980) 'The phonology and phonetics of English intonation' (Unpublished doctoral dissertation, Massachusetts Institute of Technology, Cambridge, MA).

Pierrehumbert, J. and Hirschberg, J. (1990) 'The meaning of intonational contours in discourse', in P. Cohen, J. Morgan, and M. Pollack (eds), *Intentions in Communication* (Cambridge, MA: MIT Press) 271–311.

Pike, K. (1945) *The Intonation of American English* (Ann Arbor: University of Michigan Press).

Riggenbach, H. (1991) 'Toward an understanding of fluency: a microanalysis of nonnative speaker conversations', *Discourse Processes*, 14: 423–41.

Riggenbach, H. (1999) *Discourse Analysis in the Language Classroom, Vol. I, The Spoken Language* (Ann Arbor, MI: University of Michigan Press).

Riggenbach, H. (2001) 'Hesitation phenomena in second-language fluency', in A. Wennerstrom (ed.), *Music of Everyday Speech: Prosody and Discourse Analysis* (Oxford: Oxford University Press) 252–6.

Segalowitz, N. (2000) 'Automaticity and attentional skill in fluent performance', in H. Riggenbach (ed.), *Perspectives on Fluency* (Ann Arbor, MI: University of Michigan Press) 200–19.

Selting, M. (1994) 'Emphatic Speech style – with special focus on the prosodic signalling of heightened emotive involvement in conversation', *Journal of Pragmatics*, 22: 375–408.

Skehan, P. (1998) *A Cognitive Approach to Language Learning* (Oxford: Oxford University Press).

Swales, J. (1990) *Genre Analysis: English in Academic and Research Settings* (Cambridge: Cambridge University Press).

Tarone, E. (1980) 'Communication strategies, foreigner talk and repair in interlanguage', *Language Learning*, 30: 417–31.

Tench, P. (1990) *The Roles of Intonation in English Discourse* (Frankfurt am Main: Peter Lang).

Tench, P. (1991) 'The stylistic potential of intonation', in W. van Peer (ed.), *The Taming of the Text* (London: Routledge) 50–82.

Thompson, I. (2001) 'Japanese speakers', in M. Swan and B. Smith (eds), *Learner English: A Teacher's Guide to Interference and Other Problems*, 2nd edn (Cambridge: Cambridge University Press) 296–309.

Trager, G. and Smith, H. (1951) *An Outline of English Structure* (Norman, OK: Battenburg Press).

Wennerstrom, A. (1994) 'Intonational meaning in English discourse: A study of nonnative speakers', *Applied Linguistics*, 15, 4: 399–420.

Wennerstrom, A. (1997) 'Discourse intonation and second language acquisition: three genre-based studies' (Unpublished doctoral dissertation, University of Washington, Seattle, WA).

Wennerstrom, A. (2000) 'The role of intonation in second language fluency', in H. Riggenbach (ed.), *Perspectives on Fluency* (Ann Arbor: University of Michigan Press) 102–27.

Wennerstrom, A. (2001a) *The Music of Everyday Speech: Prosody and Discourse Analysis* (New York: Oxford University Press).

Wennerstrom, A. (2001b) 'Intonation and evaluation in oral narratives', *Journal of Pragmatics*, 33: 1183–206.

Wennerstrom, A. (2003) *Discourse Analysis in the Language Classroom*, Volume 2, *Genres of Writing* (Ann Arbor: University of Michigan Press).

Wennerstrom, A. and Siegel, A. (2003) 'Keeping the floor in multiparty conversations: intonation, syntax, and pause', *Discourse Processes*, 36, 2: 77–107.

Wichmann, A. (2000) *Intonation in Text and Discourse: Beginnings, Middles and Ends* (Harlow: Longman).

Wong-Fillmore, L. (1995) 'Individual differences in second language acquisition', in D.B. Durkin (ed.), *Language Issues: Readings for Teachers* (White Planes, NY: Longman) 224–47.

Yule, G. 'Speakers' topics and major paratones', *Lingua,* 52 (1980) 33–47.

5

A Review of Recent Research on Speech Rhythm: Some Insights for Language Acquisition, Language disorders and Language Teaching[*]

Ee Ling Low

Early research on speech rhythm

Early research on speech rhythm subscribed to the notion of isochrony, which advocates that the perception of rhythm in speech is based on the regular recurrence of some form of speech unit. On the basis of whether stresses or syllables were isochronous, Pike (1945) and Abercrombie (1967: 97) distinguished between 'stress-timed' and 'syllable-timed' languages. In stress-timed languages, interstress intervals or feet are believed to be isochronous. A foot consists of a stressed syllable and any number of unstressed syllables up to, but not including, the next stressed syllable. On the other hand, in 'syllable-timed' languages, it is the syllables that are said to be perceived to recur at equal intervals in time. However, early research has shown that prefect isochrony is an idealized state and isochrony is now described as a tendency, with scholars ascribing to the notion of a rhythm continuum where languages fall somewhere along the continuum between between 'stress-based' and 'syllable-based' languages (Dauer, 1983; Miller, 1984). This section will provide an overview of early research on speech rhythm which led to the rejection of the notion of prefect isochrony, some of which can be found in the background section of a paper by Grabe and Low (2002).

In the view put forward by Pike (1945) and Abercrombie (1965; 1967), the distinction between stress- and syllable-timing was strictly categorical, with languages being classified as either stress-timed or syllable-timed. Abercrombie's classification (1967: 35) is based on how speech was produced. He believed that all spoken languages could either have chest pulses or stress pulses. Syllables are produced by chest pulses or the contractions and relaxations of the respiratory muscles which produce a succession of small puffs of air. Stress pulses, on the other hand, are reinforced chest pulses produced by extra strong muscular movement. Abercrombie suggests that it is 'the way in which the chest-pulses and stress pulses recur ... that determines the rhythm of a language.' (Abercrombie, 1967: 97). In syllable-timed rhythm, chest pulses are believed to recur at equal intervals of time while in stress-timed rhythm, it is the stress pulses that are believed to be isochronous. Examples of syllable-timed languages are French, Telugu and Yoruba, while English, Russian and Arabic typify stress-timed rhythm.

In addition to the categories of stress- and/or syllable-timing, Bloch (1942), Han (1962), Ladefoged (1975) and Hoequist (1983b) proposed a third category of rhythm, known as mora-timing. The language that exemplifies this type of rhythm is Japanese. A mora may be defined as consisting of one short vowel in the nucleus and any preceding consonants in the onset. It is therefore usually shorter than the syllable unit. In mora-timed languages, morae are believed to be isochronous. In what follows, a number of relevant studies investigating the notions of stress-, syllable- and mora-timing will be reviewed, and the difficulties in adopting this strict categorical classification of rhythm will be discussed.

Eriksson (1991: 2) states that an idealized stress-timed language would have equal interstress intervals or isochronous feet. In order to maintain the equal interstress intervals, syllable durations tend to vary according to the number of syllables in a foot. The more syllables there are in a foot, the shorter their durations have to be. On the other hand, syllable-timed languages have isochronous syllable durations.

However, studies investigating the basis of stress-timing have not, in fact, provided any evidence to support the notion of isochronous feet by measuring interstress intervals (Shen and Peterson, 1962; Bolinger, 1965; Faure *et al.*, 1980; Nakatani *et al.*, 1981; Strangert, 1985; Lehiste, 1990). Likewise, studies investigating the notion of equal syllable durations in languages perceived to be syllable-timed could not find evidence supporting the hypothesis of isosyllabicity by measuring interstress intervals (Delattre, 1966; Pointon, 1980; Manrique and Signorini, 1983). Rather, these studies found that in languages perceived as syllable-timed, the duration of stressed and unstressed syllables varies.

Cross-linguistic studies investigating the basis for a distinction between stress- and syllable-timing also measured the differences in interstress intervals (Roach, 1982; Dauer, 1983). Roach (1982) compared the interstress intervals between languages classified as stress-timed against those labelled as syllable-timed. He investigated two claims made by Abercrombie (1967) about the difference between stress-timed and syllable-timed rhythm: (i) that there is considerable variation in syllable length in a language spoken with stress-timed rhythm whereas in a language spoken with syllable-timed rhythm, syllables tend to be equal in length; and (ii) in syllable-timed languages, interstress intervals are unevenly spaced.

His findings did not support claim (i) because, in general, syllable-timed languages appeared to exhibit greater variability in syllable durations than stress-timed languages. Claim (ii) was not supported either, as there was a wider range of percentage deviations in interstress intervals in stress-timed languages than in syllable-timed languages. Roach's results led him to claim that no support for the assignment of stress- or syllable-timed rhythm can be provided on the basis of measuring time intervals in speech.

Dauer (1983) compared interstress intervals in English, Thai, Spanish, Italian and Greek and found that interstress intervals were no more regular in English, a stress-timed language than in Spanish, a syllable-timed language, and reached the same conclusion as Roach (1982); that is, that the difference between stress- and syllable-timing may not be found by measuring time intervals in speech. Thus, the results of the cross-linguistic studies carried out by Roach (1982) and Dauer (1983) led them to conclude that interstress intervals are not found to be more isochronous in stress-timed languages compared to syllable-timed ones. This has led researchers to conclude that isochrony is at best, a perceptual phenomenon (Couper-Kuhlen, 1990; 1993).

Han (1962), Port *et al.* (1980) and Port *et al.* (1987) investigated the isochrony of morae in mora-timed languages. Of these studies, only Port *et al.* (1987) found some form of support for the mora as a constant time unit. However, other researchers have questioned the acoustic reliability of the mora as a unit of timing in speech (Oyakawa, 1971; Beckman, 1982; Hoequist, 1983a; 1983b).

In summary, early experimental work did not support the strict categorical distinction of rhythm into stress-, syllable- and mora-timing. Isochrony is now described as a tendency and rhythmic variation in languages is viewed as a continuum rather than as strict categories. Consequently, researchers like Dauer (1983; 1987) and Laver (1994: 528–9) have introduced the notion of stress-based, syllable-based and mora-based languages. As pointed out by Grabe and Low (2002: 518), 'true isochrony is assumed to be an underlying constraint', while the phonetic, phonological, syntactic and lexical characteristics of a language affect the isochrony of the speech units. It is these characteristics that more recent instrumental studies have tended to investigate in their attempt to search for the acoustic correlates of rhythmic classification.

Recent research on speech rhythm

Current views of rhythm in speech

The failure of early experimental work to find acoustic evidence for the notion of isochrony has led to more current views of rhythm such as those proposed by Dasher and Bolinger (1982) and Dauer (1983; 1987). They suggest that the classification of rhythm should be based on the combinations of phonological, phonetic, lexical and syntactic properties of different languages. Dauer identified the three main influences on rhythmic patterning to be: (i) the complexity of syllable structure; (ii) the presence or absence of vowel reduction; and (iii) stress patterning of a language. Dauer proposed that stress-based languages tend to have complex syllable structures while in many syllable-based languages, there tends to be an absence of vowel reduction. In addition, Dasher and Bolinger (1982) also proposed that syllable-based languages tend not to have phonemic vowel length distinction.

Another view of speech rhythm is offered by Nespor (1990), who argued against the traditional classification of rhythm based on her analysis of what she terms as 'rhythmically mixed' or intermediate languages. She defines intermediate languages to exhibit some properties of stress-timing and some associated with stress-timing. Nespor suggested that neither the strictly categorical view nor the continuum view can account adequately for the rhythmic properties such as Polish, which is classified as stress-timed but which does not exhibit vowel reduction, a feature associated with stress-timed languages which have to compress their syllable durations in order to achieve near equal interstress intervals. Neither can the existing views on rhythm account for Catalan, which, in spite of being classified as syllable-timed, exhibits vowel reduction, a property which is lacking in a prototypical syllable-timed language.

The investigation of rhythm using rhythmic indexes

Recent research has tended to focus on attempting to find some sort of acoustic justification for previously established rhythmic categories by focusing on the phonological properties (such as vowel, syllable and consonantal length) of the languages under investigation. Several rhythm indexes have also been developed by the recent researchers in an attempt to quantify or to capture the rhythmic variation found in different languages. In this paper, I shall attempt to highlight some of indexes that have been employed in recent work on rhythm.

The Pairwise Variability Index (PVI)

Low and Grabe (1995) measured the durations of vowels in successive syllables in Singapore English (henceforth SE), which has been previously described as syllable-timed, and compared it to British English (henceforth BE), which has been classified as stress-timed. Their choice of measuring vowels stems from a suggestion by Taylor (1981: 221–2) concerning the lack of vowel length distinction between stressed and unstressed syllables in syllable-timed languages. Consequently, it is the vowels that are nearly equal in duration in syllable-timed languages. In order to test the hypothesis that vowels are more nearly equal in duration in SE than in BE, a measure referred to as the Pairwise Variability Index (PVI) was designed.[1] This measure reflects the mean absolute difference between successive pairs of vowels in an utterance, and is expressed as:

$$PVI = 100 \times \left[\sum_{k=1}^{m-1} |d_k - d_{k+1}| / (m-1) \right]$$

where m = number of vowels in utterance; d – duration of the kth vowel.

Informally, the difference in duration between successive pairings of vowels in the utterances (d1 and d2, d2 and d3) is calculated, and the absolute values taken (by discarding the negative sign where it occurs). The mean difference is calculated by summing the difference, and dividing by the number of differences (that is, one less than the number of vowels) and this is expressed as an index (the PVI). Basically, the higher the index, the greater the variability in duration between successive vowels in the utterance.

The results obtained by Low and Grabe (1995) indicated that BE subjects exhibited a significantly higher variability in duration between successive vowels than SE subjects as shown in Figure 5.1.

Low (1998) extended the enquiry of less variability in successive vowel durations in SE compared to BE by hypothesizing that the low variability is caused by a lack of alternation between full and reduced vowels in SE compared to BE, a phonological property about syllable-timed languages on which other scholars have already commented (for example, Bertinetto, 1977; Wenk and Wioland, 1982; Brakel, 1985). Two sets of sentences were designed. One containing only full vowels

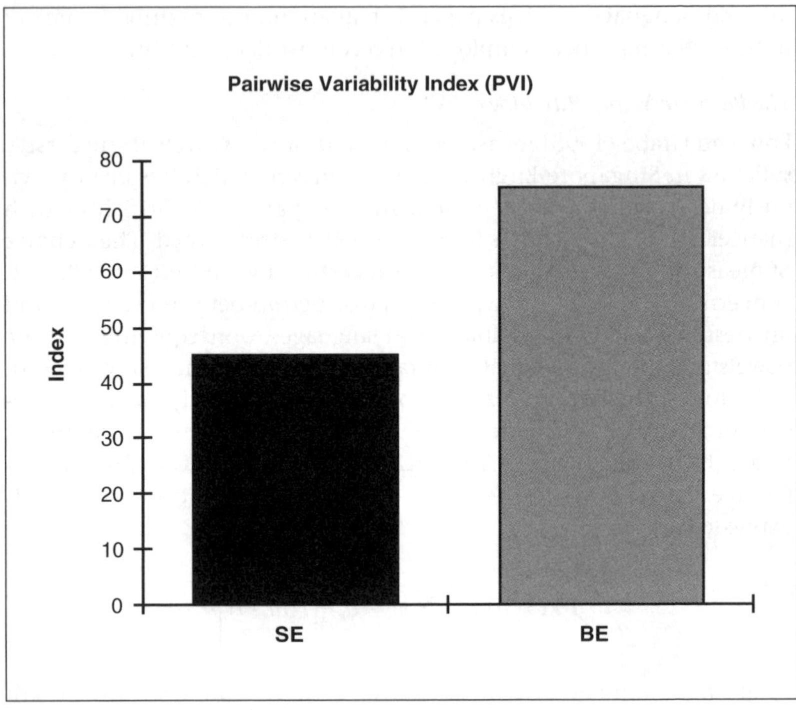

Figure 5.1   Cross comparison of PVI for SE and BE

and another set containing full and reduced vowels as they would be potentially realized in BE. Both SE and BE subjects read the sentences. Successive vowel durations were measured across the two varieties of English and their variability was captured using a modified version of the PVI (nPVI), which aims to normalize for speaking rate across each successive pair of vowels and is expressed as:

$$nPVI = 100 \times \left[\sum_{k=1}^{m-1} \left| \frac{d_k - d_{k+1}}{(d_k + d_{k+1})/2} \right| / (m-1) \right]$$

As the normalization produces fractional values, the output is multiplied by 100 to give a whole number.

The results obtained by Low (1998) showed that there was a significant difference in the PVI values between the full and the full and reduced vowel sets for BE but not for SE. This suggests that there is a difference in duration between full and reduced vowels in BE which is comparatively absent in SE. Low (1998) went on to measure the vowel spectral patterns found in the two sentence sets across BE and SE and found that the potentially reduced vowels in BE clustered in the centre of a speaker's vowel quadrilateral, suggesting a schwa-like realization.[2] In contrast, the potentially reduced vowels in SE occurred at the periphery of the speaker's vowel quadrilateral, suggesting a lack of vowel reduction. A dispersion measure was used to calculate the average distance of the vowels from the centroid (central point) and SE subjects displayed a significantly greater dispersion for reduced vowels than BE subjects (see Figure 5.2).

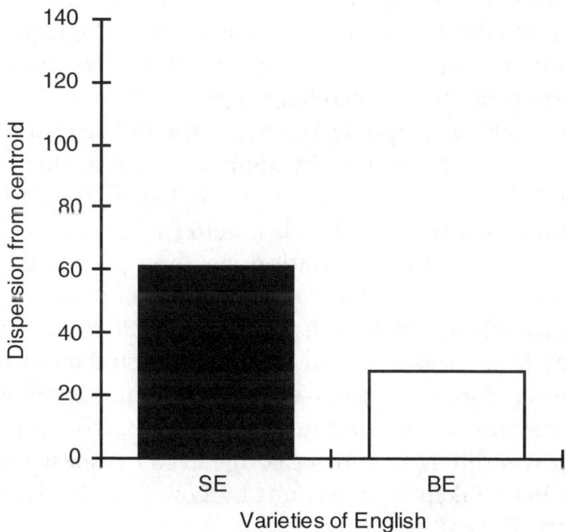

Figure 5.2   Distance from centroid in potentially reduced vowels in the two varieties

Low's (1998) findings provided acoustic validation for the perception of syllable-timing in SE; namely, that SE appears to have less of a contrast between full and reduced vowels in comparison to BE.

The studies reviewed above (Low and Grabe (1995) and Low (1998)) also show the capability of the PVI in capturing the rhythmic difference between two languages; one classified as stressed-timed (BE) and the other syllable-timed (SE).

Ramus, Nespor and Mehler's (1999) Rhyhm Index (RRI) vs the PVI (Low, Grabe and Nolan (2000)

Ramus *et al.* (1999) also set out to provide acoustic evidence for the traditional stress-timing/syllable-timing dichotomy by investigating three different properties of the durational variation in languages: %V, which they defined as the proportion of vocalic intervals in the sentence (section of speech between vowel onset and offset); ΔV, the standard deviation of vocalic intervals; and ΔC, the standard deviation of consonantal intervals (consonantal interval = section between vowel offset and vowel onset). Ramus *et al.* (1999) argue that a combination of %V and ΔC is the measure that offers the best acoustic correlate of rhythm classes. For instance, %V is smaller in French, which is said to be syllable-timed, and may therefore exhibit traits of syllable-timing like the lack of vowel reduction: ΔC was found to be larger in English and this could reflect the more complex syllable structures associated with a prototypical stress-timed language.

Low *et al.* (2000) attempted to compare the PVI against the standard deviation measures ΔC and ΔV by applying them to their data for SE, BE, English, Polish, Dutch, French, Spanish, Italian, Catalan and Japanese. They proposed that the PVI is a better indicator of rhythmicity than either of the standard deviation measures proposed by Ramus *et al.* (1999). The reason why standard deviation tends to work better for tightly controlled data such as that of Ramus *et al.* (five sentences each produced by four speakers) than the read speech data of Low *et al.* is because the standard deviation would reflect spurious variability introduced by changes in speaking rate within and across sentences, and between-speaker differences in speaking rate. Such speaking rate differences have been taken into account by Low *et al.* in the normalized version of the PVI (nPVI).

Consider a language where three successive long vowels follow three successive short vowels and another where long and short vowels alternate. Both would give the same standard deviation, although the pattern of vowel durations differs radically between the two.

Low *et al.* (2000) concluded their paper by suggesting an addition to the vocalic nPVI. The standard deviations published by Ramus *et al.* (1999) showed that rhythmically mixed languages such as Catalan and Polish exhibit complementary levels of vocalic and intervocalic variability. In Polish, the standard deviation of vocalic intervals was relatively low, making Polish similar to the syllable-timed languages in the sample. But the standard deviation of intervocalic intervals was comparatively high. The reverse applied to Catalan. Low *et al.* suggested that a combination of their vocalic nPVI with a measure of intervocalic interval variability would provide a better indicator of rhythmic class than the vocalic nPVI alone. This combination would capture the rhythmic characteristics of stress-timed, syllable-timed and mixed languages. It was predicted that English (stress-timed) should exhibit relatively high variability index values for vocalic and intervocalic intervals. Some English syllables are relatively complex and we find consonant clusters in the onset and in the coda. Others have a very simple structure. Consequently, intervocalic variability is likely to be high. Spanish (syllable-timed) should have low values in both types of interval. Successive vowels are similar in length, and a large proportion of syllables have a simple CV structure (Dauer, 1983). Polish (mixed) would be low on the vocalic axis and high on the intervocalic axis. Catalan (mixed) would be high on the intervocalic axis, and low on the vocalic axis.

Grabe and Low (2002) further tested the predictions made by Low *et al.* (2000) by applying both the normalized PVI (nPVI) on the measurements of vocalic and the raw PVI (rPVI) intervocalic interval[3] (minus pauses and periods of silence) of 18 different languages, including previously rhythmically unclassified languages. The aim was to establish whether the unclassified languages would pattern with the stress-timed or the syllable-timed group or whether some or all of them would be intermediate. Their results showed that languages that have been previously classified as prototypically stress-timed (Dutch, German and British English), syllable-timed (French and Spanish) and mora-timed (Japanese) are clearly separated out, as shown in Figure 5.3.

Prototypically stress-timed languages have high vocalic variability since many stress-timed languages possess vowel reduction. French and Spanish, which have been classified as syllable-timed, have low vocalic variability and this could be due to the relative absence of reduced vowels observed in syllable-timed languages. Japanese, a mora-timed language, appears similar in patterning with the other stress-timed languages. A mora is smaller than a syllable in structure, but in terms of rhythmic patterning it is still closer to syllable-timing than stress-timing. Figure 5.4 shows the PVI values of all 18 languages investigated.

The profile for Catalan supports Nespor's (1990) observations that it is rhythmically mixed because, although it appears to resemble a syllable-timed language, it does have vowel reduction (a property associated with stress-timed languages) and this is evident from the higher vocalic variability it exhibits in comparison to Spanish, for example, which has no vowel reduction.

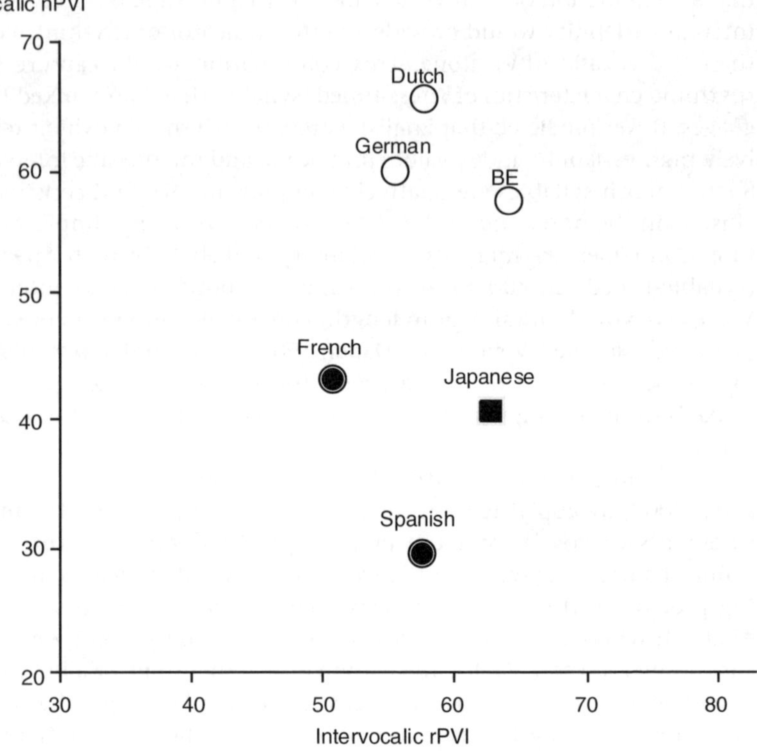

Figure 5.3 PVI profiles from prototypical stress-timed languages English, Dutch and German, syllable-timed languages French and Spanish, and mora-timed language Japanese (vocalic variability is plotted on the vertical axis against intervocalic variability on the horizontal axis)

○ = stress-timed   ● = syllable-timed   ■ = mora-timed

Low *et al.* (2000) concentrated on the rhythmic differences between SE and BE. In Figure 5.4, we see that SE has a lower vocalic variability than BE but it is no way similar to protypically syllable-timed languages like French or Spanish.

Overlapping with the edges of the stress-timed and syllable-timed group of languages are the previously rhythmically unclassified languages Welsh, Greek, Malay, Tamil and Rumanian.

Based on their findings, Grabe and Low (2002) conclude that on the vocalic dimension, prototypically stress-timed languages like German, English and Dutch are clearly separated from the syllable-timed languages French and Spanish. However, there also appears to be a gradi-

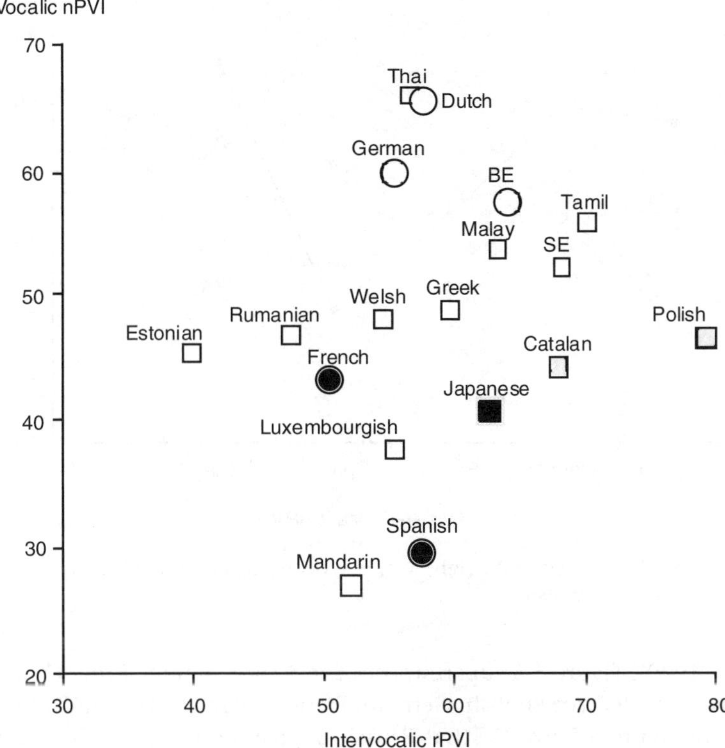

Figure 5.4   PVI profiles for data from 18 languages.
Prototypical ○ = stress-timed, ● = syllable-timed ■ = mora-timed
□ – mixed or unclassified

ent of languages that are more or less stress- or syllable-timed such that
we can consider the notion of degrees of stress- or syllable-timing. The
data also show the capability of the vocalic nPVI to separate out languages into the traditional categories of stress- and syllable-timing but
the intervocalic rPVI shows interesting differences between Polish and
Estonian, both of which, while having similar vocalic variability,
clearly exhibit a different intervocalic structure.

In addition, Grabe and Low (2002) also compared their PVI results
against Ramus *et al.*'s (1999) measures of %V and ΔC, which the latter
had earlier advocated as being able to offer the best acoustic correlate of
rhythm classes. Grabe and Low (2002) found comparable results for the
extremes of the PVI space and the %V and ΔC space obtained by Ramus

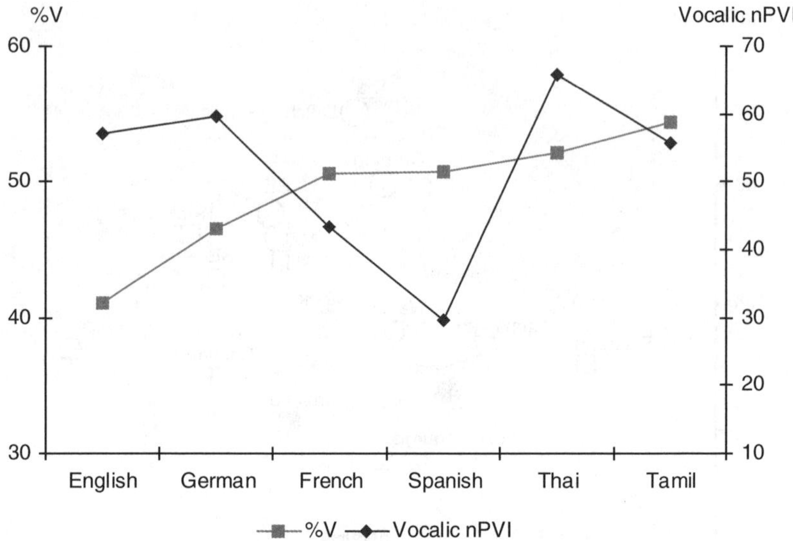

Figure 5.5   Left y-axis: %*V*; right y-axis: vocalic nPVI values (the variety of English is British English)

et al. (1999). Figure 5.5 superimposes the results obtained for %V and the vocalic nPVI for English, German, French, Spanish, Thai and Tamil.

From Figure 5.5, we see that British English and German have low %V values and high vocalic nPVI values. French and Spanish have high %V values, but low vocalic PVI values. In Thai and Tamil, %V values are higher than in French and Spanish. But unlike French and Spanish, the vocalic nPVI is high also.

This complementarity of overall vowel time (%V) and vocalic variability (nPVI) in English and German on the one hand, and French and Spanish on the other, may contribute substantially to impressions of stress- or syllable-timing. If the relationship between the two measures provides the acoustic basis for an impression of stress- or syllable-timing, then Thai would be classified as stress-timed. Although %V is high, the vocalic nPVI is even higher. Tamil would however not be classifiable.

The reliability of rhythm indexes: Variability Index (VI) (Deterding, 2001) vs PVI (Low et al. 2000) vs Rhythm Index (RRI) (Ramus et al. 1999)

Deterding (2001) developed the variability index (VI) which is based on the average of the differences between the duration of adjacent syllables instead of vowels, which have been the central focus of Low *et al.*'s PVI. The effects of speaking rate are dealt with by dividing the duration of each syllable by the average duration of all the syllables excluding the final syllable, which is often lengthened. The VI is calculated based on the following mathematical formula:

$$VI = \frac{1}{n-2} \sum_{k=1}^{n-2} |d_{k+1} - d_k|$$

Where d_k is the duration of the kth syllable and n is the number of syllables in the utterance.

Ong (2004), presented as a paper by Low, Deterding and Ong (2004), focused on a comparative study of the reliability of the rhythm indexes developed by Deterding (2001), Low *et al.* (2000) and Ramus *et al.* (1999). To recap, Deterding (2001) measured the duration of successive syllables and calculated the VI of the syllables. He found the syllables more likely to be equal in SE (a syllable-based language) than BE (a stress-based language), as he obtained a significantly lower VI for SE than BE. Low *et al.* (2000) developed the PVI, which calculates the variability of vowels in successive syllables, and found the vowels are more likely to be equal in syllable-based rather than stress-based languages. They ascribed this lower variability to the relative absence of the vowel reduction characteristic of syllable-based languages. Ramus *et al.* (1999) showed that the proportion of vocalic intervals in an utterance (%V) and the standard deviation of consonantal intervals (ΔC) provide the best cues to rhythmic classification. Syllable-based languages are found to exhibit lower intervocalic durations (low %V) compared to stress-based languages. However, stress-based languages, which generally have a more complex syllable structure, tend to have a higher standard deviation for consonantal intervals (ΔC). Low *et al.* (2004) aimed to test the reliability of these three indexes by investigating the degree of variation in results obtained by two different measurers trained in acoustic phonetics for each of these indexes, to identify the problems encountered during the measurement process for conversational speech and to find the correlation of each index with a perceptual test of rhythm. See Table 5.1 for the different measurers for each index.

Table 5.1   Different measurers for each rhythm index

	M1	M2	M3
Deterding (2001)	√		√
Low *et al.* (2000)		√	√

The data investigated comprised 45 utterances of at least seven syllables, each with no pauses in between, taken from the NIE Corpus of
spoken Singapore English (NIECSSE) of both British and Singaporean
speech in an interview setting. For the perceptual test, subjects listened
to all 45 utterances and were asked to mark each utterance on a scale of
1 to 9, 1 being syllable-based and 9 being stress-based. For each index,
there were at least two measurers. The same measurements obtained
for Low *et al.* were mapped onto Ramus *et al.*'s (1999) index since there
were no pauses in between the utterances and the consonantal intervals could safely be whatever was not measured as vocalic intervals for
the Low *et al.* measure.

In terms of the variance in results obtained between the measurers for
each index, the Pearson r value between the two measurers obtained
for Deterding's (2001) index was higher, at 0.74, than that obtained for
Low *et al.* (2000), which was at 0.60. This suggests that there was greater
agreement between the measurers for Deterding's index than for that of
Low *et al.* and consequently that it appeared easier to measure syllables
rather than vowels. Since Low *et al.* (2000) only looked at read speech,
more guidelines need to be drawn out for measuring vowels in conversational speech, since there are many more phonological processes
involved like linking and deletion for example, all of which influence a
measurer's judgement of vowel segmentation.

A few of these problems encountered by the measurers using Deterding's index will be discussed below. The first problem had to do with
the limitations of spectrographic analysis. For example, the syllable
boundary between the end of the fricative /s/ and the word-initial /h/
in the words '*price here*' is not at all discernible by looking at the spectrogram shown in Figure 5.6 below.

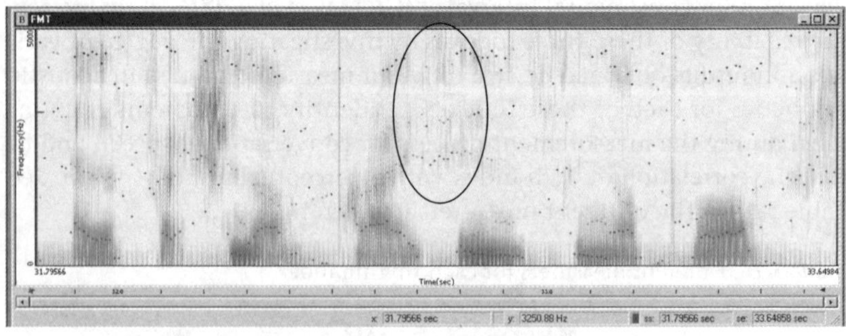

æt ə   fræk ʃ ənɒvðə   pr aɪ   s h ɪ ə ɪn   s ɪŋ ə p   ɔː

Figure 5.6 Spectrogram of the utterance '*at a fraction of the price here in
Singapore*'

The second problem encountered in the measurement involved ascertaining the number of syllables in a word. This could be due to various factors, such as the compression or deletion of syllables; for example, the final syllable of *basically* where one measurer considered it to be /beɪ sɪ klɪ/ and therefore three syllables, and another as ./beɪ sɪ kə lɪ/ and therefore four syllables. The final problem encountered in measurement was that of deciding on the boundary between adjacent vowels across word boundaries, such as the end of the vowel /ɔː/ and the beginning of the vowel /ɒ/ in the words 'more of'.

The mean VI values obtained between the measurers is shown in Table 5.2 below and the means were found to be significantly different.

Table 5.2   VI values obtained for Deterding's (2001) index

Measurers	Mean VI
M1	0.54
M3	0.59

Table 5.3 shows the means obtained for BE and SE speakers across the two measurers.

Table 5.3   VI values for BE and SE speakers for Deterding's (2001) index

Mean VI	Measurer 1	Measurer 3
BE speakers	0.60	0.62
SE speakers	0.51	0.58

While no significant difference emerged across the means for BE speakers, a significant difference was found in the means for SE speakers. What this suggests is that the measurers dealt with the SE data differently. Furthermore, while one measurer obtained a result that significantly differentiated SE from BE rhythmically, the other did not.

For Low *et al.*'s (2000) index, the utterances where great discrepancies in the results found were examined and several problems were found. Firstly, in several of the utterances, vowels were so reduced that it was virtually impossible to take measurements of these vowels. See the example highlighted in Figure 5.7 below.

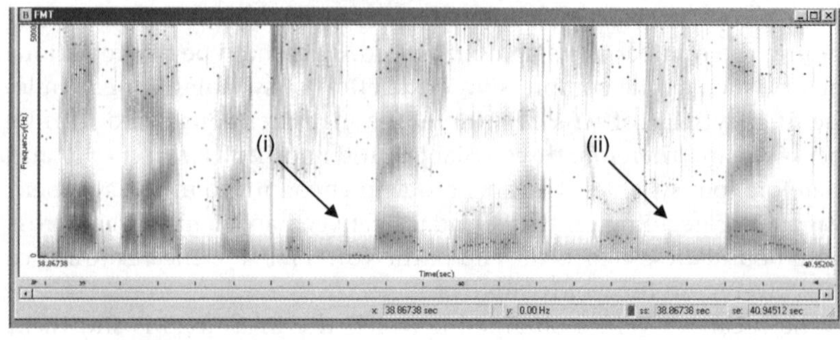

Figure 5.7   Spectrogram of the utterance '*not that I participated in that sort of thing*'

In particular, the schwa in (i) and (ii) above were not discernible from the spectrogram. The problem of discerning the number of syllables each word has was also encountered. Finally, the influence of linking /w/ and /j/ on the surrounding vowels also posed a problem in the measurement process. While one measurer disregarded their presence and kept to the phonemic transcription of the words '*two a.m.*', the other considered their presence and thus had a very different segmentation for the surrounding vowels. See Figures 5.8 and 5.9 which illustrate the difference in segmentation by the two measurers.

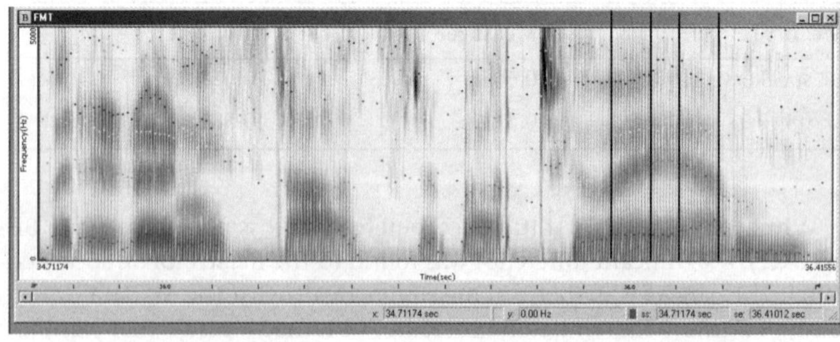

Figure 5.8   Duration of /eɪ/ and /em/ by one measurer

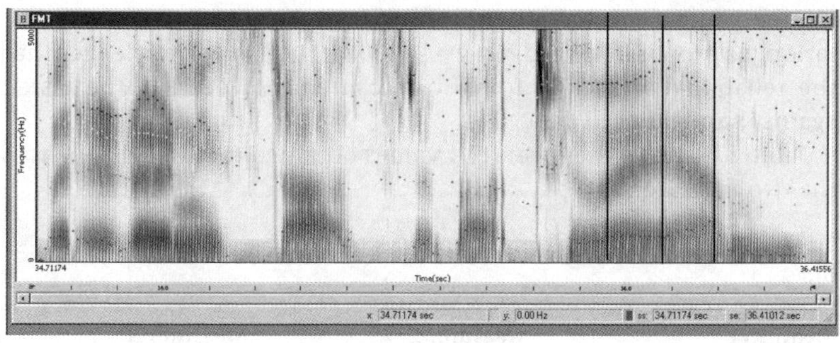

Figure 5.9   Duration of of /eI/ and /em/ by another measurer

Table 5.4 shows the mean PVI obtained for the two measurers.

Table 5.4   Comparison of mean (PVI) between measurers for Low *et al.* (2000)

Measurers	Mean (PVI)
Measurer 2	48.4
Measurer 3	51.4

No significant difference was found in the values obtained by the two measurers, unlike that obtained for Deterding's index. This could be because of the ethnicity of the measurers for Low *et al.*'s index, both of Singaporeans. Indeed, if the ethnicity of the measurers influences the measurements made, then the issue of who measures the data becomes important. This finding complements what Ramus (2002) highlighted as a major limitation that confronts all the different measurements of rhythm; that is, the manual determination of interval boundaries. He feels that this is still largely subjective and that it is virtually impossible to ensure that measurers dealing with new languages under investigation can employ exactly the same criteria. He proposes that the way forward in dealing with huge amounts of data is the automatic segmentation of speech data through algorithms, such as those developed by Pellegrino and colleagues (Farinas and Pellegrino, 2001), and the idea of an automatic calculation of the proportion of vocalic intervals in speech and the variability of consonantal intervals without segmentation, as proposed by Galves *et al.* (2002). He also acknowledges that the reliability of such automatic measurements needs to be tested against hand-labelled data.

Table 5.5 shows the mean PVI values obtained for SE and BE across the two measurers.

Table 5.5 Mean PVI for BE and SE speakers for both measurers for Low *et al.*'s index

Mean PVI	Measurer 2	Measurer 3
BE speakers	56.3	62.0
SE speakers	44.5	46.1

No significant difference was found between the measurers for either the SE or BE data. However, both measurers obtained a significant cross-variety difference for SE and BE, which is a consistent finding with the results obtained in earlier work by Low *et al.* (2000) and Grabe and Low (2002). As Ramus *et al.*'s measure was automatically converted from the vowel measurements, there is no further need to test for inter-measurer reliability.

Table 5.6 shows the correlation of each rhythm index with the perceptual test.

Table 5.6 Correlation values of each rhythm index with perceptual test

Correlation	Pearson's r value
Deterding (2001)	0.37
Low *et al.* (2000)	0.51
Ramus *et al.* (1999) %V	0.0024
Ramus *et al.* (1999) ΔC	0.07

From the r values shown in Table 5.6, it is clear that Low *et al.*'s index reflects the strongest correlation with the perception of rhythm. There appears to be virtually no correlation between the %V and ΔC with the perceptual test of rhythm. The possible explanation for this result could lie in the fact that we did not apply a normalization procedure for the data as Ramus (2002) had suggested, and that could have skewed the results. This is also an observation made by Barry *et al.* (2003), who noted that Ramus *et al.*'s measure, in particular, is very sensitive to tempo-induced processes. Furthermore, Ramus *et al.*'s index is based on phonological properties which might be better captured using different languages rather than different varieties of the same language. The findings also suggest that the measurement of vowels better embodies the rhythmic patterns in speech and agrees with the earlier findings made by Low *et al.* (2000) and Grabe and Low (2002). This could be because vowels represent the sonorous peaks of a syllable and thus provide a good cue to rhythmic class distinction, an idea extensively explored by Galves *et al.* (2002). Listeners could therefore be listening out for strong versus weak forms of vowels as cues to determine the type of rhythm being played to them.

The findings of Low *et al.* (2004) led them to conclude that Low *et al.*'s (2000) index appears to be most reliable in capturing rhythmic patterning in speech. However, unless an automatic measure of rhythm is employed, manual segmentation will need far tighter guidelines, especially with regard to the subjectivity in the judgement of the number of syllables a word contains and the question of how to deal with the phonological processes such as linking and extreme vowel reduction inherent in conversational speech. In the case of severely reduced vowels, one possibility might be to assign 0 duration to the vowels. The question of normalization to control for speech rate is another important issue that needs to be looked at in greater detail. In particular, the method of normalization needs to be considered; that is, whether there should be a pairwise normalization or one that normalizes across the entire utterance.

Applications of rhythmic indexes

In this section, we look at how rhythm indexes have been employed in research in different fields; in particular, language acquisition, language disorders and language teaching.

Language acquisition

Grabe *et al.* (1999) examined the rhythmic patterns produced by 4-year old French and English children and their mothers. The vowels in utterances that had minimally four syllables each were measured and the PVI as it first appeared in Low (1998) and which later appeared in Low *et al.* (2000) was applied. It contained the normalization component to control for speech rate. The comparison between French and English was carried out because of the traditional classification of French as syllable-timed and English as stress-timed. The aim of the experiment was to test whether English children had acquired the rhythm of English by age four and to contrast these against comparable data from French.

Grabe *et al.*'s hypothesis was that the syllable-timed rhythm of French appears to be easier to acquire because there is no need to compress syllables to achieve the foot isochrony that is required for a stress-timed language like English. In other words, the rhythm of a syllable-timed language ought to be more easily acquired than a stress-timed one. Their results provided support for their hypothesis as the PVI obtained for English children and their mothers differed significantly, but the values obtained for French children and their mothers did not. More data are needed from languages belonging to the different rhythmic groups and also data from different varieties of a language to further verify this hypothesis. For example, it would be interesting to find out whether the rhythm of SE, which has been classified as syllable-timed is easier to acquire than BE, which is described as stress-timed.

Ramus *et al.*'s (1999) measurements of vowel/consonantal segmentation for eight different languages suggest that rhythmic classification more accurately reflects specific phonological properties such as syllable structure and these are, in turn, signalled by the acoustic/phonetic properties such as consonantal and vowel durations. Based on their findings, they suggest that the existence of rhythm classes allows for the simulation of infant language discrimination. Their finding is consistent with the hypothesis that newborn infants do rely on a coarse segmentation of speech.

Thus, the rhythm indexes developed in recent years have proved to be a useful tool in examining the acquisition of rhythm cross-linguistically.

Language disorders

Peter and Stoel-Gammon (2003) applied Low *et al.*'s (2000) PVI to the measurement of the speech rhythm of imitated sentences produced by two children suspected of childhood apraxia of speech, a condition that has been identified as being responsible for impaired speech prosody. The same measurements were repeated and calculated for two matched-age controls. Results showed that for the sentence imitation task, children with apraxia did not differ significantly from their unimpaired counterparts but in all other tasks set (that is, singing a familiar song, imitating clapped rhythms and repetitive tapping), the unimpaired peers obtained a significantly higher accuracy score compared to their peers with apraxia. Oh *et al.* (2004) applied Low *et al.*'s PVI to the speech produced by schizophrenic patients with formal thought disorder (FTD) against those without formal thought disorder (NFTD) and compared the results against a healthy control, all matched for intellectual functioning. Previous research showed that, syntactically, both groups of patients exhibited more errors than the healthy controls but, semantically, FTD patients contained significantly more intra-sentential semantic anomalies compared to the healthy controls. Oh *et al.* (2004) measured successive vowel durations across five utterances for each speaker and found that no significant differences emerged between FTD and NFTD patients as well as against the healthy controls. They suggest that since all three subjects were matched for accent (Southern British English), it is not surprising that their speech rhythm is not significantly different. Since rhythmic patterning is dependent on the phonological properties of speech material such as syllable structure, it can be suggested that the segmental properties of the subjects are not affected by the schizophrenic condition (either FTD or NFTD).

The PVI may be used as a yardstick for unimpaired versus impaired speech rhythm as in Peter and Stoel-Gammon's (2003) study. Ultimately, deviation from the 'target' PVI value can be used as a diagnostic test to ascertain whether children are sufferers from childhood apraxia. The application of the PVI to diagnose rhythmic deviation between two groups of schizophrenic patients (FTD and NFTD) was found to be less successful. In fact, Oh *et al.* (2004) found that other temporal aspects such as periods of silence and articulation rate were found to be more reliable as diagnostic cues to signal the type of schizophrenic condition suffered.

Language teaching

The importance of rhythm indexes to language teaching is evident from their application to native and non-native varieties of a language since they shed light on the rhythmic differences between native and non-native learners of a language. Such differences can then become the key areas of focus for a teacher in the classroom.

Indeed, the seminal works comparing native varieties of English against nonnative varieties of English where the PVI was first used a tool for investigating rhythmic variation are Low and Grabe (1995), Low *et al.* (2000) and Deterding (2001), all of which compared the rhythm of SE (a nonnative variety) compared to BE (a native variety). It was shown that vowel and syllable variability was lower in SE than in BE and this explains why the former has been described as syllable-timed and the latter as stress-timed. The relative absence of vowel reduction compared to BE was also found to be characteristic of SE.

Gut and Milde (2002) applied the PVI to measure the rhythm of standard Nigerian English. Previous descriptions have classified Nigerian English as syllable-timed rather than stress-timed, and vowel reduction has been found to be less prevalent compared to BE. They found significantly less vowel-to-vowel variability in Nigerian English than in BE but there were no significant differences in syllable-to-syllable variability between the two varieties of English.

Thomas and Carter (2003) employed the PVI to compare the rhythm of the English spoken by the African Americans and the Hispanics. The Hispanics also spoke Spanish, which has been described as a syllable-timed language. Results showed that Hispanics exhibited more syllable-timed rhythm, compared to African Americans. Interestingly, the African Americans had PVI values similar to BE and this suggests that they spoke a more stress-timed variety of English.

Moving away from English, the PVI has also been applied to compare the rhythm of Latvian spoken by native speakers against Russian speakers of Latvian (Bond *et al.*, 2003). Latvian has been described as syllable-timed whereas Russian is stress-timed. Interestingly, their results showed that while the PVI values between proficient Russian speakers of Latvian and native Latvians were similar, differences were found in the rhythm of the Latvian spoken by the less proficient Russians. The less proficient speakers had high PVI values characteristic of stress-timed languages rather than the syllable-timed rhythm of Latvian.

I would like to move away now from the applications of the PVI to the native and nonnative varieties of a language to consider the possible implications of such findings for the language classroom. It is important to note that the PVI is based on a calculation of vowel-to-vowel variability. The PVI has been shown to be a powerful tool in capturing the rhythmic differences between a stress-timed language (which displays a high PVI) and a syllable-timed language (which has a low PVI). In addition, several studies on nonnative varieties of English reviewed above have alluded to the relative scarcity of reduced vowels in attempting to explain why nonnative varieties veer towards syllable-timing rather than the stress timing associated with native varieties such as BE and American English. What, then, are the implications for pronunciation teaching?

I would first like to consider the question of where and when reduced vowels occur in a native variety of English such as BE. Low *et al.* (2000) had considered this point in their paper and suggested, based on the review of related literature, that reduced vowels appear to be correlated with speaking style and stress. In particular, unstressed words are potential carriers for weak or reduced forms of vowels (Tiffany, 1959).

Furthermore, speaking style also influences the realization of reduced vowels, as there are many more reduced vowels in connected speech than in citation forms of words (Shearme and Holmes, 1962). Kohler (1990) noted that in unstressed positions, function words in English tend to be realized as reduced vowels. Since the presence or absence of reduced vowels or weak forms influences the rhythmic patterning of a language, teachers wishing to help students to understand how to veer towards the stress-timing of native Englishes can choose to focus on the concept of weak forms in the classroom. Liang (2003) raises two reasons why weak forms ought to be taught. First, it is to allow students to acquire a more native speaker oriented rhythm (though it is arguable within each teaching context whether the teaching model ought always to be the native variety of English). Second, she feels that the production of weak forms can help nonnative speakers to sound more intelligible when interacting with native speakers of English. In her article, she also outlines a clear and reasonable lesson plan for the teaching of weak forms in the language classroom. She suggests that instead of providing a long list of weak forms for memorization, it is better to introduce the weak forms according to the grammatical category of function words such as articles, pronouns, auxiliary verbs, prepositions and so on. She then suggests sentence drills where both the strong and weak forms of the words are presented. For example, '*Can you go?*' versus '*You can go*'. She advocates choral drilling since Kelly (2000) has suggested that this can help provide a chance for students to practice anonymously. Liang (2003) also suggests listening exercises where students are asked to identify all weak forms in a passage read to them. Finally, the importance of communicative practice is not neglected since it is important for students to apply what they have learnt in real life communicative situations. To achieve this, Liang suggests the interview technique which focuses on getting students to interview each other about their abilities to do certain things. In so doing, the focus is on '*can*'; for example, '*Can you use the Powerpoint software?*' The interviewees, in providing answers to such ability-related questions, would ultimately have to respond with the weak forms of '*can*'; for example, '*I can't use Powerpoint but I can learn to use it.*'

Conclusion

This chapter has reviewed current research into speech rhythm. In so doing, it has highlighted the multi-disciplinary impact of such research. In line with the theme of the rest of the book, the implications of rhythmic research for classroom practice in terms of what ought to be the focal areas, and a suggestion of how these can be taught was also presented. Needless to say, as the research into speech rhythm proceeds at a neck-breaking pace, it is necessary for the language teacher not only to be cognizant of these latest findings but to constantly reflect on how this may impact everyday classroom practice.

Notes

* This work is partially funded by the NIE Academic Research Project RI 1/03 LEL: Theoretical Speech Research and its practical applications.
1 The PVI was first designed based on a suggestion by Dr Francis Nolan of the Phonetics Laboratory at the University of Cambridge.
2

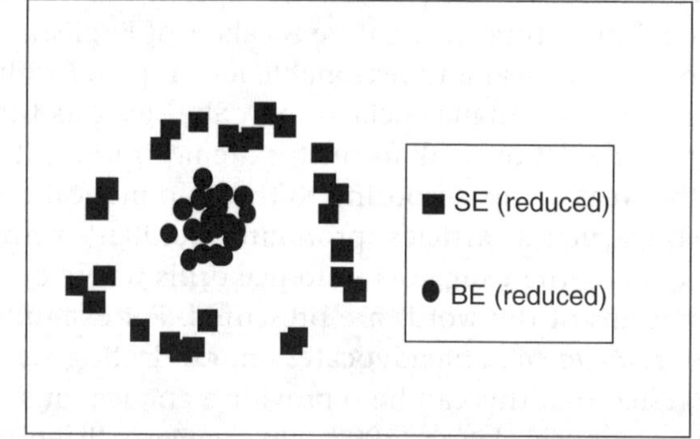

Figure 5.10   A schematic representation of the reduced vowels found in SE and BE

3 For a justification of why the nPVI was applied to vocalic intervals but the rPVI on intervocalic intervals, please refer to Grabe and Low (2002: 526–7).

Bibliography

Abercrombie, D. (1965) *Studies in Phonetics and Linguistics* (London: Oxford).
Abercrombie, D. (1967) *Elements of General Phonetics* (Edinburgh: Edinburgh University Press).
Barry, W. J., Andreeva, B., Russo, M., Dimitrova, S. and Kostadinova, T. (2003) 'Do rhythm measures tell us anything about language type?', *Proceedings of the 15th International Congress of Phonetic Sciences*, 2693–6.

Beckman, M. (1982) 'Segment duration and the "mora" in Japanese', *Phonetica*, 39: 113–35.

Bertinetto, P.M. (1977) 'Syllabic blood, oveero l'italiano come lingua ad isocronismo sillabico', *Studi di Grammatica Italiana*, 6: 69–96.

Bloch B. (1942) 'Studies in colloquial Japanese IV: phonemics', *Language*, 26: 86–125.

Bolinger, D.L. (1965) *Forms of English: Accent, Morpheme, Order* (Cambridge: Harvard University Press).

Bond, Z.S., Markus, D. and Stockmal, V. (2003) 'Prosodic and rhythmic patterns produced by native and non-native speakers of a quantity-sensitive language', *Proceedings of the 15th International Congress of Phonetic Sciences*.

Brakel, A. (1985) 'Towards a morphophonological approach to the study of linguistic rhythm', *Chicago Linguistic Society*, 21: 15–25.

Couper-Kuhlen, E. (1990) 'Discovering rhythm in conversational English: perceptual and acoustic approaches to the analysis of isochrony', *KontRI Working Paper*, 13.

Couper-Kuhlen, E. (1993) *English Speech Rhythm. Form and Function in Everyday Verbal Interaction* (Amsterdam: Benjamins).

Dasher, R. and Bolinger, D. (1982) 'On pre-accentual lengthening', *Journal of the International Phonetic Association*, 12: 58–69.

Dauer, R.M. (1983) 'Stress-timing and syllable-timing re-analysed', *Journal of Phonetics*, 11: 51–62.

Dauer, R.M. (1987) 'Phonetic and phonological components of language rhythm', *Proceedings of the 11th International Congress of Phonetic Sciences*, 447–50.

Delattre, P. (1966) 'A comparison of syllable length conditioning among languages', *International Review of Applied Linguistics in Language Teaching*, IV, 3: 183–98.

Deterding, D.H. (2001) 'The measurement of rhythm: a comparison of Singapore English and British English', *Journal of Phonetics*, 29: 217–30.

Eriksson, A. (1991) 'Aspects of Swedish speech rhythm', *Gothenburg Monographs in Linguistics*, 9 (Sweden: University of Gothenburg).

Farinas, J. and Pellegrino, F. (2001) 'Automatic rhythm modeling for language identification', *Proceedings of Eurospeech*, 2539–42.

Faure, G., Hirst, D.J. and Chafcouloff, M. (1980) 'Rhythm in English: isochronism, pitch and perceived stress', in L.R. Waugh and C.H. van Schooneveld (eds), *The Melody of Language* (Baltimore: University Park Press) 71–9.

Galves, A., Garcia, J., Duarte, D. and Galves, C. (2002) 'Sonority as a basis for rhythmic class discrimination', *Proceedings of Speech Prosody*.

Grabe, E. and Low, E.L. (2002) 'Durational variability in speech and the rhythm class hypothesis', in C. Gussenhoven and N. Warner (eds), *Laboratory Phonology*, 7 (Berlin: Mouton de Gruyter 515–46.

Grabe, E., Post, B. and Watson, I. (1999) 'The acquisition of rhythmic patterns in English and French', *Proceedings of the 14th International Congress of Phonetic Sciences*.

Gut, U. and Milde, J.T. (2002) 'The prosody of Nigerian English,' *Proceedings of Speech Prosody*, 367–70.

Han, M.S. (1962) 'The feature of duration in Japanese', *Onsei no kenkyuu*, 10: 65–80.

Hoequist, C.J. (1983a) 'Durational correlates of linguistic rhythm categories', *Phonetica*, 40: 19–31.

Hoequist, C.J. (1983b) 'Syllable duration in stress-, syllable- and mora-timed languages', *Phonetica*, 40: 203–37.

Kelly, G. (2000) *How to Teach Pronunciation* (London: Pearson).

Kohler, K.J. (1990) 'Segmental reduction in connected speech in German: phonological facts and phonetic explanations', in W.J. Hardcastle and A. Marchal (eds), *Speech Production and Speech Modelling* (Dordrecht: Kluwer) 62–92.

Ladefoged, P. (1975) *A Course in Phonetics* (New York: Harcourt Brace Jovanovich).

Laver, J. (1994) *Principles of Phonetics* (Cambridge: Cambridge University Press).

Lehiste, I. (1990) 'Some aspects of the phonetics of metrics', in K. Wiik and I. Ramo (eds), *Nordic Prosody*, V (Turku: University of Turku) 206–18.

Liang, W.X. (2003) 'Teaching weak forms', *Forum*, 41: 32–6.

Low, E.L., Deterding, D. and Ong, P.K. (2004) 'Rhythm indexes: a comparative study of their reliability', Paper presented at the British Association for Academic Phoneticians (BAAP) Colloquium, Cambridge.

Low, E.L. (1998) *Prosodic prominence in Singapore English*, PhD thesis (University of Cambridge).

Low, E.L. and Grabe, E. (1995) 'Prosodic patterns in Singapore English', *Proceedings of the 13th International Congress for Phonetic Sciences*, 636–9.

Low, E.L., Grabe, E. and Nolan, F. (2000) 'Quantitative characterizations of speech rhythm: syllable-timing in Singapore English', *Language and Speech*, 43, 4: 377–401.

Manrique, A.M.B. and Signorini, A. (1983) 'Segmental reduction in Spanish', *Journal of Phonetics*, 11: 117–28.

Miller, M. (1984) 'On the perception of rhythm', *Journal of Phonetics*, 12: 75–83.

Nakatani, L.H., O'Connor, J.D. and Aston, C.H. (1981) 'Prosodic aspects of American English speech rhythm', *Phonetica*, 38: 84–105.

Nespor, M. (1990) 'On the rhythm parameter in phonology', in I. Roca (ed.), *Logical Issues in Language Acquisition* (Dordrecht: Foris) 157–75.

Oh, T., Low, E.L. and Ong, P.K. (2004) 'Rhythm and other temporal aspects in the disorganized speech of schizophrenic patients: a preliminary study', Paper presented at the British Association for Academic Phoneticians (BAAP) Colloquium, Cambridge.

Ong, P.K. (2004) 'Rhythm: a comparative study of indexes', Academic Exercise, National Institute of Education, Singapore .

Oyakawa, T. (1971) 'On the directionality of segmental conditioning in Japanese', Monthly Internal Memo (University of Berkeley, California 81–103.

Peter, B. and Stoel-Gammon, C. (2003) 'Rhythm production in speech and music tasks in childhood apraxia of speech and normal development', Paper presented at the Child Phonology Conference, University of British Columbia, Vancouver.

Pike, K.L. (1945) *The Intonation of American English* (Ann Arbor: University of Michigan Press).

Pointon, G.E. (1980) 'Is Spanish really syllable-timed?', *Journal of Phonetics*, 8: 293–304.

Port, P.F., Al Ani, S. and Maeda, S. (1980) 'Temporal compensation and universal phonetics', *Phonetica*, 37: 235–52.

Port, P.F., Dalby, F. and O'Dell, M. (1987) 'Evidence for mora-timing in Japanese', *Journal of the Acoustical Society of America*, 81: 1574–85.

Ramus, F. (2002) 'Acoustic correlates of linguistic rhythm: perspectives', *Proceedings of Prosody*.

Ramus, F., Nespor, M. and Mehler, J. (1999) 'Correlates of linguistic rhythm in the speech signal', *Cognition*, 73, 3: 265–92.

Roach, P. (1982) 'On the distinction between '"stress-timed" and "syllable-timed" languages', in D. Crystal (ed.), *Linguistic Controversies* (London: Edward Arnold) 73–9.

Shearme, J.N. and Holmes, J.N. (1962) 'An experimental study of the classification of sounds in continuous speech according to their distribution in the formant, 1-formant two plans', *Proceedings of the 4th International Congress of Phonetic Sciences*, 233–40.

Shen, Y. and Peterson, G.G. (1962) 'Isochrony in English', *University of Buffalo Studies in Linguistics Occasional Papers*, 9: 1–36.

Strangert, E. (1985) *Swedish Speech Rhythm in a Cross-Linguistic Perspective*, (Umea: Umea Studies in Humanities, 9).

Taylor, D.S. (1981) 'Non-native speakers and the rhythm of English', *International Review of Applied Linguistics in Language Teaching*, 19, 3.

Thomas, E. and Carter, P. (2003) 'A first look in Southern African American and European English', Paper presented at NWAV32 New Ways of Analyzing Variation, University of Pennsylvania, Philadelphia.

Tiffany, W.R. (1959) 'Nonrandom sources of variation in vowel quality', *Journal of Speech and Hearing Research*, 2: 305–17.

Wenk, B. and Wioland, F. (1982) 'Is French really syllable-timed?', *Journal of Phonetics*, 10: 193–216.

6
Factors Affecting Turn-taking Behaviour: Genre meets Prosody

Rebecca Hughes and Beatrice Szczepek Reed

The orderly distribution of opportunities to participate in social interaction is one of the most fundamental preconditions for viable social organization. For humans, conversation and other more specialized or context-specific forms of talk-in-interaction ... are species-distinctive embodiments of this primordial site of sociality (Schegloff, 2000: 1).

Introduction

This chapter looks at work on turn-taking from the perspective of what a speaker must know in order to participate in Schegloff's 'primordial site of sociality'. After a brief overview of the existing literature, we propose a set of broad hypotheses about what speakers must know in order to accomplish successful turn-taking in conversation. We then go on to offer analyses of two extracts from a native/non-native interaction which demonstrate the impact of knowledge about conversational genre on the local negotiating work accomplished by the speakers in the realms of prosody and syntax. We conclude by suggesting a broader interpretative framework for future analysis of turn-taking behaviour.

Previous literature on turn-taking

Turn-taking is a complex and still not wholly understood part of speech behaviour, and is centred in linguistic and social mechanisms where several levels of communicative activity work simultaneously and dynamically: intonation, syntax, semantics, pragmatic knowledge, sociolinguistic knowledge. This makes turn behaviour potentially a rich vein for speech research.

The basic mechanisms of turn-taking have been studied in some detail for at least 30 years in the conversation analysis (CA) tradition, and, in fact, Schegloff (2000) situates the beginnings of work in this area as far back as the mid-1950s in the work of Erving Goffmann on face work. Over the years, different studies have reached diverse conclusions as to the key features of turn-behaviour. Many studies have suggested that prosody plays a central role in turn-taking. For example, Schegloff (1998), Wells and Macfarlane (1998) and Fox (2001) discuss the relevance of the pitch pattern on the last major accent in a turn as relevant for potential turn transition. Local *et al.* (1985) describe the prosodic resources with which speakers of London Jamaican demarcate turn endings, including tempo, loudness, duration, vowel quality and pitch. Local *et al.* (1986) do the same for Tyneside English, and Wells and Peppè (1996) for Ulster English. Ogden (2001; 2004) shows voice quality to be a central feature of turn-taking in Finnish, while Tanaka (2004) demonstrates how Japanese utilises pitch in turn transitions which are lacking in a turn-final object.

Other studies have suggested that syntax plays more of a role, but is supported by prosody (Caspers, 2003). Auer (1996) argues that, while prosody is extremely relevant in the local fine tuning of transition organization, syntax is the main factor for the predictability of turn taking opportunities:

> If, then, the independence of prosody from syntax is considerable, the priority of syntax nonetheless cannot be denied either. The discussion ... suggests a model in which syntax and prosody cooperate in very delicate ways, each of them on the basis of its particular semiotic possibilities. Into this model of a division of labour, syntax brings its capacity to build relatively far-reaching gestalts, the completion of which becomes more and more projectable in time; prosody, particularly intonation, brings in its local flexibility to revise and adjust these gestalts while they are 'put into speech'. Thus, syntax retains its priority, but prosody/intonation is nevertheless independent from it (p. 75).

Others have conducted quantitative analyses and suggested that while 'syntax has a stronger contribution than any individual prosodic feature ... the whole prosody contributes as strongly as, or even more strongly than, syntax' (Koiso *et al.*, 1998: 295). Some studies have acknowledged that prosody and syntax may have different levels of importance in different languages. For example, Wells and Macfarlane

(1998) show that while the occurrence of a final major accent in a turn constructional unit may signal upcoming turn completion in many varieties of English, the exact prosodic realization varies across dialects, and may not be crucial to participants' monitoring turns for transition spaces. Similarly, Szczepek Reed (2004) shows that a wide variety of different intonation patterns occur on and after the last accented syllable in English, suggesting that it is 'a broad cluster of prosodic, syntactic and pragmatic cues' which is involved in the negotiation of turn transition, rather than a single linguistic feature alone. Tanaka (1999) shows that in Japanese conversation the vast majority of turn endings (71.8%) rely on grammatical cues, whereas in the remaining cases, prosody is employed as the main factor (Tanaka, 2004).

Some studies have shown that turn-taking protocols that emerge when speakers have no access to prosodic cues lead to a doubling in the time it takes to complete the same task (Johnstone *et al.*, 1994). The implication here is that although it is possible to communicate and exchange turns using syntactic and semantic cues alone, prosody enhances the interactive efficiency to a dramatic extent. More controversially, some have suggested that there is no such thing as a turn-taking mechanism, speakers simply 'alternate', and that the elaborate investigations of turns to pin down rule-like correlates are part of a futile, formalist conspiracy to reduce language to 'sequences of word-based forms' (Cowley, 1998: 541). Others have shown consistently and experimentally that speakers, or rather, listeners, have a remarkable capacity to predict the end point of a given utterance, both in terms of number of words and duration (Grosjean and Hirt, 1996). Such predictability, or projection, of an upcoming turn-ending has also been described by Auer (1996) (above), and Selting (1996), who differentiates four linguistic signalling resources for the projection of turn-finality:

> Syntactic projection, which is done by the initiation of syntactic schemata; prosodic projection, which is accomplished by the use of prosodic means of unit and/or turn holding or yielding; semantic projection, which is realized by the use of particular lexical constructions such as *either … or, first … second*, etc., or by starting to provide a piece of information that needs to be completed; discourse-pragmatic or sequential projection, which is achieved by the formulation of announcements, prefaces or other kinds of initiation of recognizable activity types which are thus being made expectable (p. 359).

Similarly, Ford and Thompson (1996) show that participants orient to syntactic, intonational and pragmatic features of talk in their prediction of an upcoming transition relevance place.

Thus, any brief literature of turn-taking research leads to the conclusion that more than one linguistic signal affects a listener-speaker's ability to understand when they should, or should not, speak. That is to say, it is not enough to simply listen for syntactic closure, or to wait for another person to stop, or sound as if they are stopping. The ability to maintain or change turn depends on many simultaneous factors. In spontaneous conversation speakers manage and process multiple levels of language knowledge and processing ability simultaneously. While any model of spontaneous speech must simplify the data, this processing phenomenon should eventually, we argue, be acknowledged as a defining characteristic of the mode.

This chapter reports an attempt to uncover a little more about the necessary conditions for successful turn-behaviour and to position these in a wider debate about speech research. Rather than pursuing the tradition of starting from linguistic evidence in the form of utterances that both the CA approach and the more quantitative work uses, the study begins outside any specific interactional data and asks some basic questions about what speakers must know in order to hand-over and initiate speech properly.

Towards an understanding of what speakers must know

This section gives a set of broad hypotheses about turn-taking inferring what speakers must know. The hypotheses are as follows:

(1) Speakers know that speakers alternate;
(2) Speakers know that there are, and can easily recognize, genres and contexts in which it is expected that speakers will alternate, others where varying degrees of monologue are the norm;
(3) Speakers know that there are appropriate patterns of alternation that are expected in a particular genre or context;
(4) Speakers know, in a given language, the syntactic, semantic, and prosodic cues that signal turn-hold and turn-change intentions;
(5) Speakers know, for a given interlocutor, how turn-taking cues will be realized by that speaker.

These hypotheses move from the most general and basic conception of what a speaker must believe about the nature of speaking to the real-time processing of the stream of speech of a particular instance of talk. The hypotheses can be annotated and given rationales as follows. The most fundamental hypothesis we can form about turn-taking is that, to use Cowley's (1998) very neutral term:

Speakers know that speakers alternate

That is to say, speakers know that other speakers speak for a finite period and that there is an expectation that another speaker will, in due course, respond and initiate an utterance. In dyadic or multi-party contexts, therefore, which are the basis of most work on turn-taking, the onus falls on the recipients continually to monitor a speaking turn for transition relevance places and be ready to speak. However, in thinking about this we quickly see it is not the case that listeners are always listening in a 'primed to speak' state. For example, the audience of a lecture is carrying out appropriate turn-behaviour precisely by *not* seeking to initiate or respond. This indicates that speakers must also have knowledge of speech genres to inform their decision to speak. Therefore, a second hypothesis might be framed as:

Speakers know that there are, and can easily recognize, genres and contexts in which it is expected that speakers will alternate, others where varying degrees of monologue are the norm

Even during spontaneous conversation participants negotiate spates of talk in which one acts as primary speaker whereas others engage in listening activities only. One such conversational environment is storytelling. In more regulated genres of talk, such as interviewing, turn-taking takes place under the broad knowledge that one participant will do the asking and another will answer; however, individual instances of transition still have to be negotiated locally. Further along the scale, genres such as lectures and speeches allow for no spoken turns by any other than the allocated speaker.

Once this is recognized, a further layer of knowledge can be seen to be relevant. Speakers must know not only that genres and contexts can be distinguished by the interactive responsibility placed on them, but also for a specific type of talk they must have a sense of the interactional and sequential patterns of that context. This will range from a knowledge of high level discourse, sociolinguistic and conversational norms (who is allowed to speak, how much, and about what) to utterance level knowledge of patterns of talk (for instance, formulaic sequences and appropriate pair-parts). This type is summed up in hypothesis 3:

Speakers know that there are appropriate patterns of alternation that are expected in a particular genre or context

For example, once a speaker has set up an upcoming narrative by saying something along the lines of 'you'll never believe what happened to us in the car park the other day', the remaining participants must know that this speaker is about to deliver a narrative, and will therefore require a longer turn space than someone who says, for example: 'What is everybody having for drinks?' Hierarchical issues in interactions such as doctor/patient or student/professor bring their own social preconceptions about turn allocation and conversational actions. Furthermore, different conversational topics, activities and sequence types depend on speakers' knowledge about turn-holding priorities.

However, these three hypotheses do not cover enough scope to help us explain turn-behaviour. Knowing that alternation can take place and knowing appropriate patterns of turn-taking in a variety of contexts will not be enough to allow the speaker to participate appropriately. In fact, these first three hypotheses may, in effect, be mapped onto the state of the advanced second language learner who has excellent proficiency, but feels unable to participate in spontaneous conversation. The listener must also gain an understanding of the signals that a speaker sends out to show whether they are ready to hand over the conversational baton, or not. Therefore a fourth hypothesis is:

Speakers know, in a given language, the syntactic, semantic, and prosodic cues that signal turn-hold and turn-change intentions

While most English varieties are fairly consistent in their deployment of syntactic and semantico-pragmatic turn-taking signals, the shapes of prosodic cues for turn transition differ across dialects, and other languages rely on different combinations of linguistic features. Therefore, knowledge about which language parameters to use and to listen out for, and an understanding of the form in which those parameters are employed for turn-taking, is vital for accomplishing smooth floor transition.

Finally, and perhaps most interestingly, a focus on how turn-taking is managed brings *speaker idiolect* into the modelling of speech behaviour. Much of the research on turn-taking implies that a listener is able to project utterance endings, and that they have a sense of the speech rate, pitch, and rhythm of a stream of speech to which they are attending. Loudness and speech rate in particular are signals of turn-hold and turn-change intentions. However, the implication of this ability to signal and to recognize changes in prosody on a second-by-second basis is that a listener must have an acute awareness of what even a total stranger's norms of voice are. That is to say, even at the start of a conversation with someone whose voice has never been heard before a listener will need to know almost instantaneously how 'loud', 'high' or 'quick' are realised by this interlocutor. If, as has been suggested by previous work, frequency, intensity and timing all play a part in cueing the desire to hold or release a turn, then a listener must quickly have a sense of what is louder, higher, or quicker for this particular speaker. This therefore brings us to the final hypothesis, as we must infer that knowledge of idiolect in terms of voice quality and production play a key part in appropriate turn behaviour:

Speakers know, for a given interlocutor, how turn-taking cues will be realized by that speaker

This hypothesis also may indicate that in looking at unsuccessful turns between near strangers we may find more evidence for what is crucial to effective turn behaviour than in the material on which much of the classic work on turn-taking is based (transitions between family members or close friends).

Exploring the hypotheses through instances of turn-behaviour

The data on which the research in this paper is based are a corpus of spoken English created at the National Institute of Education, Singapore which we are using with the kind permission of its creators, David Deterding and Ee Ling Low. Further details can be found in Deterding and Low (2001). The methodology, details about the incidence of turn-taking, rationale for choosing certain speakers, and explanation of how successful and unsuccessful turns were defined can be found in Hughes (2005). The work we are reporting here looked in some detail at instances of overlapping talk between interviewer and interviewee and used these to further the discussion in relation to the hypotheses mentioned earlier. The hypotheses are dealt with in reverse order in the analysis, beginning from examples of what occurred at points of turn change and turn hold in the data and moving to a broader discussion of genres and speaker expectations.

Caspers (2003) posits the notion of turn change being the norm, and speakers having to signal turn hold. As the data in question are all taken from interviews in a one-to-one semi-structured format, this starting point for an analysis of successful and unsuccessful turn behaviour seems particularly appropriate. That is to say, both Caspers's assumption and the interview format itself suggest a predictable pattern of turn change taking place. Where violations occur – for example, interviewer not realizing that a speaker has ended, or difficulty between interviewer and interviewee in deciding who should take the floor – there may be particularly strong evidence for a breakdown in the signalling of turn transition intentions.

The data in Hughes (2005) were analyzed in terms of collaborative versus non-collaborative overlaps, similar to the distinction between turn-competitive and non-competitive interruptions made by French and Local (1986), who find that

> the positioning of interruptor's speech at a non-completion point in current turn does not alone make for a hearing of that speech as directly competitive for the turn. (p. 162)[1]

The instances were further analyzed in terms of whether the original speaker had been attempting to relinquish or retain the floor. The full transcripts from which these extracts are taken, together with relevant sound files can be found at: http://www.arts.nie.edu.sg/ell/davidd/niecsse/index.htm under the codes f16-a and f16-c respectively. The first extract comes from an interaction in which a non-native student of English is being interviewed about past holidays by a lecturer, who is an English native-speaker:[2]

(1) Langkawi, extract f-16a

```
1   S:      okay the las::t er vacAtion (.) me and my hUsband wen:t to
2           <<all> langKAwi?>
3           (-)
4           erm
5           (-)
6   ->      [most
7   -> I:   [how
8           how long did you go THERE for;
```

The interviewer (*I*) and interviewee (*S*) overlap on the words 'most' and 'how'.

Previous to this overlap, *S* has replied to *I*'s question where she went for her last vacation with the turn in lines 1–5 in the transcript. Her answer comes in a single sentence, and on the last accent and following unstressed syllable -*KAwi*, line 2, she produces a high rising pitch curve, which can be seen in Figure 6.1. This intonation contour is followed by an unfilled macro-pause, a hesitation marker, and another macro-pause (lines 3–5). It is at this point that *I* decides to come in, treating *S*'s hesitation as an opportunity for transition. The brief overlap on the two monosyllabic words *most* and *how* (lines 6f.) is quickly resolved by *S* giving up the floor to *I*, who repeats the part of his turn that was produced in overlap, and continues (line 8).

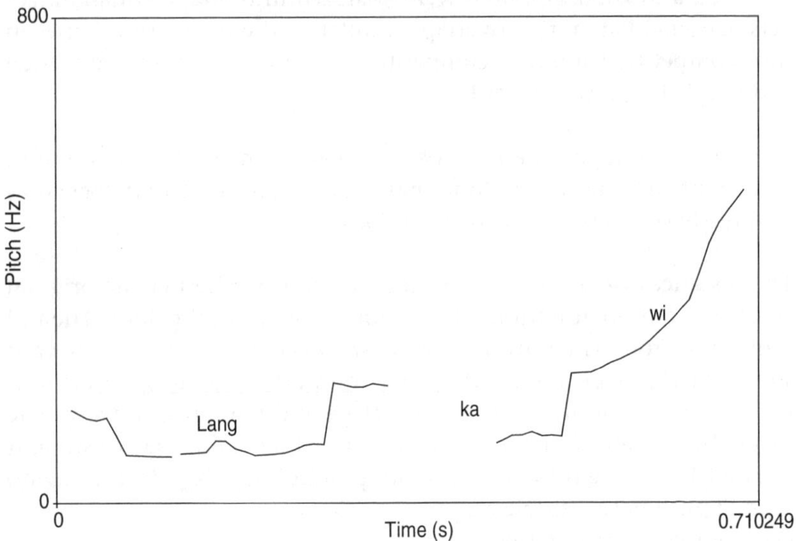

Figure 6.1   Fundamental frequency: Langkawi

The transition between the two speakers is not a smooth one: *S*'s pausing, combined with her immediate relinquishing of the floor once she has started again in overlap with *I*, shows that she had attempted to give up the floor after *Langkawi*. However, something in the delivery of the end of her turn seems to have signalled to *I* that she was planning to continue, and indeed her rising intonation contour can be heard as try-marking, inviting a minimal recipient response (Sacks and Schegloff, 1979), rather than contextualizing turn completion. *I* does not provide any back channelling, and after a relatively long hesitation period, *S* decides to continue – in overlap with *I*, who at this point has also decided to take over.

In combination with local prosodic signalling cues, the broader issue of conversational genre may play a role in this misunderstanding. Despite being syntactically complete, *S*'s turn is a very brief response to

a question posed to her in an interview situation, in which the interviewer asks a question, and the interviewee is then allocated extended
turn space for her response. *I* may be waiting for elaboration on *S*'s
part, and may therefore be reluctant to come in. From *S*'s perspective,
the try-marking intonation at the end of her turn invites *I* to give back
channelling. However, in the genre of professional interviewing it is
not customary for the interviewer to give recipient responses, and *I*
indeed refrains from doing so. This seems to trigger her uncertainty as
to how to continue, and therefore put both of them in a conversational limbo.

Thus, both participants' difficulties can be explained with reference
to conversational genre: *S*'s unfulfilled expectation of a recipient
response from *I*, and *I*'s unfulfilled expectation of more elaboration
from *S* both have their roots in the genre 'interview' in which this
interaction takes place. This, therefore, shows the need to extend the
analysis of turn behaviour from the micro to the macro level, and
understand better the relationships between them.

The following extract is different in nature from the first example
analyzed; it occurs later in the same interview:

(2) New experience, extract f16-c

```
1   I:    have you ever BEEN DIVing before,
2   S:    N::::: <<f> ˆˋNO!>
3         (.)
4   I:    so this is a NEW expErience for [you.
5   S:                                    [YES.
6         <<creaky> yea- >
7         [be-
8   I:    [how long does it TAKE you;
9         to get a DIVing cert.
```

F16-c shows two instances of overlapping talk. In passing, it can be
mentioned that the first instance is one of non-competitive overlap. In
line 3, *I*'s turn *so this is a new experience for you* is overlapped near its
completion in the middle of the last adverbial phrase *for you*. Syntactically, the sentence is complete before the adverbial phrase, and semantically, nothing is added that could not have been predicted from the
turn so far. Thus, this is a 'friendly take-over' in that *I* is already within
his transition relevance space when *S* comes in to begin her next turn.

For our purposes, however, it is the second of these instances of overlap that is of interest. This is an example of an unsuccessful attempt by
a speaker to hold a turn. In order to successfully analyze it, we have to

take a look at the previous exchange in the same sequence, where *S* replies to *I*'s Yes/No question *have you ever been diving before* (line 1) with the strongly accented single token *no* (line 2), which carries a pronounced rising-falling intonation contour and higher volume than surrounding speech. She does not continue her turn after this, and there is a micro-pause before *I* comes back in with his next Yes/No question (line 4). To this *S* replies again with a single token, *yes* (line 5), however with a less marked prosodic pattern. Probably with respect to the previous overlap (lines 4f.), *S* repeats her affirmative as a clipped and creaky *yea-* (line 6). Following this, she attempts to continue; however, *I* overlaps with her first syllable *be-* (line 7) and takes over the floor to ask a follow-up question (lines 8f.).

Although we have seen in extract (1), which takes place earlier in the same conversation, that the interviewer may initially have had a preference for longer replies to his questions, he does not allow for enough turn space in this extract. The exchange in lines 1–4 immediately before the interrupting sequence offers a possible interpretation. *I* has asked a Yes/No question and was given a short, type-conforming response (Raymond, 2000)[3] in the form of *NO!*. The ensuing pause shows that *I* would have given *S* more room to speak, had she chosen to do so. In the sequence that follows (lines 5–9), *I* shows orientation to that previous exchange and treats *S*'s type-conforming response – this time a yes – as complete, only allowing her to produce a repeated version in the clear after previous overlap. Even though this second *yea-* is clipped and quite obviously not designed for turn completion, *I* takes over the floor as if he had 'learned' from the prior sequence that short, type-conforming responses mean TRPs in his co-participant's speech.

Thus, in this instance it is not so much knowledge about conversational genre that seems to influence turn-taking activity, but knowledge about a co-participant's behaviour acquired during ongoing interaction. This shows the importance of including individual speakers' idiolects into the description and analysis of turn-taking.

Conclusion

These two examples from early and later in the same interview show the delicate interaction between factors at the different levels hypothesized above. At the level of idiolect and prosodic signalling, the interviewee's intonation patterns and slightly 'choppy' delivery with long pauses after short responses influence the interlocutor's turn-taking behaviour early in the interview. Later, having perhaps developed the impression that the speaker will only give short responses, and since no turn-holding signals are forthcoming, *I* begins to move more quickly from one question to the next to keep the conversation flowing. Wells and Corrin (2004) describe such development of participants' expectations of each others' turn-taking behaviour within the span of one interaction between a child and his caretaker. They show that certain behaviour by the caretaker earlier in the talk can trigger modified turn-taking moves by the child later on, thus making up a small step in the child's learning curve of prosodic patterns for turn-taking. Adult interaction between speakers of different varieties of English, such as native/non-native, may be another interactional environment in which participants monitor each others' turn-taking and modify their own behaviour at transition relevance places accordingly.

The semi-structured interview context of the speech data in the NIE corpus provides a useful instance of how turn-taking idiosyncrasies, and also the wider conversational genre, lead to expectations about turn behaviour in the speakers. We are arguing that this effect has been under-researched in the previous work. In the interview genre, for instance, there will be an assumption that the Sacks *et al.*'s (1974) turn-taking rule of 'first speaker selects' will generally be the norm. The pattern we may expect to see is that of question, answer to question and next question. There is a higher-order framework for turn-taking behaviour in place. This higher-order discourse pattern is an example of what we raised in hypotheses 2 and 3: the suggestion that speakers must know which genres lead to speaker alternation and what the expected patterns of alternation are. However, when we see and hear the speakers in action, despite the expectations of the genre, the interviewer is at times singularly hesitant about asking the next question. Thus, even in a semi-regulated conversational structure such as an interview, participants have to negotiate turn transition on a moment-to-moment basis at the local points of potential speaker change.

Our argument is that when looking at the data in a more fine-grained way – for example, the pitch curves and timing of some speakers sending mixed signals to the interviewer – it is not enough to retain the focus solely at that level of analysis. These analyses suggest that at least two, inter-related, aspects can be regarded as impacting on the turn-taking behaviour of these speakers: genre and idiolect. While previous work has almost always acknowledged that more than one primary signal affects turn-taking behaviour, few have seen this as a defining characteristic of the spoken mode. To speak is to know how to begin to speak and whether or when one should end. To answer these primary questions a speaker, we suggest, needs to be able to assess several signals simultaneously. A further tentative conclusion of this chapter is that situating turn-taking analyses in a broader context that takes in genre and idiolect may affect the conclusions one reaches about turn mechanisms.

These hypotheses suggest a framework that may provide a better understanding of turn behaviour than has been possible when we take the stream of speech and its syntax and prosody alone. Fully understanding turn-behaviour may require us to look beyond the stream of speech – the locus of the majority of work on turn-taking – and to look in two directions. The first, as we have hinted, is towards the constraints on turn behaviour that are imposed by socio-cultural and genre norms. Little or no work has been done on turn-taking signals from an inter-lingual perspective, and this would be a source of fascinating research in the future.

Appendix

GAT transcription conventions[4]

Sequential structure:

[]	
[]	overlap
=	quick, immediate connection of new turns or single units

Pauses:

(.)	micro-pause
(-), (–)	short, middle or long pauses (0.25–1 second)

Accents:

ACcent	primary, or main accent
Accent	secondary accent

Lengthening:

:,: :,:::	lengthening, according to duration

Final pitch movements:

?	high rise
,	mid-rise
-	level pitch
;	mid-fall
.	low fall

Pitch step-up/step down:

↑	pitch step up
↓	pitch step-down

Change of pitch register:

<<l>>	low pitch register
<<h>>	high pitch register

Volume and tempo changes:

<<f>>	forte
<<p>>	piano
<<all>>	allegro
<<len>>	lento

Notes

1 French/Local show that the prosodic design of high pitch and raised volume identifies an incoming turn as competing for the floor at a non-completion point, whereas incoming utterances at non-completion points that are lacking in those features are not treated as turn-competitive by co-participants.
2 See Appendix for transcription conventions.
3 In his thesis 'Type-conforming and non-conforming responses to yes/no type interrogatives', Raymond (2000: 17) defines type-conforming responses as 'responses designed for the constraints embodied in the grammatical form of a FPP (First Pair Part, B.S.R.) ... For yes/no type interrogative FPPs, such type-conforming responses are overwhelmingly accomplished by turns that contain either a "yes" or "no".'
4 Cf. Selting *et al.* (1998).

Bibliography

Auer, P. (1996) 'On the prosody and syntax of turn-continuations' in E. Couper-Kuhlen and M. Selting (eds), *Prosody in Conversation* (Cambridge: Cambridge University Press) 57–101.

Caspers, J. (2003) 'Local speech melody as a limiting factor in the turn-taking system in Dutch', *Journal of Phonetics*, 31: 251–76.

Cowley, S.J. (1998) 'Of timing, turn-taking and conversations', *Journal of Psycholinguistic Research*, 27, 5: 541–71.

Deterding, D. and Low, E.L. (2001) 'The NIE Corpus of Spoken Singapore English (NIECSSE)', *SAAL Quarterly*, 56: 2–5.

Ford, C.E. and Thompson, S.A. (1996) 'Interactional units in conversation: syntactic, intonational, and pragmatic resources for the management of turns', in E. Ochs, E.A. Schegloff and S.A. Thompson (eds), *Interaction and Grammar* (Cambridge: Cambridge University Press) 134–84.

Fox, B.A. (2001) 'An exploration of prosody and turn projection in English conversation', in M. Selting and E. Couper-Kuhlen (eds), *Studies in Interactional Linguistics* (Amsterdam/Philadelphia: Benjamins) 287–315.

French, P. and Local, J. (1986) 'Prosodic features and the management of interuptions' in C. Johns-Lewis (ed.), *Intonation in Discourse* (London/Sydney: Croom Helm) 157–80.

Grosjean, F. and Hirt, C. (1996) 'Using prosody to predict the end of sentences in English and French: normal and brain-damaged subjects', *Language and Cognitive Processes*, 11, 1/2: 107–34.

Hughes, R. (2005) 'Investigating turn-taking in the NIE Corpus of Spoken Singapore English' in Deterding, *et al.* (eds), *English in Singapore: Phonetic Research on a Corpus* (New York: McGraw Hill) 115–25.

Johnstone, A., Berry, U. and Nguyen, T. (1994) 'There was a long pause: influencing turn-taking behaviour in human–human and human–computer spoken dialogues', *International Journal of Human–Computer Studies,* 41: 383–411.

Koiso, H., Horiuchi, Y., Tutiya, S., Ichikawa, A. and Den, Y. (1998) 'An analysis of turn-taking and backchannels based on prosodic and syntactic features in Japanese map task dialogs', *Language and Speech,* 41, 3/4: 295–321.

Local, J.K., Kelly, J. and Wells, B.H.G. (1986) 'Towards a phonology of conversation: turn-taking in Tyneside English', *Journal of Linguistics,* 22: 411–37.

Local, J.K., Wells, B.H.G. and Sebba, M. (1985) 'Phonology for conversation. Phonetic aspects of turn delimitation in London Jamaican', *Journal of Pragmatics,* 9: 309–30.

Ogden, R.A. (2001) 'Turn-holding, turn-yielding and laryngeal activity in Finnish talk-in-interaction', *Journal of the International Phonetics Association,* 31: 139–52.

Ogden, R.A. (2004) 'Non-modal voice quality and turn-taking in Finnish', in E. Couper-Kuhlen and C.E. Ford (eds), *Sound Patterns in Interaction* (Amsterdam/Philadelphia: Benjamins) 29–62.

Raymond, G. (2000) 'The structure of responding: conforming and non-conforming responses to yes/no type interrogatives', Unpublished PhD Thesis (University of California, Los Angeles).

Sacks, H. and Schegloff, E.A. (1979) 'Two preferences in the organization of reference to persons in conversation and their interaction', in G. Psathas (ed.), *Everyday Language: Studies in Ethnomethodology* (New York: Irvington) 15–21

Sacks, H. Schegloff, E.A. Jefferson, G. (1974) 'A simplest systematics for the organization of turn-taking for conversation', *Language,* 50: 696–735.

Schegloff, E.A. (1998) 'Reflections on studying prosody in talk-in-interaction', *Language and Speech,* 41, 3/4: 235–63.

Schegloff, E. A. (2000) 'Overlapping talk and the organization of turn-taking for conversation', *Language in Society,* 29: 1–63.

Selting, M. (1996) 'On the interplay of syntax and prosody in the constitution of turn-constructional units and turns in conversation', *Pragmatics,* 6, 3: 357–88.

Szczepek Reed, B. (2004) 'Turn-final intonation in English', in E. Couper-Kuhlen and C.E. Ford (eds), *Sound Patterns in Interaction* (Amsterdam/Philadelphia: Benjamins) 97–119.

Tanaka, H. (1999) *Turn-taking in Japanese Conversation: A Study in Grammar and Interaction* (Amsterdam/Philadelphia: Benjamins).

Tanaka, H. (2004) 'Prosody for marking transition-relevance places in Japanese conversation: the case of turns unmarked by utterance-final objects', in E. Couper-Kuhlen and C.E. Ford (eds), *Sound Patterns in Interaction* (Amsterdam/Philadelphia: Benjamins) 63–97.

Wells, B. and Corrin, J. (2004) 'Prosodic resources, turn-taking and overlap in children's talk-in-interaction', in E. Couper-Kuhlen and C.E. Ford (eds), *Sound Patterns in Interaction* (Amsterdam/Philadelphia: Benjamins) 119–47.

Wells, B. and Macfarlane, S. (1998) 'Prosody as an interactional resource: turn-projection and overlap', *Language and Speech,* 41, 3/4: 265–94.

Wells, B.H.G. and Peppè, S. (1996) 'Ending up in Ulster: prosody and turn-taking in English dialects', in E. Couper-Kuhlen and M. Selting (eds), *Prosody in Conversation* (Cambridge: Cambridge University Press) 101–30.

Part III

Spoken Discourse and Language Pedagogy

7
Spoken Discourse, Academics and Global English: a Corpus Perspective

Anna Mauranen

Introduction

Analyzing spoken language as it occurs in natural interaction provides radically new insights into language: in the last few decades, research traditions that have focused on speaking (notably discourse analysis, conversation analysis, and pragmatics) have revitalized linguistics and challenged the adequacy of sentence-based models which have developed from analyzing written language – or invented sentences. The traditional concept of clause may go far (even if not all the way) in describing written text, but as anyone working with speech notices, its usefulness as an analytical tool of speaking is limited.

Spoken discourse has turned out to be much more organized than it would seem in the light of sentence-based models, which make it look chaotic. New categories of linguistic items which have made their way to linguistic description, such as discourse particles (for example, Aijmer, 2002), require redefining the boundaries of pragmatics and semantics; the analysis of dialogues has questioned descriptions of lexical (for example, Tao, 2001) and grammatical items (for example, Ford *et al.*, 2003) as well as the role of grammar in the light of unfolding discourse (DuBois, 2003). Many new departures from conventional descriptions are based on corpus data, which has enabled us to obtain large-scale evidence of linguistic patterning.

At the same time as our views of language have been revised in the light of research, the need for spoken communication in foreign-language teaching has rocketed. In principle, general purpose language curricula have long prioritized spoken over written skills, even though the appropriateness of the depictions of speech can be questioned. In contrast, tailor-made teaching such as English for academic purposes has strongly concentrated on reading and writing. Recently, however, this field has come under new pressure on account of accelerating globalization and academic mobility. It is not enough for academic discourses to keep to the written mode.

Clearly, if we want to prepare learners for the requirements of real-world language use with any efficiency, we cannot afford to rely on inadequate or outmoded descriptions of language. To meet current demands, we need models that can be applied to a variety of communicative goals, and that also impart procedural rather than declarative knowledge of the language to learners. An important step towards this objective consists in making use of corpora of spoken academic discourse, such as the Michigan Corpus of Academic Spoken English (MICASE, www.hti.umich.edu/m/micase), its British counterpart The British Academic Spoken English (BASE, www.rdg.ac.uk/slals/base), and the English as a lingua franca corpus ELFA (www.uta.fi/laitokset/kielet/ engf/research/elfa). This chapter looks into spoken academic discourse, and addresses issues of modelling spoken language and its consequences on language teaching from this angle. The main foci are on spoken corpora and the use of English as an international language.

Speaking and language

Natural languages exist primarily as speech – even languages that have never been codified in writing serve the fundamental human need to communicate. Speaking is the first mode in which children acquire language, it constitutes the bulk of most people's daily engagement with linguistic activity, and it is the prime motor of language change. It also provides our main data for understanding bilingualism and language contact, since mechanisms like code-switching, code mixing, or borrowing appear in speech earlier and to a larger degree than in writing. For linguistic theory, it is therefore crucial to be able to account for spoken language. While nobody is likely to deny the primacy of speech in principle, linguistic theory does not always take this principle seriously. Formal linguistics has not been too particular about the mode of language it deals with – given that it tends to operate with constructed examples, the distinction may not matter after all. Nevertheless, it is to spoken language that theories of language need to turn to in order to get to the roots of language.

For the last two or three decades or so, attention to language in use has expanded the linguist's domain of interest far beyond the clause, into text and the context of situation. Linguistic phenomena pertaining to the level of discourse have been observed to possess both regularity and meaning, and cannot be written off as defective or incomplete reflections of the ideal language that native speakers possess and recognize despite the contingencies of online processing; performance has begun to occupy centre stage.

Pragmatic aspects of language reveal major differences between writing and speaking. Many hedges are quite specific to speaking (*sort of*, *kind of*), others to the written mode (*it is reasonable to assume*), and even though some are shared (*somewhat, a little bit*), they tend to favour one or the other mode. For example *a little bit* occurs rarely in writing, and most of the few occasions are in speech quotations in fiction or news. Moreover, some linguistic items also assume different kinds of uses and prioritize different senses in speaking as compared to writing. Dictionaries and other reference works tend to be built on the written mode so strongly that even if the senses and uses typical of speaking are given, they are usually given less priority. A case in point is *just*, where dictionary meanings heavily emphasize the 'righteous' sense, the temporal sense of very recent past, or a very small amount (*just 0.77 of a second*). Yet in speech, *just* is predominantly a mitigator and tends to co-occur with reflexive discourse *if we could just move on to the second issue* (see Lindemann and Mauranen, 2001).

Careful descriptions of categories like discourse particles (for example, Östman, 1981; Aijmer, 2002) have also contributed to a redefinition of the boundaries of pragmatics and semantics. Discourse particles carry systematic meanings that cannot be captured without analyzing real speech – although they are characteristically multifunctional, each seems to have their own associations with a particular set of functions – for example, *now* with topic-changing, and *actually* with expectation (Aijmer, 2002).

In contrast to the work on discourse particles, which has usually taken a particular expression as its point of departure and proceeded to its functions, pragmatic phenomena can also be tracked down by starting from a broad function and mapping its expressions. This can be illustrated by criticism and disagreement. In speech, an expression like *I disagree* is not used in general conversation (McCarthy, 1998) or in academic contexts (Mauranen, 2003b). *I disagree* occurred only four times in a million words in the MICASE corpus of academic speaking, and *I don't agree* six times. Instead, expressions of critical intent seem to fall into three main types in academic speech:

1. cognitive verbs: *it seems to me, what puzzles me, I was wondering* or similar expressions (**to me** *A is like B...*),
2. reflexive discourse *say (what I'm saying, trying to say, you're saying), argue, point,...*
3. others: *but, why...*
(Mauranen, 2003b)

These are clearly different from those in found in written academic discourse (see Hunston, 1993; 1994). Discourse reflexivity also seems to be involved in both positive and negative evaluation, implying that it plays an important role in secondary socialization; that is, in socialization that follows primary socialization in the family, and takes place in schools, universities, hobbies, workplaces and so on.

In all, research from the recent US-based corpora of academic speaking (the MICASE and the T2K-SWAL, The TOEFL 2000 Spoken and Written Academic Language Corpus) has already shown that academic speaking is very different from academic writing; that is to say, academic speaking is more like speaking than it is like academic writing. This is not the assumption on which courses in academic speaking have traditionally been based (and still are, see Mauranen, 2004): without an empirical basis, our intuitions concerning academic speech have turned out to be unreliable, as is so often the case with linguistic intuition.

A fundamental difference between speaking and writing is, of course, in the nature of interaction; in spoken encounters, the flow of discourse is interactively co-constructed, which demands a broader range of skills in the construction of meaning than in written discourse. The co-construction of expressions in ongoing interaction appears to be typical of L2 speakers just as it is of native speakers; similar processes seem to be going on in L1–L2 dyadic encounters (see Kurhila, 2003) as well as in L2–L2 multi-party encounters (Mauranen, forthcoming): for example, self-repairs are frequent, whereas other-repairs are not. Skilful speakers in L2–L2 interaction seem to make use of both *proactive strategies*, such as self-repairs, which look ahead in the discourse and aim at preventing misunderstandings, and *retroactive repair strategies*, following the recognition of a communication problem. All interactive repairs (that is co-constructed repairs and self-repairs) are highly co-operative means of ensuring the flow of intelligible and mutually satisfactory discourse.

One of the most intriguing claims by discourse analysts is expressed by Du Bois (2003: 54) as follows: 'spoken discourse most transparently reveals grammar in use'. This is a direct challenge to the most sacred domain of linguistic research based on the written clause: grammar. McCarthy (1998) also discusses grammatical structures (subject–verb inversion in reporting clauses; conditionality in *if*-clauses) which have distinctive uses in spoken English discourse. It seems possible to think that some characteristics of spoken grammar, such as rules of the Preferred Argument Structure are universal, as Du Bois (2003) suggests, because they are firmly rooted in human cognitive processing, while others (see, for example, Ford *et al.*, 2003) may be language specific. If this is so, the latter obviously need teaching to L2 learners, the former not. But the teaching cannot be based on the traditional descriptions of writing-based grammars, because pedagogic grammars, for obvious reasons, restrict themselves to that which is perceived to be the most fundamental in the language structure. It matters very much, therefore, where we begin to look.

Leech (2000) is one of those scholars who strongly object to giving special treatment to spoken language. He participates in the debate of what he presents as two schools of thought, those in favour of a separate speech grammar (what he calls the 'Nottingham school'), and those (like himself) in favour of an integrated approach. His integrated approach postulates a common grammar for speech and writing, but accepts that empirical findings on speaking can enrich the common grammar. Leech nevertheless dismisses the difference between the separatist and the integrated approaches, somewhat unexpectedly, as a 'matter of rhetorical emphasis' (2000: 690). He builds his own rhetoric on narrowing down the scope of grammar at the expense of discourse, and concludes that most of what might be specific to a spoken grammar can in fact be handled elsewhere in a model of language, therefore we can get by with one grammar. He thus recognizes the special character of speech – as long as it is kept outside grammar.

Without going into the details of internal inconsistencies in his argument, I would simply like to point out two things here: first, winning the battle for a restricted domain of grammar seems to mean losing the war over separate treatment, since now we need to account for speech characteristics outside grammar. This is hardly likely to offer the learner the 'comfort' Leech conjures up (p. 690) of only having to learn one grammar, because other components in the total learning load have now grown. Second, Leech's proposal implies that we do not question the primacy of writing in grammatical description, but merely patch it up with new findings from speaking. The problem with this is that although it is possible, even plausible, that there is a strong and relevant common core to spoken and written grammar, the priorities of the two modes in this suggestion are wrong and ought to be reversed. Given the primacy of speech in human language, surely we should base our models and descriptions on spoken language in the first place, and only then see where writing fits in and to what extent it needs special description.

Speaking, the corpus and the classroom

Foreign language teaching has embraced the practical goals of learning spoken communication for as long as we have evidence of language teaching, but, as McCarthy points out, the models of grammar and vocabulary that were the basis for the input were based on the written mode (McCarthy, 1998: 18). This emphasis on spoken language has remained much the same in general purpose English teaching, such as school curricula, where communicative teaching has been the generally accepted basis since the 1970s. Language teaching for specific purposes has been on a different track, because its rationale is based on learners' immediate or foreseeable needs, and tailoring courses to cater to those. In English for Academic Purposes (EAP) this has overwhelmingly meant an emphasis on written skills.

However, the needs-based, instrumental thinking that characterizes the EAP world is facing new challenges. The academic world, just as the worlds of business, entertainment, and tourism, is increasingly demanding good spoken skills in international encounters. Students, researchers and teaching staff engage in more and more international activities as a normal part of their academic life. Clearly, if we want to prepare learners for the requirements of real-world language use with any efficiency, we need descriptions of the target language that reflect its actual current use. Ideal models of either the language or the user do not meet learners' needs. There is not much point in wasting time with inadequate and unhelpful models of speaking that have to be unlearned and revised in the face of real-world experience. The revision of language models for all applicational purposes is a never-ending task, insofar as we believe linguistic theory and description make progress and learners' goals change; one of the fundamental challenges right now concerns the modelling of speech.

A similar shift from a written bias towards spoken language is in evidence in corpus studies: spoken corpora have received more attention and there have been more attempts to compile them – the results can be seen in the emergence of a number of fairly new corpora entirely or to a large part dedicated to speaking. Moreover, these tend to include applied purposes, mainly that of L2 teaching or testing. Examples of such corpora are CANCODE (http://uk.cambridge.org/elt/corpus/cancode), MICASE (Simpson *et al.*, 1999), T2K-SWAL (Biber *et al.*, 2001), and some more are in preparation, such as BASE (Nesi and Thompson, 2002) and the two English as lingua franca corpora, the academic ELFA (Mauranen, 2003a), and the multi-genre VOICE in Vienna (see www.univie.ac.at/Anglistik/voice; Seidlhofer, 2002a).

Many of the radical departures from conventional linguistic descriptions have originated in corpus study, and although the written mode has dominated much corpus-based research, as spoken corpora are becoming increasingly available, they enable us to obtain large-scale evidence on patterning in speech. Whether this implies that spoken language is in need of separate descriptions from those of the written mode, is a matter of debate in corpus linguistics, where some scholars advocate the former view (for example, Butler, 1998; McCarthy, 1998), while others, such as Leech, prefer to emphasize that which speech and writing have in common.

Since the main strength of a corpus is that it can show what is typically or commonly used in a language, based on what David Brazil (1995) called 'used language', it allows us to replace normative recommendations which draw on tradition or teacher intuition only. It is quite common to find examples showing that what has been taught as functional language use need not be the same as that which is frequent in the language, or even something that appears at all. Such findings seem to be particularly typical of speech, possibly because less research has been available. Even simple and 'well-known' phenomena get questioned: for instance, the most frequent meaning of *think* is 'have an opinion' (*other than that **I think** your proof is more credible than the Berkeley proof*) rather than 'mental process', and the typical use of *pretty* is as an intensifier (*it's a **pretty** straightforward procedure*) rather than as an adjective. Such things can be seen in a corpus and shown to students by a teacher, or be discovered by students on their own, and we can expect corpus data to provide us with relevant information to build pedagogical practices on.

The least we can hope to achieve with corpus-based descriptions of spoken language is better reference works such as grammars and dictionaries as well as renewed syllabus design, even though the path from linguistic research and pedagogical descriptions tends to be long and winding. It is, moreover, by no means obvious what all the implications of corpus research are to language teaching, as Widdowson has pointed out several times (recently for example 2003). What the implications are specifically for the teaching of spoken language are not much clearer, because these have been explored even less.

We can distinguish three pedagogically relevant ways that distinguish spoken and written corpora. First, because spoken corpora tend to consist of transcribed speech, they undergo an extra step of removal from their origins; this may bring about problems in their face validity or 'authenticity' in some rather mundane sense. Nevertheless, a corpus helps freeze speech for observation, and thereby helps one to notice and make sense of repeated patterning, which may subsequently become easier to observe in ongoing, complex and unpredictable interaction. Second, they cannot be used for immediate productive tasks, as written corpora can to provide help with composition or comprehension; they are therefore restricted to observation and learning for delayed use. Yet prepared talks are a common task in academic contexts, which needs to be kept in mind. Third, because spoken language has been less exhaustively described, it is harder to think of appropriate strings to search for – so, for example, the kinds of spoken idioms textbooks have cherished tend to be based on fiction dialogues or 'language pedagogical mythology' (*it's raining cats and dogs*; *you can say that again*), and are not likely to be found. The repeated sequences that we do find are less fixed but often crucially conducive to successful discourse (**let me just** *tell you a little bit about it*). And it can be argued that if these units are indeed those used by speakers in memory storage and access, as is suggested, for example, in Bybee and Hopper (2001), they are surely better candidates for units of teaching and learning than descriptions that ignore such units in favour of separate syntax and lexis, such as we usually have. Much more research on such units and their relevance to processing needs to be carried out; recent research has made remarkable progress in modelling the mechanisms of chunking in second-language learning (Ellis, 1996; 2002; Wray, 1999; 2002), but we shall ultimately need extensive, applicable descriptions in addition to models.

Clearly, it is impossible to emulate the unpredictability of real-life language use in the classroom. But what be can done is to show that there is more order and pattern in the apparent chaos than appears at first sight. It is important to engage learners' own activity and assist them in making their own observations, as was suggested in the early days of corpus pedagogy by Tim Johns (1991) in his 'data-driven learning'. Even if linguistic models come up with improved descriptions of spoken language, it is clear that pedagogical descriptions will have to be radically reduced and brief. It will therefore always be important to provide learners with means of making their own observations, however good our normative rules are; learners are better off with procedural tools than facts about products.

Transcribed speech corpora can help learners make observations that are their own, and answer their own questions. Soon we can also expect soundtracks to be made available with speech corpora. One of the main attractions of corpus data is that it allows learners to make genuinely novel observations on language, and for speech the field is wide open. However, real spoken data is, to many teachers, much less accessible than written text in large quantities. Applied linguists are needed for providing not only good descriptions but also good data.

But it is not only learners who may entertain notions of speech that derive from written dialogues read aloud. Many teachers are still unfamiliar with authentic transcribed speech. Textbook dialogues in the normal stylized manner do not give teachers or learners a realistic view of what speaking is like. Transcribed speech looks amusing to first-timers, and it seems to be hard to believe that this is how we go about speaking. Surprisingly, many practising teachers are ignorant of the nature of ongoing speech, and the detachment from online processing offered by a transcription can act as an eye-opener better than recorded sound. A transcript does not invite us to engage in the sense-making process, which comes naturally but draws our attention away from the components that go into the whole. While many useful expressions can no doubt be taught with some pruning of the hesitations, false starts and repetitions of true speaking, it is helpful, on occasion, to show the 'dysfluencies' as well.

Speaking English in today's world

On one point 'the Nottingham School' and Leech are firmly placed on the same side, and this is the prioritization of, in fact the exclusive reliance on, the native speaker as the relevant model for the foreign learner. Reading their texts, I take these native speakers to match Kachru's (1985) 'inner circle' speakers. However, I wish to question this on account of the current position of English as a global language, and argue that we also need to take on board Kachru's outer and expanding circles if we want to convey a realistic picture of English as it is used today.

A recent and much discussed development in the world of English is its dominant position in international communication. This has caused much worry, and the development has often been seen as a threat – either to other languages, or to Standard English. One debate has concerned the origin of this spread as a consequence of deliberate linguistic imperialism (Phillipson, 1992; Pennycook, 1994), although this view has also been criticized (Brutt-Griffler, 2002). However, whether English is a threat or a blessing and whether its spread resulted from deliberate policy or a more complex process, it is generally agreed that its unprecedented spread is a fact of the world we live in (Crystal, 1997; Graddoll, 1997), and as things stand, we are not likely to see the end of it soon.

The consequences of this state of affairs to the teaching of English have lagged surprisingly far behind. Widdowson (1994) set out to question the primacy of the native speaker in the use of English and, for example, Seidlhofer (2002a; 2002b) has argued in favour of adopting the lingua franca use of English as a crucial component of English language pedagogy. Empirical support for questioning many of the standard beliefs on what is important in teaching English pronunciation comes from Jenkins's (2000) important study on English phonology in international communication. Despite these voices, and growing interest among teachers of English, there is astonishingly little practical work oriented towards English as lingua franca (ELF), and very little research into it (see, however, papers in Knapp and Meierkord, 2002). Recent results already suggest that students learning English as a foreign language may also prefer to learn an international variety of English rather than any of the national varieties they are usually offered at school (Lepistö, 2004). In this, they are more radical than their teachers. All this should alert us to the significance of ELF.

This increasing use of English as a global lingua franca has implications for teaching spoken English. ELF is possibly even more heterogeneous than native Englishes – and, indeed, it is probably better to talk about different varieties within it from the outset. ELF speakers' command of English is highly variable both in terms of the degree to which they have acquired the target from their education, and also in terms of the quality of the command, as it were, deriving from the enormous variety of first language backgrounds. These characteristics are also likely to persist. ELF speakers typically maintain their first languages, with English kept largely for restricted purposes in various professional contexts. Although English is also common in many recreational contexts, such as tourism, spectator sports, entertainment, and the like, it is not likely to be granted an official status in many countries where it is taught as a foreign language – as, for example, in

Europe. Despite the many functions that international English has, then, it is mostly not used for the kinds of everyday purposes for which people use their first language. This obviously needs to be taken into account in teaching – immigrants to English-speaking countries have very different needs for English from international speakers, while the latter are the larger group.

As is generally known, language change takes place primarily through speech. Therefore, it is to spoken language that we should turn our primary attention when describing the emerging international varieties of English. Writing is not only more conservative, but it is in certain respects less of a problem for an international speaker of English. Written text can be planned and produced with more time, consulting reference works and other texts as models. For publishing texts, professional help is also available, usually by native speakers (see, for example, Ventola and Mauranen, 1991; Burrough-Boenisch, 2002). For communication in the written mode, then, speakers of International English have relatively little to worry about. It is also in the spoken language that speakers need most of those skills that are unique to English as a foreign language compared with other foreign languages – namely, coping with the unpredictability of the linguistic and cultural background of your interlocutors.

Learners also get less help for spoken language from standard peda gogic descriptions than they do for writing, and therefore often need to work out the use of linguistic features for themselves. For instance, discourse markers have not entered language teaching materials adequately (see Zorzi, 2001). On this point, one source of help is provided by speech corpus data – if it is available. Because there is much less of spontaneous speech data available for teachers or learners than there is of written corpus data, learners' (as well as teachers') opportunities of finding out for themselves how speech is patterned and how it differs from corresponding written language are seriously restricted. Understanding the differences between speech and writing is more of a hurdle than it might seem, as came out very clearly in an experiment with a highly experienced oral skills teacher (Mauranen, 2004): the teacher as well as the students assumed that written academic texts would supply them with suitable 'difficult items' to look for in a corpus of spoken academic discourse (MICASE), and the surprise, even disappointment, was great when this turned out to be a mistaken assumption.

Preliminary corpus findings from the ELFA corpus (English as a Lingua Franca in Academic Settings, University of Tampere; see, Mauranen, 2003a) suggest that international academic discourse contains relatively few misunderstandings and that of these even fewer are primarily language-based (Mauranen, forthcoming). The success strategies employed by skilful ELF speakers could be utilized in teaching. Many are interactive strategies: some resemble any L1 interaction, such as co-construction of expressions; others are more like L1-L2 interaction, such as frequent self-repairs, clarifications and repetitions, or active signalling of comprehension. Repairs appear more common than in comparable L1 speech, but many of them are similar in kind; for example, rephrasing the content (*the ethnic people and eh* **minorities Russian minorities)** lexical choice (*then it will be no* **questions** *eh it will be no* **conflicts)** or pragmatic features, such as adding hedges *(will eh at f-* **maybe** *at first they will)*. Others again, most conspicuously grammatical repairs (*main roles eh* **the** *main roles;* **to have** *a big influence* **to make** *big influence)*, seem to be absent from native speakers' speech. Grammatical repairs are not co-constructed; that is, interlocutors do not seem to participate in formulating grammatical form, but orient themselves to the contents of what is being said.

Whether successful strategies can be directly taught remains an open question, but an idea of what works in real international communication should be helpful to teachers as well as students, as support and encouragement for their own efforts. It is also important to include recent major developments in the language in our descriptions, which currently includes international Englishes. This is the kind of speech students are likely to encounter, and therefore this is what we must prepare them for.

Conclusion

I have been arguing in this chapter that spoken language should take precedence over written in our descriptions of language. Whether this description should be incorporated in the grammar rather than somewhere else is a moot point. There is increasing evidence that the most interesting units of language as it is employed in constructing meanings can be complex combinations of lexis, grammar, and pragmatics (see, for example, Fillmore *et al.*, 1988; Sinclair 1991; 1996; Wray, 2002; Barlow, 2003) and that these are likely to be equally relevant in foreign language processing (Ellis, 2002; Wray, 2002). Whatever shapes our models will eventually take, it is crucial that they adopt the spoken language as their point of departure, making appropriate additions as the need arises to accommodate written language as well.

It seems that spoken discourse for a foreign-language user involves expectations of interactive behaviour, knowledge of pragmatic items and their semantics as well as uses of grammar that diverge from that which is describable on the basis of written language data, and that require the recognition that the rules of use cannot be applied across modes.

Above all, the cooperative manner of co-constructing discourse is something that we ought to draw learners' attention to, in order to teach them to help each other out, and invite help efficiently from their interlocutors.

The 'balanced' view of emphasizing the commonalities of speech and writing bears a certain resemblance to the evolution vs creationism debate in the United States: the two are posited as equal alternatives, although they rest on entirely different bases. Spoken and written modes are not alternatives, but writing is a kind of epiphenomenon of human language, which is fundamentally spoken. This is not to question the virtues of writing, but just to point out that it can never be on an equal footing with speech.

It is important to remember that most learners of English as a foreign language will use the language as a lingua franca with other foreign speakers. Consequently, our teaching should seriously consider successful lingua franca use as providing valuable models for communication strategies. I am not suggesting that ELF data is the only viable linguistic model for learners; what I am suggesting is, first, that data of successful ELF discourse is indispensable for modelling communication strategies – in authentic speech. Second, I am suggesting that in order to keep up with current developments in the target language we must complement our existing databases with English in international use. Native-speaker English can continue to be described separately by those who wish to do so, and it is of fundamental significance to any description of the language as a whole, but at the same time, we must respond to change.

Bibliography

Aijmer, K. (2002) *English Discourse Particles* (Amsterdam: John Benjamins).
Barlow, M. (2003) 'Chunks, blends, and the individual speaker', Paper given at the ICAME conference, Guernsey, April 23–27.
BASE corpus (www.rdg.ac.uk/slals/base)

Biber, D. Reppen, R., Clark, V. and Walter, J. (2001) 'Representing spoken language in university settings: the design and construction of the spoken component of the T2K-SWAL Corpus', in R.C. Simpson and J.M. Swales (eds), *Corpus Linguistics in North America* (Ann Arbor: University of Michigan Press) 48–57.

Brazil, D. (1995) *A Grammar of Speech* (Oxford: Oxford University Press).

Brutt-Griffler, J. (2002) *World English: A Study of its Development* (Clevedon: Multilingual Matters).

Burrough-Boenisch, J. (2002) *Culture and Conventions: Writing and Reading Dutch Scientific English* (Utrecht: LOT).

Butler, C. (1998) 'Collocational frameworks in Spanish', *International Journal of Corpus Linguistics,* 3, 1: 1–32.

Bybee, J. and Hopper, P. (2001) 'Introduction to frequency and the emergence of linguistic structure', in J. Bybee and P. Hopper (eds), *Frequency and the Emergence of Linguistic Structure* (Amsterdam: John Benjamins) 1–24.

CANCODE corpus (http://uk.cambridge.org/elt/corpus/ cancode.htm)

Crystal, D. (1997) *English as a Global Language* (Cambridge: Cambridge University Press).

Du Bois, J.W. (2003) 'Discourse and Grammar', in M. Tomasello (ed.), *The New Psychology of Language, Vol. 2,* (Mahwah: Lawrence Erlbaum) 47–87.

ELFA corpus (www.uta.fi/laitokset/kielet/engf/research/elfa)

Ellis, N.C. (1996) 'Sequencing in SLA. Phonological memory, chunking, and points of order', *SSLA,* 18: 91–126.

Ellis, N.C. (2002) 'Frequency effects in language processing', *SSLA,* 24: 143–88.

Fillmore, C.J., Kay, P. and O'Connor, M.C. (1988) 'Regularity and idiomaticity in grammatical constructions: the case of "let alone"', *Language,* 64, 3: 501–38.

Ford, C.E., Fox, B.A. and Thompson, S.A. (2003) 'Social interaction and grammar', in M. Tomasello (ed.), *The New Psychology of Language, Vol. 2,* (Mahwah: Lawrence Erlbaum) 119–43.

Graddoll, D. (1997) *The Future of English?* (London: The British Council).

Hunston, S. (1993) 'Evaluation and ideology in scientific writing', in M. Ghadessy (ed.), *Register Analysis. Theory and Practice* (London: Pinter) 57–73.

Hunston, S. (1994) 'Evaluation and organization in a sample of written academic discourse', in M. Coulthard (ed.), *Advances in Written Text Analysis* (London: Routledge) 191–218.

Jenkins, J. (2000) *The Phonology of English as an International Language* (Oxford: Oxford University Press).

Johns, T. (1991) 'Should you be persuaded: two examples of data-driven learning', in T. Johns and P. King (eds), *Classroom Concordancing,* ELR Journal, 4: 1–16.

Kachru, B.B. (1985) 'Standards, codification, and sociolinguistic realism: the English language in the outer circle', in R. Quirk and H. Widdowson (eds), *English in the World: Teaching and Learning the Language and the Literatures* (Cambridge: Cambridge University Press) 11–30.

Knapp, K. and Meierkord, C. (eds) (2002) *Lingua Franca Communication* (Frankfurt: Peter Lang).

Kurhila, S. (2003) *Co-constructing Understanding in Second Language Conversation* (Helsinki: University of Helsinki).

Leech, G. (2000) 'Grammars of spoken English: new outcomes of corpus-oriented research', *Language Learning*, 50, 4: 675–724.

Lepistö, S. (2004) *Ambitious Americans and Educated Britons: A study on upper secondary school students and their preferences and attitudes towards different varieties of the English language*, Unpublished MA thesis, University of Tampere, Department of English.

Lindemann, S. and Mauranen, A. 2001 '"It's just real messy." The occurrence and function of *just* in a corpus of academic speech', *English for Specific Purposes*, Special Issue (1): 459–76.

Mauranen, A. (2003a) 'The corpus of English as lingua franca in academic settings', *TESOL Quarterly*, 37, 3: 513–27.

Mauranen, A. (2003b) '"But here's a flawed argument". Socialisation into and through Metadiscourse', in P. Leistyna and C.F. Meyer. (eds), *Corpus Analysis. Language Structure and Language Use* (Amsterdam: Rodopi) 19–34.

Mauranen, A. (2004) 'Speech corpora in the classroom', in G. Aston, S. Bernardini and D. Stewart (eds), *Corpora and Language Learners* (Amsterdam: John Benjamins) 197–213.

Mauranen, A. 'Signalling and preventing misunderstanding in ELF communication', *IJSL*, Special Issue, ed. by Christiane Meierkord, forthcoming.

McCarthy, M. (1998) *Spoken Language and Applied Linguistics* (Cambridge: Cambridge University Press).

MICASE corpus (www.hti.umich.edu/m/micase)

Nesi, H. and Thompson, P. (2002) 'Building BASE: an introduction to the British Academic Spoken English Corpus', Paper presented at TALC 2002, 26–31.7, Forli, Italy.

Östman, J.-O. (1981) *You know. A discourse-functional approach* (Amsterdam: John Benjamins).

Pennycook, A. (1994) *The Cultural Politics of English as an International Language* (London: Longman).

Phillipson, R. (1992) *Linguistic Imperialism* (Oxford: Oxford University Press).

Seidlhofer, B. (2002a) 'Basic questions', in K. Knapp and C. Meierkord (eds), *Lingua Franca Communication* (Frankfurt: Peter Lang) 269–302.

Seidlhofer, B. (2002b) 'Closing a conceptual gap: The case for a description of English as a lingua franca', *International Journal of Applied Linguistics*, 11, 2: 133–58.

Simpson, R.C., Briggs, S.L., Ovens, J. and Swales, J.M. (1999) *The Michigan Corpus of Academic Spoken English* (Ann Arbor, MI: Regents of the University of Michigan).

Sinclair, J.M. (1991) *Corpus, Concordance, Collocation* (Oxford: Oxford University Press).

Sinclair, J.M. (1996) 'The search for units of meaning', *Textus*, IX: 75–106.

Tao, H. (2001) 'Discovering the usual with corpora: the case of remember', in R.C. Simpson and J.M. Swales (eds), *Corpus Linguistics in North America* (Michigan: University of Michigan Press) 116–44.

The TOEFL 2000 Spoken and Written Academic Language (T2K-SWAL) Corpus, Princeton, NJ: Educational Testing Service.

Ventola, E. and Mauranen, A. (1991) 'Non-native writing and native revising of scientific articles', in E. Ventola (ed.), *Functional and Systemic Linguistics. Approaches and Uses* (Berlin: Mouton de Gruyter) 457–92.

VOICE corpus (www.univie.ac.at/Anglistik/voice)

Widdowson, H. (1994) 'The ownership of English', *TESOL Quarterly*, 28: 377–89.

Widdowson, H. (2003) *Defining Issues in Foreign Language Teaching* (Oxford: Oxford University Press).

Wray, A. (1999) 'Formulaic language in learners and native speakers', *Language Teaching*, 32: 213–31.

Wray, A. (2002) *Formulaic Language and the Lexicon* (Cambridge: Cambridge University Press).

Zorzi, D. (2001) 'The pedagogic use of spoken corpora: introducing corpus concordancing in the classroom', in G. Aston (ed.), *Learning with Corpora* (Bologna: CLUEB) 85–107.

8
Spoken Grammar: Vague Language and EAP

Joan Cutting

Introduction

Studies of spoken English have traditionally focused on language with explicit meaning, and the reports dealt cursorily and unsystematically with implicit or vague language with highly context-dependent meaning. The result is grammar reference books and English as a Foreign Language text-books with little emphasis on this aspect of informal spoken language. Yet, in daily communication, a great deal of what is intended to be communicated is implicit and can be taken for granted. Crystal and Davy (1975: 111–12) acknowledged that 'lack of precision is one of the most important features of the vocabulary of informal conversation' and 'the use of lexical vagueness is undoubtedly a main sign of social and personal relaxation ... the "choice" of the vague lexical item is conducive to maintaining the informal atmosphere of the situation'. This chapter argues that implicitness is an essential feature of spoken grammar, lexis and discourse structure, that it demands a systematic study of its inter-related parts, and that it should be a central part of the model taught to students of English as a Foreign Language, so that they can be helped to communicate on all levels with their interlocutors.

The chapter starts with the history of discourse analysis approaches taken to examining implicitness and a description of the model of the implicit language of the in-group (Cutting, 2000). Then it moves on to a summary of how pedagogical grammars have described implicitness, to arrive finally at an exploration of the way it has been portrayed in EFL methodology and practiced teaching books.

Discourse analysis

The history

Firth (1957), Garfinkel (1967: 3) and Bernstein (1971) were amongst the first to note that speakers intend and hear more than what is said, and to look for grammatical and lexical markers of implicitness. Garfinkel simply talked of 'unstated understandings' (p. 3), but Bernstein (1971), observing that the restricted code of social groups contains context-dependent language based on unspoken assumptions not available to the outsider, included context-dependent grammatically simple sentences in his list of restricted code features. His context-dependent language is in part exophoric reference, which Halliday and Hasan (1976: 34–6) explained depends on both the context of common experience and the context of culture. None of these studies examined the exact nature of the language whose meaning depended on unstated understandings and unspoken assumptions.

Interactional sociolinguistics began to look at implicit meaning in the 1960s; their model also focused on lexico-grammatical features, but here the relation between highly context-dependent language and social context and the behaviour of social groups was more central to their theoretical framework. Sociologist Goffman (1963) examined the way that social and interpersonal contexts 'provide presuppositions for the decoding of meaning' (Schiffrin, 1994: 105), although he did not look at the code itself. Gumperz did focus on the locution; his 'contextualization cues' are central to the model of analysis to be proposed in this chapter. He explained that members of social groups use language with implicit meaning: 'exclusive interaction with individuals of similar background leads to reliance on unverbalized and context-bound presuppositions in communication' (1982: 131). Here again we are talking about exophoric reference but the description itself is vague. Tannen (1984: 31) highlighting the function of implicitness in-group cohesion, does list some of the linguistic features involved. She mentioned ellipsis, indirectness, implicature and unstated meanings as interpersonal involvement signals of 'high involvement style'. She claimed, 'the more work ... hearers do to supply meaning, the deeper their understanding and the greater their sense of involvement with both text and author' (1989: 23). None of these linguists explored in any great depth the linguistic features carrying unstated meaning, or suggested how the features relate to each other or to the context. None of these descriptions are longitudinal or developmental.

Since the 1980s, linguists also discussed implicitness at the mode and genre level, but painting the differences with a broad brush, they have risked over-simplifying and over-generalizing the case. Chafe (1982) describes the written mode as explicit and context-free, and the spoken mode as implicit and context-dependent. Biber (1988) claims that in-explicit references, defined as those that are decoded with recourse to situation, occur more in popular lore texts such as informative texts found in popular magazines than in academic prose.

Just as interactional sociolinguistics relates implicitness to high involvement, pragmatics relates unstated reference to cooperative behaviour. Grice (1975) saw referring items as pragmatic processes through which the hearer infers the speaker's intentions, guided by the cooperative principle: the maxims of quantity, quality, manner and relevance which constrain the speaker's choice of referring terms. He described the principles for communicating implicit assumptions and underlying meaning in his theory of maxim-flouting and conversational implicature. Brown and Levinson (1978), outlining positive politeness strategies, mentioned ellipsis amongst their in-group identity markers. On the whole, these linguists see implicitness as running over stretches of discourse, expressed in speakers' intentions as they show cooperativeness and solidarity, and not linked to any particular linguistic features.

Critical discourse analysis takes quite a different view of implicitness. Fairclough (2003: 55) sees implicitness in all modes and genres: 'Implicitness is a pervasive property of texts, and a property of considerable social importance.' More importantly, although he agrees with those who hold that implicitness correlates with expressions of claims of common ground, asserting that:

> All forms of fellowship, community and solidarity depend upon meanings which are shared and can be taken as given, and no form of social communication or interaction is conceivable without some such 'common ground'. (Ibid: 55)

He is mainly concerned with the way that assumptions are used to exercise social power. For him, implicitness is related to ideology, in that those with power can shape the nature and content of this common ground; texts with power can carry implicit assumptions that they impose upon the reader or listener by making them bring the assumptions into the process of interpretation (1989: 82–3). Wodak (1996: 2) also examines the effect of speakers in a position of power using implicit language; she explains that confusion can result when there are 'gaps between distinct and insufficiently coincident cognitive worlds,' since these can separate 'insiders from outsiders, members of institutions from clients of those institutions, and elites from the normal citizen uninitiated in the arcana of bureaucratic language and life.' She says that hearers and readers lacking the background knowledge assumed in the media can be prevented from understanding by imprecise references and pronominalizations, and by intertextuality being only barely explicit (ibid: 101–29). Wodak gets a little closer to describing the linguistic features.

In the field of Second Language Acquisition, Roberts (2003: 117) follows on with the view that language dependent on inference and in-group knowledge is associated with social differences and the assertion of power. She makes the point that socialization relies on negotiating local meanings through conversational inference, and that contextualization cues call up background knowledge that relates to social relations, rights, obligations and ideologies. This, she says is a problem for second language acquisition of minority language speakers, as:

> Knowing how to use and interpret a particular cue means at least for that interactional moment that you are a 'belonger'. And in contrast, the failure to pick up on a cue not only creates misunderstanding but sets the minority linguistic speaker apart. She is not in that interactional moment an emergent member of the same communicative community. As a result, small interactive differences can contribute to large social consequences. (Ibid: 118)

Roberts feels that analysts should 'participate in everyday routines of a particular group in order to understand conventionalized ways of interpreting meaning' (ibid: 119) and redefine the process of second language acquisition as second language socialization, even though learners may want to take up an ambiguous position in relation to the discourse. Once again, there little attempt to analyze the language involved.

Recent sociolinguistic studies of spoken English and casual conversations seem to have moved away from discussions of vague and implicit language altogether. Eggins and Slade's (1997) analysis of the characteristics of casual conversations makes no mention of it. Malone (1997: 43) gives attention to the implicitness of pronouns:

> Conversations are populated with a cast of actors, present and absent, whose explicit characterizations and implicit known identities give shape and meaning to talk.

but takes this issue no further. Coupland's (2000) collection of essays on small talk touches on service encounters, chat and casual conversations, but no mention is made of vague language. Similarly, Cameron's (2000) description of spontaneous talk lacks a reference to implicit language.

Corpus linguistics seems to have bypassed the issue of grammar and lexis with low semantic content so far. Corpora have helped linguists analyze spoken discourse, but virtually none of them have looked into the frequency and use of vague language. Stenström (in Svartvik, 1990) looks at the lexical items peculiar to spoken discourse, but focuses on the discourse function of words such as 'really' and 'right'. Altenberg (in Svartvik, 1990) also looks at spoken discourse items such as hesitators and softeners. Sinclair (1991) simply mentions conventional implications and inferences in passing. Hunston (2002) limits her discussion to concordances and collocation of semantically contentful words (as one might call words with explicit and transparent semantic meaning), even in her exploration of the applications to language teaching and English for Academic Purposes (EAP).

McCarthy and Carter (1997), experts in the field of spoken grammar, lexis and discourse features, who base their analysis on CANCODE (Cambridge and Nottingham Corpus of Discourse in English), are the exception. They say:

> General words enable a speaker to express attitudes and feelings without needing to locate an exact or precise referent. They are widely used in spoken discourse ... general words *thing* and *stuff* are among the most frequent words in spoken English. (p. 16)

About vague language, they say:

> Vague expressions are more extensive in all language use than is commonly thought and they are especially prevalent in spoken discourse. ... In most informal contexts most speakers prefer to convey information which is softened in some way by vague language. (p. 19)

McCarthy (1998: 108–18) mentions that deliberately vague and imprecise language, as in 'this *sort of* slide and sound sequence' and 'this picture *thing*' are frequent in everyday talk, and that they 'make an important contribution to naturalness and the informal, convergent tenor of everyday talk.' Carter in Seidlhofer (2003: 92) gives 'See you *around* six' and 'Oh, seven thirty *or thereabouts*' as examples of vagueness, and explains that 'vague language is non-authoritarian and puts the speakers on an immediately casual and equal footing with their interlocutors'.

Linguists who have analyzed vague language in great detail are Channell (1994) and Cutting (2000). Channell has explored implicit lexis in depth. Her model includes vague additives (for example, 'round ten'), approximators and vague quantifiers (for example, '1,500 died'), vague 'placeholder' words (for example, 'thingy' and 'whatsis-name'), 'tags' (for example, 'or something', 'and things' and 'and so on'). Channell affirms that an expression or word is vague if (a) it can be contrasted with another word or expression that appears to render the same proposition, if (b) it is 'purposely and unabashedly vague', or if (c) the meaning 'arises from intrinsic uncertainty'. Her analysis of vague expressions 'shows that their meanings are themselves vague', that 'speakers share knowledge of how to understand them', and that 'it is apparently impossible to describe their meanings independently of consideration of context and inference' (1994: 196–8). She states that hearers can go beyond the given information because they share pragmatic assumptions about likely category members. Channell says that imprecision can be a way of being polite, avoiding being offensive, derogatory and pretentious.

The model of the implicit language of the in-group

Influenced by interactional sociolinguistics, pragmatics and corpus linguistics, Cutting (2000) analyzed the language used by the academic discourse community of Edinburgh University MSc Applied Linguistics students in casual conversations in the common room. Her analysis helped her devize a model of vague language (see Figure 8.1) containing implicit contextualization cues (non-anaphoric definite implicit reference and vague lexis), and implicitness over utterances (clausal ellipsis and humorous conversational implicature).

Let us start with an explanation of grammatical implicit contextualization cues. All of these are non-anaphoric definite referring expressions whose meaning was not immediately interpretable from something concrete in the text. In this category are general nouns, demonstrative pronouns and adverbs and personal pronoun. 'That thing', 'a thing', 'the person' or 'people' have as much contentfulness as non-anaphoric 'that', 'he' or 'they'. Implicit reference also includes colloquial forms of general noun, such as 'whatsit', and vague noun clauses such as 'what you said you'd do'. The following is an example of the non-anaphoric general noun:

The in-group code of implicit contextualization cues

- Grammatical

- implicit non-anaphoric definite reference

- general nouns	eg: 'the thing'
- demonstrative pronouns	eg: 'that'
- demonstrative adverbs	eg: 'now'
- third person personal pronouns	eg: 'she'

- Lexical

- course proper nouns - actual use	eg: 'Chomsky'
- metonymical use	eg: '[their] Chomsky'
- unique course noun	eg: 'exam'
- limited range course nouns	eg: 'project'
- general 'do' verbs	eg: 'done [their Chomsky]'

Implicitness over utterances

- unfinished sentences

- with interlocutor completion	eg: 'the mental and the...'
- with conjunctions and vague fillers	eg: '...or something'

- humorous conversational implicature

- public flouting	eg: 'His book right!'
- private flouting	eg: 'Not that you'd notice!'

Figure 8.1   The implicit language of the in-group

(1)   15041 CM   Can't remember the last time I handed in any-
                              thing late.
            15042 DM   (heh heh // heh heh)
            15043 CM   // Usually it's three months early.
            15044 DM   (heh heh) Right. (8)
  →   15045 DM   So I typed **that thing** up again after you'd gone.
            15046 CM   Oh yeah.

Only those sharing the common background knowledge would know
what this refers to. In the following example, the non-anaphoric personal pronoun's referent would only be known to interlocutors:

(2)   15159 DM   I'm going to give out a questionnaire.
            15160 DM   And I'll give you one as well.
            15161 DM   Sometime this week I hope t- tomorrow I'll get
                              them all done.
            15162 AF   What your core project?
            15163 DM   Yeah. ((0.5))
  →   15164 CM   Did **he** like did he like the idea?
            15165 AF   That's very energetic.
  →   15166 DM   Well you know what **he's like**.
            15167 DM   It's difficult to tell isn't it?

And in the next, a non-anaphoric demonstrative adverb co-occurring
in the same utterance as a non-anaphoric demonstrative pronoun
doubles the implicit nature of discourse:

(3)   26102 CM   // You- you don't have the processor to do it.
            26103 BM   Bu- but why don't I?
            26104 CM   Cos (0.5) in technical terms you own an // Eighty-
                              Eight.
            26105 BM   // Say.
  →   26106 BM   You shouldn't be **here**.
            26107 FF   I got the job.
            26108 BM   How come she got back so early? (0.5)
  →   26109 BM   **That** was yesterday.
            26110 CM   In technical (1) terms you own a what's called an
                              eighty-eight six processor and you need an eighty-
                              three eighty-six processor which is two models
                              newer and better than yours.

Moving on now to lexical implicit contextualization cues, the following is an example of a proper noun with metonymical use (in which the proper noun refers to something other than the person or thing named in the proper noun) co-occurring with a general verb, which would doubly obscure the meaning to an outsider:

(4)→   08031 AM   Though though I haven't I haven't **done** any **Chomsky.**
        08032 AM   Probably a bit late // now.
   →   08033 CM   // **Chomsky** doubles up in **Psycholinguistics.**

In this example, 'I haven't done any Chomsky' means 'I haven't studied any of Chomsky's theories for the exam'. Unique course nouns refer to entities of which there is only one in the course; for example, 'the external' and 'the exam'; limited range nouns are ones that refer to a class of nouns related to the course, as in 'the article' or 'the project'. All of these carry unstated meaning because they are superordinates with specific referents, only understood by the interlocutors. The general 'do' verb is the exophoric pro-verb, as in 'What was she doing?' and 'What am I to do?', and the lexical verb 'do', as in 'do a question' meaning 'write a question', in which 'do' carries its own meaning. Not in the 'do' verb category was the auxiliary, or the endophoric pro-verb, as in 'I did that'. In the next example, 'do' features with general noun 'people', making the implicitness of the exchange double:

(5)   10066 DM   So did you **do** everything?
       10067 DM   // Or sort of choose a few **people**?
       10068 CM   // Em. (0.5)
       10069 CM   No I**'ve done** all **the people.**
       10070 DM   // Really?

Although the general words themselves carry almost zero semantic content, their referents are specific, and known to the interlocutors.

Looking finally at implicitness over utterances, part of this category is unfinished sentences, left open by choice, as in:

(6)   12091 AM   Because (0.5) I mean they had the same kind of divide didn't they?
       12092 AM   same axis.
   →   12093 AM   // They had the er mental and **the** ...

> 12094 CM   // **Yeah**. (0.5)
> 12095 CM   **What you what you know and what you do.**
> 12096 AM   Yeah.
> 12097 AM   It was just that Saussure concentrated on the mental and Bloomfield concentrated on the on the // physical.

In this example, the hearer has enough in-group knowledge to be able to predict correctly how the utterance was to end. This category also includes both public flouting humour, in the case of in-jokes based on a cooperative maxim being flouted and the knowledge shared by the whole group, and also private flouting humour, which depends on interpersonal knowledge shared only by the interlocutors. In the following example, BF flouts the maxims of quantity and manner, indulging in a little banter:

> (7)   14021 DM   More than I did this weekend I'm telling you.
>   14022 BF   You had friends didn't you?
> →   14023 BF   **I can imagine why you wouldn't want to.**
>   14024 DM   Resting.
> →   14025 BF   **Yeah**.
> →   14026 BF   **Sure.** (heh heh)

The result is an exclusive in-joke, which reinforces the assertion of in-group membership. In the next example, NF flouts the maxim of quality, being ironic:

> (8)   29051 NF   I'd better go to my class. ((2))
>   29052 AF   You did this last week didn't you? // (heh)
>   29053 NF   // Yeah.
> →   29054 NF   **I really like the teacher very much.**
>   29055 AF   (heh heh)
>   29056 DM   It's very relaxing. (1)

Only an in-group member would know for sure whether NF was sincere or joking. Cutting's (2000) study was longitudinal: it looked at the way that vague language developed as members of an in-group got to know each other, and the way that this varied according to the topic under discussion. She found that the only language features that increased consistently regardless of topic area were the ones included in the implicit grammatical reference category (general nouns, non-anaphoric demonstrative pronouns, demonstrative adverbs and third person personal pronouns). In dialogues on topics closely related to the course, the increase in implicit grammatical reference was steeper than in dialogues on non-course topics, and there was also an increased density of course limited range nouns (for example, 'the article'), metonymical proper names (for example, 'how's your Chomsky?'), general 'do' verbs (for example, 'I've done the people') and unfinished sentences. That is to say, the type of implicit features that occurred varied with the length of time the interlocutors had known each other, and also according to the type of topic in the conversation.

When Cutting examined the function of implicit language, she found that it was used mostly in exchanges with an interactional function. The use of implicit language in utterances with a socially cohesive function suggests that using it was a high involvement strategy for asserting in-groupness. Only certain features of implicit language are likely to have been chosen consciously (metonymical proper names, limited range course nouns, general words, unfinished sentences and implicit humorous utterances). Most of the features of grammatical implicitness (choice of pronouns and adverbs) are more a reflection of in-groupness, respecting the maxim of quantity.

Further research on the model of the implicit language of the in-group

Cutting's model could be extended to other social groups. It could be tested in other linguistics departments and, indeed, language schools around the world. Research into the casual conversations of non-academic discourse communities could be undertaken using the model, so long as they meet frequently in informal circumstances and tend to talk about their common interest. These could be (a) people united by a common activity, such as a team of cleaners from a work place or a group of peace protesters; (b) people united by common interests who meet frequently in order to discuss their mutual passion, such as football team supporters, science fiction buffs or computer nerds; or (c) people, such as regular cronies in a local pub or neighbors who always meet over the garden fence, who are united by neither a common activity nor a common interest but by frequent physical proximity in circumstances in which they chat informally about entities in a well-established common background knowledge. The language of the family, couples and would-be couples could be analyzed along similar lines. Shalom (1997: 187) has found that the personal advertisement in lonely hearts columns 'resonates with ambiguity' and that 'the most "stereotypical" lexis is imbued with a vagueness'. Finally, work could be done to discover whether the implicit language model is generalizable to other languages. If parallels and equivalents could be drawn up between languages, this could help language teaching, as well as business and other relationships between countries.

The social dimensions of Cutting's model require investigation. Cutting (1998) looked into the influence of different social contexts on implicit language and its function, using as a database a random selection of dialogues from CANCODE.

Beginning with the variable of situational context type, she found that the grammatical contextualization cue occurred in all contexts, regardless of the level of formality; this is to say, the degree of formality did not affect the density of grammatical cues. Thus, for example, even in a service encounter about setting up a mortgage, the client uses a general verb, a general noun and a non-anaphoric personal pronoun: 'but I'm **doing** a PhD and there's various **things they** want'. However, analysis did show that the context that contained the highest density of implicit language was the informal conversation between friends. This suggests that depth of relationship did correlate with the density of cues. The following example comes from a gossip session between friends:

> A: 'You know when we were in the pub that time with Stuart, and John was saying to Stuart **what you said**. I told you that Stuart told Ed, didn't I?'
> B: 'I- I shouldn't have told him **all the stuff I did**, cos I told him so much.'

In this particular example, it could also be that the topic was such that the language chosen was aimed to intentionally exclude outsiders.

Turning now to the analysis of function in this sample of CANCODE dialogues, it emerged that the most frequent function of implicit language was that of giving little importance to the referent, either to be friendly or to be critical. To take an example, when three friends are talking informally as they organize the sale of second-hand goods, they show a friendly attitude by being vague about each one's task, 'Cos I'm thinking if we got that then Alison could start **doing her stuff**.' Similarly, when friends are shopping together, they show their disgust of the prices by reducing the value of the referent, 'seven pounds for **that little thing**?'

There are other social dimensions, not dealt with in the CANCODE study, that merit investigation. The first is the relationship between implicit language and gender. Some studies have been done on indirectness and gender, but none have examined the choice of grammar and lexis in this field. Tannen (1994: 23–34) found that North Americans associate indirectness with female style, and that men and women tend to interpret ambiguity differently, whereas Mills (2003: 142) notes that it is stereotyping males to say that males are more direct than females, and that indirectness and politeness are not associated in all cultures. Other areas that require investigation are the relationship between implicit language and socio-cultural groupings such as class and age, and between implicit language and power.

Approaches taken to the analysis of language are reflected in the descriptions of language then compiled for students of linguistics and learners of language. Predictably, the scarcity of studies in implicit language can be seen in the scant attention paid to this aspect of language in pedagogical grammars.

Pedagogical grammars

Traditionally, grammar reference books have tended to describe written grammar outside the social context, with little mention of vagueness. Huddleston (1988: 84–91), for example, contented himself with saying that central members of the noun class denote persons or concrete objects, that non-specific noun phrases are usually indefinite, and generic noun phrases are non-specific. He did not entertain the fact that one genre may have more generic noun phrases than others, or that generic noun phrases may have a social function.

Even since the 1990s, text-books describing grammar have mostly ignored the implicit in spoken grammar and lexis. Yule (1996) prefers to describe written grammar, limiting discussion of vagueness to the areas of conversational implicature and indirect speech acts. Batstone (1994: 25) mentions that the choice of grammar reflects knowledge of the world, and that incompleteness in the form of initial clausal ellipsis, as in 'Got a light?', requires schematic knowledge (knowledge of the world) and systemic knowledge (knowledge of the language system) for its interpretation, but he does not mention incompleteness of words themselves, in the sense of low semantic content.

Biber *et al.* (1999), in their monumental description of the grammar of spoken and written English, explain that approximators, typically modifiers of numerical or quantifying expressions, convey imprecision, and that hedges, such as 'like', can indicate imprecision of word choice. The closest that they get to discussing implicit reference is in their explanation of indirect anaphoric reference, in which 'the connection is inferred rather than signaled by repetition' (p. 263), and generic reference (p. 265), in which the noun 'refers to a whole class rather than to an individual person or thing', otherwise known as higher-order superordinates. They do not mention general words 'thing' or 'person', or non-anaphoric pronouns 'they' or 'this' as part of their indirect anaphora or generic reference.

Linked to approaches of discourse analysis and pedagogical grammars is language learning theory; from these stem approaches to language teaching methodology and course books for students of language. The influence of psychological, sociological and linguistic theory has always been in evidence in language learning theory and teaching methodology. The result is again predictable.

Language learning theory, teaching methodology and EFL course books

The history

Foreign language learners often sound 'bookish and pedantic' because they do not know how to use vague expressions (Brown, 1979). Brown said that one aspect of acquiring a second language is 'learning to be imprecise'. It could be that language learners look for the most explicit way of expressing themselves in order to ensure that they communicate their meaning; generally speaking, EFL books aim to teach vocabulary with content and so encourage them to expand their stock of semantically contentful vocabulary. Theories about inexplicit language and hidden meaning did not reach language learning theory books in the 1970s, 1980s or 1990s. Cook (1991), for example, discusses the theory of vocabulary learning and teaching, and says that learners learn superordinates after basic level terms, but he does not go on to describe their acquisition of general nouns, which are at a higher level than superordinates, despite his affirmation that the most frequently used words in the target language are usually taught first. Hatch (1992) discusses the features of cohesion and coherence and how to teach them, and refers little to the pronoun with no apparent cohesion, or the 'incoherent' noun.

Present-day literature about language learning theory and research in the field of EFL/EAP continues, on the whole, to ignore the informal spoken side of the students' life. Coxhead and Nation (2001: 257–63) analyze the vocabulary needed by EAP students and conclude that they need technical vocabulary and academic words such as 'argue', 'process' and 'expansion', stating that 'The "context-independent" vocabulary is

an important tool of the writer in doing learned and scientific things.'
This is the formal end of the spectrum and it refers only to written language. Starfield (2001) looks at the notion of discourse community in
EAP and focuses on verbal exchanges. She concludes that the community has more inequality, power relations and discursive struggles than
previously argued, but she does not look into the grammar and lexis
used by those who establish the rules of group behaviour.

With the growth of computational research and corpus linguistics,
the findings of linguistic analyses of real language in corpora are available to writers of language course books. As McCarthy and Carter say:

> By studying the natural patterns of everyday situations, we can
> come to a much better understanding of what each one demands of
> participants in terms of cultural and linguistic behaviour. With such
> information, we are better placed to design syllabuses and materials,
> evaluate existing ones and, perhaps most important of all, to understand the interpersonal and inter-cultural areas of language learning
> that are most sensitive to subtle differences in the manipulation of
> interpersonal grammars. (1994: 123)

However, Eggins and Slade say that 'there is still a paucity of adequate
materials for teaching casual conversation to learners of English as a
second or foreign language' (1997: 8). Carter in Seidlhofer (2003: 92)
goes further:

> Several English language coursebooks do not exhibit many examples
> of vague language, even though it is always pragmatically highly
> significant, and nearly always enables polite and non-threatening
> interaction.

Counteracting the view that corpus linguistics should feed EFL course
books, McDonough (2002: 37–8) says that although corpus linguistics
provides course book writers and teachers with a database of actual language, he questions 'how "real" the English presented for learning purposes actually needs to be'. He says:

> The greater the precision of the description of contemporary language, the greater the pressure on the learner to conform to that
> 'real English': however, the English the learner needs to know is
> primarily the English that will do the jobs that he or she needs to
> perform in the language.

In 1988, Beebe pointed out:

> Second language learners may never attain native-like proficiency to the best of their ability because they may find that the reward of being fluent in the target language is not worth the cost in lost identification and solidarity with their own native language group. (p. 63)

The question is whether international students want to produce implicit language themselves, whether they want to sound more like native speakers of English in order to make their own language more acceptable for their colleagues and claim in-group membership. It could be that the solution is for books to sensitize students and help them to understand the features, without actually training them to use or produce vague language themselves. On the other hand, if one is to follow the learning-by-doing philosophy, one could argue that only by trying to produce vague language themselves can students fully internalize the forms and social functions.

Methodology books purporting to train EFL teachers to teach spoken English mainly ignore the informal side of spoken English. Bygate (1987) and Dörnyei and Thurrell (1992) are examples. They describe conversational rules and structure but do not train students to recognize informal grammar and lexis.

A limited number of EFL/EAP methodology books (Cook, 1989; Channell, 1994; Jordan, 1997) do, however, put forward some methodological advice to make students aware of vague language. Channell suggests that students could be given practice in using vague language by asking them to locate vague words in a text, explain their meaning and note the changes to the text when more precise words are substituted for the vague words. Cook recommends the use of exercises that oblige the student to evaluate the known information and remove superfluous information from passages. This implies removing complete phrases and words from sentences. Jordan suggests that EAP teachers make their students aware of informal spoken language so that they can understand the shifts to colloquial register in their lectures (p. 186), and of vague written language (pp. 240–3) so that they can write using hedges such as modals expressing possibility, probability adverbs and approximators, and so that they can understand and speak using colloquialisms such as 'thingy' and 'whatsisname'. He advocates exercises that raise student awareness of the correspondence between vagueness and hedging, and caution or tentativeness in academic writing, such as asking them to re-write hedged sentences in a non-tentative way. He also suggests exercises that would help them avoid informal, conversational English in their writing, by asking them to recognize vague and colloquial features in written sentences. He advocates extending this formality to spoken English. All of these ideas are useful for writing English and speaking in the tutorial domain, but they are not helpful for training students to understand and speak naturally in the informal setting, and thus cohere socially and even enter the discourse community, should they aspire to do so.

EFL/EAP course-books rarely prepare learners to chat in order to pass the time, keeping the conversation going in groups in which 'nothing is happening' at the time. Lynch's *Study Listening* (1983), Lynch and Anderson's *Study Speaking* (1992), and Flowerdew's *Academic Listening* (1994) train students to listen and speak in formal academic situations, to take notes in lectures, give presentations in seminars and so on. They do not prepare them to interact socially with their colleagues, referring in an informal way to aspects and components of their academic life.

McCarthy and Carter's (1997) *Exploring Spoken English* does have as its objective the training of teachers and students of linguistics in the analysis of naturalistic conversational data, from the point of view of general words as in 'thing' and 'business' and vague language as in 'or something' or 'kind of'. McCarthy and Carter pick out these features, along with all the other features that they list, in a series of authentic spoken texts. Although they prepare students to recognize the characteristics of conversational English, their book does not contain exercises that train them to use it actively.

Interesting and encouraging is the growth of language descriptions and advice about language in the internet, that take into account the importance of vague language, even if they do not provide exercises to practice using it. The Appendix, p. 177, contains a sample of pages from *Linguarama International* (1992–2002) http://www.linguarama.com/ps/297-4.htm.

The potential applications of studies in vague language for EFL books and courses are, in fact, endless. Controlled exercises could be devized to train students to remove content from words and leave less contentful words in their place, thereby removing explicitness and leaving implicitness. They could then be given free practice in using the discourse community implicit language, talking in interactional conversations about their course subjects. Students could be trained to guess what is being talked about by piecing together vague expressions and using the context. If they were trained to recognize the features of in-group code, they might appreciate when the cause of their lack of comprehension is because of their own linguistic or cultural gaps, and when it is because of the implicit language. However, it should be kept in mind that not all students may want to sound quite so British as they would if they used this form of speaking. They may feel that they wish to preserve more of their own cultural identity. It is possible that they have different ways of expressing in-groupness in their own cultures that they will prefer to reflect.

Nunan (2003: 195) advocates 'encouraging learners to become active explorers of language' so that they can learn about grammar in context, saying that 'Students can bring samples of language into class, and work together to formulate their own hypotheses about language structures and functions.' The next section describes a study carried out with an EAP class, using samples of vague language brought into EAP class by students and a linguistic exercise running over several classes, aimed at developing an awareness of implicitness and its social function.

Teaching the implicit language of the in-group

In order to test whether EAP students can be trained to recognize vague language and appreciate its function, Cutting (1999) organized a series of activities with authentic data in their normal class time, in the University of Sunderland. The students were told about the features of in-group code and were helped to find them in a sample dialogue from the MSc common room data. They were then asked to go with a cassette recorder and record any group of home students who appeared to have known each for some time and were talking informally. In the next class, they were trained to transcribe, and they then analyzed the dialogues to find features of in-group code in their dialogues. Their analyses were successful.

A questionnaire showed that many students did not understand their dialogues but realized that the implicit reference was partly to blame. A significant proportion of the students agreed that implicitness was a marker of intimacy. One said, 'it is very often the case within my group of friends. I think we developed something like a group code which is probably difficult to understand for outsiders.' When asked if studying this language closely had helped them in their socializing with British students, some offered answers such as, 'if I don't understand a conversation between two persons that's because they have a closed talking'. The exercise itself had proved enjoyable: comments such as 'I found this project really thrilling since I had never done such a study on language' abounded. This suggests that students can be made aware of the function of in-group code, and that they can be reassured that it is not always their own language competence level that makes conversations difficult to understand.

Conclusion

This chapter has shown that implicitness is an essential feature of spoken grammar, lexis and discourse structure, and that it is a system of interrelated parts, and it has suggested that it should be a central part of the model taught to students of English as a Foreign Language. It has described a longitudinal study of the formation of the implicit language of an academic discourse community and argued that to use implicit language is to assert the in-group membership and show solidarity. It has suggested ways of developing an awareness of vague language in EFL students.

The model of implicit language is hoped to contribute to the field of applied linguistics, to provide a model and a stimulus for further investigation. The model needs adding to and refining; more social variables need to be taken into account. Above all, this chapter hopes to inspire EFL course book designers to include mastery of this important aspect of natural spoken language in the syllabus.

Appendix: http://www.linguarama.com/ps/297-4.htm

Vague language

Vague language is not totally accurate or clear. Although some people think this is 'bad' English, all native English speakers use vague language when they are unable or unwilling to give accurate information, or they think it is either unnecessary or socially inappropriate to do so. A good example of vague language is rounding up numbers when telling the time. Twenty-six minutes past two becomes:

> It's **about** half past two.
> It's **almost** half past two
> It's half two-**ish**.
> It's **nearly** half past two.

Often, speakers use vague language not because they do not have accurate information, but because they feel it is more polite to make a less definite statement. 'That is wrong' becomes: 'I'm not sure that's completely correct.' As short definite statements sometimes sound too assertive to native English speakers, they often add extra vague language to a sentence. This extra language has no extra meaning, it is just a social softener.

The use of vague language differs from language to language and is an important cultural consideration when doing business in a foreign language. Native English speakers, for example, can find Germans direct because German uses little vague language. On the other hand, for Germans, native English speakers can sound indecisive, inaccurate and lacking authority. In both cases they are reacting to characteristics of the language, not their business partner. Here are some more examples of vague language commonly used by native speakers of English.

List completers

Sometimes a speaker might start a list of some kind and then cannot remember the rest of the list or does not think the other items are important enough to mention. In these cases, list completers are ideal:

> 'I typed some letters, reports *and other things like that.*'
> 'You have to ask a doctor or a lawyer *or someone like that.*'

List completers are very common and use words such as things and stuff. Here are some more list completers:

> and stuff like that
> and things / stuff
> or something like that
> or stuff like that
> or what / where / whoever

Placeholders

Placeholders are for when a speaker does not know or cannot remember the name of something or someone.

> 'I need a *thingummy* for the slide projector.'
> 'I gave it to *whatsisname* in the accounts department.'

Grammatically these simply replace the name of the person or object that the speaker cannot remember and never change their form. Other placeholders include:

> whatsername (for a woman)
> whatsit
> thingy
> thingummyjig

Quantities

Vague language is very common with numbers when expressing quantity, frequency or the time. Low numbers are often substituted by phrases such as *a couple of*/*a few*, whereas larger numbers are rounded up with *about*/*around* or replaced with *lots of*/*loads of*.

Bibliography

Altenberg, B. (1990) 'Spoken English and the Dictionary', in J. Svartvik (ed.), *The London-Lund Corpus of Spoken English* (Lund: Lund University Press).

Batstone, R. (1994) *Grammar* (Oxford: Oxford University Press).

Beebe, L.M. (1988) 'Five sociolinguistic approaches to second language acquisition,' in L.M. Beebe (ed.), *Issues On Second Language Acquisition. Multiple Perspectives* (Rowley, Massachusetts: Newbury House).

Bernstein, B. (1971) *Class, Codes and Control, Vol.1* (London: Routledge and Kegan Paul).

Biber, D. (1988) *Variation Across Speech And Writing* (Cambridge: Cambridge University Press).

Biber, D., Johansson, S., Leech, G., Conrad, S. and Finegan, E. (1999) *Grammar of Spoken and Written English* (Harlow: Longman Pearson).

Brown, J. (1979) 'Vocabulary: learning to be imprecise', *Modern English Teacher*, 7/1: 25–7.

Brown, P. and Levinson, S. (1978) *Politeness* (Cambridge: Cambridge University Press).

Bygate, M. (1987) *Speaking* (Oxford: Oxford University Press).

Cameron, D. (2000) *Good to Talk?* (London: Sage).

Carter, R. (2003) 'Orders of Reality: CANCODE, Communication, and Culture', in B. Seidlhofer, *Controversies in Applied Linguistics* (Oxford: Oxford University Press).

Chafe, W.L. (1982) 'Integration and involvement in speaking, writing, and oral literature', in D. Tannen (ed.), *Spoken And Written Language: Exploring Orality And Literacy* (Norwood, NJ: Ablex) 261–72.

Channell, J. (1994) *Vague Language* (Oxford: Oxford University Press).

Cook, G. (1989) *Discourse* (Oxford: Oxford University Press).

Cook, V. (1991) *Second Language Learning and Language Teaching* (London: Arnold).

Coupland, J. (2000) *Small Talk* (Harlow: Pearson Education).

Coxhead, A. and Nation, P. (2001) 'The specialised vocabulary of English for academic purposes', in J. Flowerdew and M. Peacock (eds), *Research Perspectives on English for Academic Purposes* (Cambridge: Cambridge University Press).

Crystal, D. and Davy, D. (1975) *Advanced Conversational English* (London: Longman).

Cutting, J. (1988) 'Opening lines from the floor', *Language at Work*, 13: 123–6.

Cutting, J. (1998) 'The function of inexplicit language in "CANCODE" casual conversations', conference presentation, Sociolinguistics Symposium 12 (University of London).

Cutting, J. (1999) 'The Grammar of Spoken English and its Application to English for Academic Purposes', *Papers from Seminar of the British Association of Applied Linguistics* (Sunderland: Sunderland University Press).

Cutting, J. (2000) *Analysing the Language of Discourse Communities* (Oxford: Elsevier Science).

Dörnyei, Z. and Thurrell, S. (1992) *Conversation and Dialogues in Action* (Hemel Hempstead: Prentice Hall International).

Eggins, S. and Slade, D. (1997) *Analysing Casual Conversation* (London: Cassell).

Fairclough, N. (2003) *Analysing Discourse: Textual Analysis for Social Research* (London: Routledge).

Firth, J.R. (1957) *Papers In Linguistics. 1934–51* (Oxford: Oxford University Press).

Flowerdew, T. (1994) *Academic Listening* (Cambridge: Cambridge University Press).

Garfinkel, H. (1967) *Studies in Ethnomethodology* (Engelwood Cliffs, New Jersey: Prentice Hall).

Goffman, E. (1963) *Behaviour in Public Places* (New York: Free Press).

Grice, H.P. (1975) 'Logic and conversation', in P. Cole and J. Morgan (eds), *Pragmatics. Syntax and Semantics, Vol. 9* (New York: Academic Press).

Gumperz, J. (1982) *Discourse Strategies* (Cambridge: Cambridge University Press).

Halliday, M.A.K. and Hasan, R. (1976) *Cohesion in English* (London: Longman).

Hatch, E. (1992) *Discourse and Language Education* (Cambridge: Cambridge University Press).

Huddleston, R. (1988) *English Grammar: An Outline* (Cambridge: Cambridge University Press).

Hunston, S. (2002) *Corpora in Applied Linguistics* (Cambridge: Cambridge University Press).

Jordan, R.R. (1997) *English for Academic Purposes: A Guide and Resource Book for Teachers* (Cambridge: Cambridge University Press).

Linguarama International (1992–2002) http://www.linguarama.com/ps/297-4.htm

Lynch, T. (1983) *Study Listening* (Cambridge: Cambridge University Press).

Lynch, T. and Anderson, K. (1992) *Study Speaking* (Cambridge: Cambridge University Press).

Malone, M.J. (1997) *Worlds of Talk: The Presentation of Self in Everyday Conversation* (Cambridge: Polity Press).

McCarthy, M. (1998) *Spoken Language and Applied Linguistics* (Cambridge: Cambridge University Press).

McCarthy, M. and Carter, R. (1994) *Language as Discourse: Perspectives for Language Teaching* (London: Longman).

McCarthy, M. and Carter, R. (1997) *Exploring Spoken English* (Cambridge: Cambridge University Press).

McDonough, S. (2002) *Applied Linguistics in Language Education* (London: Arnold).

Mills, S. (2003) *Gender and Politeness* (Cambridge University Press).

Nunan, D. (2003) 'Teaching Grammar in Context', in C. Candlin and N. Mercer (eds), *English Language Teaching in its Social Context* (London: Routledge).

Roberts, C. (2003) 'Language acquisition or language socialisation in and through discourse? Towards a redefinition of the domain of SLA', in C. Candlin and N. Mercer (eds), *English Language Teaching in its Social Context* (London: Routledge).

Schiffrin, D. (1994) *Approaches To Discourse* (Oxford: Blackwell Publishers).

Seidlhofer, B. (ed.) (2003) *Controversies in Applied Linguistics* (Oxford: Oxford Unversity Press).

Shalom, C. (1997) 'That Great Supermarket of Desire: attributes of the Desired Other in personal advertisements', in K. Harvey and C. Shalom (eds), *Language and Desire* (London: Routledge).

Sinclair, J. (1991) *Corpus Concordance Collocation* (Oxford: Oxford University Press).

Starfield, S. (2001) '"I'll go with the group": rethinking "Discourse Community" in EAP', in J. Flowerdew and M. Peacock (eds), *Research Perspectives on English for Academic Purposes* (Cambridge: Cambridge University Press).

Stenström, A.-B. (1990) 'Lexical items peculiar to spoken discourse', in J. Svartvik (ed.), *The London-Lund Corpus of Spoken English* (Lund: Lund University Press).

Svartvik, J. (ed.) (1990) *The London-Lund Corpus of Spoken English* (Lund: Lund University Press).

Tannen, D. (1984) *Conversational Style: Analyzing Talk Among Friends* (New Jersey: Ablex).

Tannen, D. (1989) *Talking Voices* (Cambridge: Cambridge University Press).

Tannen, D. (1994) *Gender and Discourse* (Oxford: Oxford University Press).

Wodak, R. (1996) *Disorders of Discourse* (London: Longman).

Yule, G. (1996) *The Study of Language*, 2nd edn (Cambridge: Cambridge University Press).

9
Reflecting on Reflections: the Spoken Word as a Professional Development Tool in Language Teacher Education

Fiona Farr

Introduction

The struggle for English Language Teaching (ELT), and by default language teacher education (LTE), to become recognized as a fully-fledged profession is a continuing one (Wallace, 1991: 4–6). However, increased professionalism in LTE has contributed greatly to its quest for independent disciplinary status in recent years. Some of these professional practices have occurred as a result of emerging philosophies, others because of empirical findings, and yet more due to technical advances. The present chapter firstly provides an up-to-date profile and contextualization of LTE. This includes brief discussions of theoretical and practical issues such as reflective practice, action research, critical approaches, the role of language and genre, and participation in language teaching communities of practice (Wenger, 1998). It then examines in detail how a spoken language corpus is vital for the successful critical reflection on one component of LTE programmes; teaching practice reviews, one of the most crucial aspects of what we do on teacher education programmes. As part of this discussion it will consider the part that computerized spoken language corpora can play in supporting and advancing some of the emerging paradigms. The focus is on the use of spoken corpora for professional development and introspection for those attending and conducting LTE programmes. The aim is to furnish detail on the nature of linguistic interactions in this specific arena in the belief that such deliberations are an integral part of the continuous professional development of LTE. Analytical linguistic examples, where provided, are based on a spoken language corpus of approximately 80,000 words, consisting of dyadic interactions between university-based ELT trainers and trainees discussing teaching practice (hereafter, the POTTI corpus).

Reflective practice and action research

Traditionally, up until the 1960s and 1970s, the predominant educational research framework was 'process-product' (Fang, 1996: 48; Freeman and Johnson, 1998: 399), and this was very much in line with behavioural philosophies of learning at that time. Research sought to describe the effects of teachers' actions (behaviours) on what students produced. 'In this basic paradigm, teachers' thoughts motivated their actions, which triggered students' thoughts, which motivated students' actions' (Freeman, 1996: 736). There was a disparity between the researcher and the classroom. Researchers assumed the role of the 'outside observer looking in' (Widdowson, 1993: 263). This role isolation overlooked the social and contextual complexities involved and researchers who were aloof and lacking in insider perspectives were responsible for creating 'an abstract, decontextualized body of knowledge that denies the complexities of human interaction and reduces teaching to a quantifiable set of behaviours' (Freeman and Johnson, 1998: 399 citing Smyth 1987). Consequently, LTE operated from a 'technical rationalist' perspective (Korthagen and Russell, 1995; Carter and Doyle, 1996; Crookes, 1997; Boote, 2001), which assumes that teachers need discrete amounts of predetermined knowledge in terms of subject content and delivery skills in order to develop effective teaching behaviours (Day, 1991: 38; Golombek, 1998: 447; Wideen *et al.*, 1998: 160). Language teacher educators taking this approach necessarily employ retrospective practices to transmit what teachers need to know and how they can be trained, versus what they already know and how this shapes their practice (Freeman and Johnson, 1998: 398).

With the advent of cognitive psychology (Fang, 1996: 48) and the much-cited publication of 'Schoolteacher: A Sociological Study' (Lortie, 1975) came a move in research to examining teachers' views and cognitions of their teaching and practices as they themselves interpret and represent them. A new body of research emerged describing teachers' thoughts, judgements and decisions as the cognitive processes that determined their behaviour (Freeman, 1996; Freeman and Johnson, 1998). Initially the focus of such research lay in uncovering the conceptual models of teacher thinking so that it could be used as a knowledge base in LTE (for example, Shavelson and Stern, 1981), using almost exclusively hermeneutically-oriented methodologies. Teachers were seen as mere informants and the researcher's job was to interpret and analyze the elicited language data. For various reasons, soon there was a move towards an examination of teachers' personal practical knowledge, using a variety of complementary data gathering tools and techniques. Therefore, since the 1990s, while the source of investigation has not necessarily changed (the teacher and the context of teaching), the method of investigation has altered considerably. We now have more co-construction and interpretation of teacher narratives with the teacher often being the primary investigator within a participant-researcher or action research framework, and we also have data emanating from a multiplicity of sources such as journals, classroom observations, questionnaires and so on. An extensive discussion of this type of research is not feasible in this chapter but good examples and reviews can be found in Carter and Doyle, 1996, Freeman and Johnson, 1998, Byrnes, 2000, Kramsch, 2000, Lantolf, 2000, Freeman, 2001b, Lantolf, 2001.

Findings from this type of research dictate that instead of using received or scientific knowledge as the primary focus in LTE programmes, we should start with teachers' existing schema and experiential knowledge, practical and informal theories (Wallace, 1991: ch. 1; Kinginger, 1997: 7) and bring this to the level of conscious awareness by fostering practices of reflection that can help them to 'contextualise their personal practical knowledge' (Golombek, 1998: 461). Such an awareness can then lead to appropriate development and relevant change or innovation in practice (Schön, 1983: 7; Pennington, 1995; Kennedy, 1997; Kramsch, 1998). It has been suggested that giving trainees a 'voice' (Elbaz, 1991: 10) validates their experiences (Kinginger, 1997: 8), recognizes them as persons with knowledge and cognition (Elbaz, 1981: 45), gives a feeling of ownership and individuality (VanPatten, 1997: 4), and provides a tool for continued professional development, which should be the aim of teacher education courses if we accept their limitations in terms of immediate impact. More fundamental, however, is the thesis that teaching experience and practice (apprenticeship) does not promote efficiency without the added dimension of reflection to allow for the appropriation of theory to real teaching situations (Oxford, 1997: 47). The integration of reflective activities has become central in many LTE programmes with many training materials available (see, for example, Tanner and Green, 1998) and some have even developed models for assessing the quantity and quality of reflection among trainees (Johnson, 1996; Bax and Cullen, 2003). Such reflection can also effectively be focused in the paradigm of action research with teachers as researchers or joint collaborators involved in the processes of building appropriate theory and teaching development strategy (Lieberman, 1986; see also Breen, 1989; Widdowson, 1993: 262; Burns, 1996; Crookes, 1997; Edge and Richards, 1998), and links the worlds of personal practical knowledge and empirical knowledge in a more holistic sense (Golombek,

1998: 461). Beyer, (1991) on a cautionary note, suggests that 'a careful analysis of reflection – one that helps us understand the nature, aim and process of the activities associated with a particular view of reflection – is needed if this alternative to technical training is to be viable' (p. 114). In many ways the type of research that the present chapter reports on the POTTI context is exactly this, an analysis of how we conduct reflection. Of course, the place and integrity of theoretical knowledge is not denied by the refocus suggested for LTE. Instead, the 'important elements of the future of educational practice and theory lie in the development of praxis, the theorized practice of specific situations' (Edge and Richards, 1998: 574), in a more bottom up, reflective, research-based paradigm with the teacher and teaching context at the centre in a more holistic model which integrates received and experiential knowledge (see Wallace, 1991: 15 for a diagrammatic representation of his reflective model for LTE).

The reflective practices of language teacher educators

There is an added dimension to the implementation of reflective practices, which I alluded to briefly in the previous section. In view of the fact that trainee learning can take place from what educators say and what they do, we need to be careful of 'inconsistencies between our message and our example' (Gore, 1991: 253). In the same publication, Gore distinguishes between the pedagogy we talk about (what we teach) and the pedagogy of our talk (how we teach) and how the former has had much attention to the detriment of the latter in LTE, despite both being important in the production of teachers. If we are to expect trainees to place value on and show enthusiasm for ideas and activities, then we should demonstrate our commitment to them by practising them and by doing all that we ask our students to do. This means a commitment to critical reflection running through the entire LTE programme (Beyer, 1991: 120; Korthagen and Russell, 1995: 187). Edge and Richards, (1998: 574), suggest that if we can't find time to practise what we preach, even in the face of the many demands on our time, then it is difficult to justify our position as educators of future teachers as we ourselves are at risk of becoming aloof and isolated (Duff, 1988: 111; Rossner, 1988: 108). There is also the inherent societal role of teacher trainers as 'potential *agents of change* in the creation of "learning" teachers' (Kennedy, 1997: 129, emphasis added), one that demands that we also assume the role of a learning trainer. In addition, any such neglect would mean that we continue to acquire our professional knowledge 'through unsupported processes of trial and error, and intuition' (Bailey *et al.*, 1998: 537), in the absence of formalized trainers' training courses. It has been cautioned that such example and integration at all levels is vital if 'reflective teaching is to avoid becoming simply another in a long line of slogans within educational theory and practice' (Beyer, 1991: 128). It has been suggested that this paradigm is vital to avoid the mistake of operating 'Do as I say, not as I do' regimes which advocate progressive practices within their own traditional structures. After all, how can we expect trainee teachers to challenge models to which we may be conforming?

The emerging role of teacher educators

Findings from the lenses of cognitive and personal practical knowledge research, coupled with social constructivist educational philosophies have led many to question the traditional norms of teacher education (Boote, 2003: 257; see also Wideen *et al.*, 1998). If it is even partially true that we teach the way we were taught rather than the way we are taught to teach, then one might conclude that we are bound to perpetuate the models we have been exposed to in our learning histories. It has been suggested that in order to begin breaking the cycle we can 'bring our past experience to the level of conscious awareness' (Bailey *et al.*, 1996: 11), through reflective practice and research techniques as discussed above. Therefore, learning to teach is no longer just about obtaining credentials and acquiring skills but about 'transforming an identity, adapting personal understandings and ideals to institutional realities, and deciding how to express one's self in classroom activity' (Carter and Doyle, 1996: 139). This refocus necessarily creates an emerging role for teacher educators as facilitators in the process of moulding and changing the beliefs and attitudes of trainees in using autonomous and collective procedures. Gore, (1991: 260) indicates the paramount role of interpersonal relationships between trainer and trainee in a TP context and the time needed to nurture this (see also Mann, 2003). Pennington, (1995) in her examination of teacher change refers to teachers' cognitive-affective filters as determined by their personal experiences, and philosophies decide how much innovation is converted into intake allowing for continual development in teaching practices. In fact, it seems that all arrows are pointing towards the internal worlds of teachers, both cognitively and affectively, being the appropriate focus for LTE. One of the resultant roles of teacher educators would seem to be akin to that of belief and attitude therapists. That is, they see themselves primarily working with beginning teachers' existing beliefs and attitudes. This new role is quite a departure from their more traditional roles: expert pedagogues who teach teaching skills, educational researchers who teach educational knowledge, or critics of dominant schooling practices. (Boote, 2003, p. 258)

In this and an earlier publication (2001), Boote suggests that there are many overlooked issues in relation to this newfound role such as ethical concerns and questions of appropriate competence to handle the type of invasive interventions required, both of which beg for further reflexive consideration and research. And at the heart of his discussions in both papers is what he calls the 'dilemma' (2001) or 'double-bind' (2003) inherent and irresolvable in this role. He claims that the aims of achieving meritorious belief change in a way that fits with the teacher educators' social and educational goals to improve the school system as *they* see fit is incompatible with the newly attested aim of enabling professional autonomy. In other words, it is impossible to be both facilitators of professional development and gatekeepers to the profession. Nonetheless, many of the models promoted for use in LTE, especially in the context of TP review, have their origins in talk therapy. Given the pivotal part that the spoken word plays in this equation, the following sections will examine the various theoretical approaches to the research of language and social practice before moving on to illustrate some of the more grounded work on genres and how these are manifest in various communities of practice. Both of these theoretical discussions lead us to the actual source of data for language analysis in context, which comes in the form of corpus evidence and specific to this research, the POTTI corpus.

The role of language

It is apparent in discussions so far in this chapter that language plays a major role as a tool in the development of cognitive skills (Vygotsky, 1978) and is also a form of data that encodes thoughts, philosophies and practices, as well as evidence of the progression of same, all vital in LTE. Discourse analysis, interaction analysis, conversation analysis, and content analysis have therefore been employed as appropriate methodologies in reflective practice and action research. Freeman (1996) traces the historical development of lines of inquiry using language as a way into the mind and as a vehicle for thought, through metaphor, story, personal history narratives and so on (see also Wallace, 2003; Warford and Reeves, 2003: 50). The 'representational view' of language prevalent in the 60s and 70s focused on *what* was said and assumed that our words represent our thoughts. In this framework 'words are taken as isomorphic to mental worlds' (Freeman, 1996: 734) in an individualistic sense. However, it has been argued by Freeman that this type of extraction and analysis provides only part of the story and needs to be complemented by a more 'presentational view' based on a social approach to language emanating from work by Bakhtin (1981) and Gee (1989) and others (these are discussed in more detail in the following section). The focus in presentational paradigms is on *how* something is said, thereby preserving the socio-political origins of language while at the same time 'working more fully with the complex nature of language data as language' (Freeman, 1996: 734). This allows researchers to trace processes of learning and development evidenced in the language used by those under investigation.

According to Freeman (1996: 744–50), there are three central tenets to the presentational stance: systematicity, relationship, and source. The notion of systematicity comes from structural linguistics and makes paradigmatic contrasts (what is said versus what is not said) and also syntagmatic contrasts (what is said in relation to what precedes and follows it), both of which are interdependent and gain and hold agreement through social conventions. Speech communities create and sustain relative meanings on both axes. Relationship refers to the integration of the individual and the language as a 'socially constructed voice' in Bakhtinian tradition. The idea here is that voice exists only as part of social milieu and is constructed through social dialogue (Wertsch, 1998). Researchers must therefore interpret what they hear as a representation of individuals within social communities and not as a neutral object. And finally, source of language refers to the speech community from which it is produced. The presentational approach therefore emphasizes the collective nature of language but in order to account for the place of the individual within this, Freeman (1996: 735) suggests a combination of representational and presentational approaches to language data as complimentary and inseparable, 'their integration enhances and deepens data analysis and the understandings that result', and provides two empirical examples of how this works in practice. All of these theoretical stances can help in the framing of specific spoken language analysis, and have done so in the case of the POTTI data in later sections.

Language in context: genre and communities of practice

Analysts can better interpret spoken discourse through a careful consideration of the context in which it occurs as well as the speakers who
produce it. In this paradigm, language is seen as a social product.
Socio-cultural theorists agree on the need to go beyond the isolated
individual when trying to understand the relationship between mind
and action (Burke, 1969; Vygotsky, 1978; Lantolf and Appel, 1994;
Mercer, 1995). We also need to take account of the 'instruments'
(Wertsch 1998: 24) or 'cultural tools' (Vygotsky, 1978) that individuals
use to achieve their actions. These tools come in many forms, especially language. What is acceptable and appropriate in our utterances is
determined historically and contemporarily by the culture (in the
broadest sense) in which we are operating. Bakhtin's work is especially
relevant here (Bakhtin, 1981; 1986) in many ways and has been prominent in the development and understanding of 'genre' (McCarthy,
1998; see also Jaworski and Coupland, 1999). In his writings, he considers utterances to be potentially unique, individually styled and un-
repeatable, but on the other hand, 'each sphere in which language is
used develops its own *relatively stable types* of these utterances. These
we call *speech genres*' (Bakhtin, 1986: 60, emphasis in original). Genres
are born historically, culturally, and socially through repeated echoings
and reverberations of others' utterances and are also filled with
'dialogic overtones' that take account of and reflect the prior thoughts,
expressions, and 'voices' of these present and non-present others.
Wertsch (1998: 293–4) explains 'that each word tastes of the context
and contexts in which it has lived its socially changed life; all words
and forms are populated by intentions', and he continues, 'the word in
language is half someone else's. It becomes one's own only when the
speaker populates it with his own intention, his accent, when he
appropriates the word, adapting it to his own semantic and expressive
intention'. Bakhtin postulates that, although uniquely moulded, no
utterance is new in the absolute sense. It is a composite of generic features and co-construction with other participants in the specific interaction. Such combinations give rise to a distinction between the
'referential' (semantic) and 'expressive' (emotive, evaluative) content of
utterances indicated in Baktinian abstractions.

Genre analysis has most obviously found a home in the study and
classification of various types of written discourse, and notable in the
study of academic writing (for example, Bakhtin, 1981; Kress, 1990;

Swales, 1990; Nystrand, 1992; Coxhead, 2000; Hyland, 2002; Johns and Swales, 2002), which has triggered a discussion of the role of genre relative to power, access, knowledge both socially and in education (Gee, 1989; Kress, 1990). However, concepts of 'intertextuality' (Fairclough, 1992; 1995; Candlin and Maley, 1997), and 'intersubjectivity' (Rommetveit, 1985; Wertsch, 1998), both emanating from Bakhtin's theories, have immediate relevance to spoken language. Intertextuality refers to an inherent property of a text in how it evidences the histories of other texts and hence shares its meaning with them. In other words, how individual texts 'manifest a plurality of text sources' (Candlin and Maley, 1997: 203), associated with some relatively normative institutional and social meaning. Thus, we can see commonalities and convergences within genres. The related notion of intersubjectivity is most often used to refer to 'the degree to which interlocutors in a shared communicative situation share a perspective' (Wertsch, 1998: 111); they move from their private worlds into a 'shared social reality' (Rommetveit, 1985) establishing a focus of joint attention. Reciprocal and mutual commitment is therefore a necessary condition, with bi-directional attention to the others' perspective.

Co-emergent with considerations of genre is the inevitable attention to those communities engaged in its embryonic development and perpetuation. In a thirty year period we have witnessed, through formal published accounts, a conceptual broadening evolution from Labov's notion of a 'speech community' (Labov, 1972), through Swales' and Nystrand's 'discourse community' (Nystrand, 1992; Swales, 1998), to Lave and Wenger's 'community of practice' (Lave and Wenger, 1991), with ancillary discussions of 'small cultures' from Holliday (1999). Gee's contemplation of 'Discourses' with a capital 'D' as 'forms of life which integrate words, acts, values, beliefs, attitudes, and social identities as well as gestures, glances, body positions, and clothes' (Gee, 1989: 6–7), sees the amalgamation of socio-cultural perspectives inherent in Vygotskian notions of scaffolding combine with linguistic perspectives of genre and discourse through processes of socialization in what Lave and Wenger, entitle 'legitimate peripheral participation' (Lave and Wenger, 1991). In this 1991 publication, we see an early mention of 'community of practice', a concept and framework later elaborated by Wenger (1998). Gee's original idea is that while one can overtly teach a body of knowledge, for example linguistics, one cannot teach another how to be a linguist, 'the most you can do is to let them practice being a linguist with you' (Gee, 1989: 7). This fits well with the extended idea of a learning curriculum as something that cannot 'be considered in isolation, manipulated in arbitrary didactic terms, or analyzed apart from the social relations that shape legitimate peripheral participation. A learning curriculum is thus characteristic of a community' (Lave and Wenger, 1991: 97). We therefore arrive at the abstraction of a community of practice (CoP) as a complex and dynamic entity that involves the frequent mutual engagement, joint enterprise and shared repertoire of its members. According to Wenger, (1998: 125–6), there are common indicators that a CoP has formed. The most relevant of these for present purposes include the use of specific tools, representations, and other artefacts, local lore, shared stories, inside jokes, knowing laughter, jargon and shortcuts to communication as well as the ease of producing new ones, and a shared discourse reflecting a certain perspective on the world. As an approach, it is compatible with social-constructivism because of its dynamism and mutual and cooperative engagement (Holmes and Meyerhoff, 1999: 179), and in many ways is reminiscent of a modern paradigm of apprenticeship. Having discussed theoretical approaches to language and a structured consideration of its context (through notions of genre) and use (through notions of communities of practice), it is now necessary to consider the methodological tools and procedures that are most conducive to the efficient organization and extraction of the language for analytical purposes. This brings us to corpus-based approaches.

The place of computerized spoken corpora

Corpus linguistics is a methodology (for a discussion of its methodological status see Tognini-Bonelli, 2001) which can be, and has been, used as an approach in many disciplines. Corpus software has a number of advantages for users: it produces word lists and counts occurrences of individual search items, it allows for the presentation and (re)organization of data in a way that facilitates the identification of patterns, it automatically produces cluster and collocation lists, and most software has a 'key word' tool which allows a comparison of lexis between corpora to identify relatively significant items. On the other hand, it gives easy access to spoken interactions for examples of language which can be used in a more interpretative way. Two broad approaches have developed within the field of corpus linguistics. McCarthy *et al.* (2002: 70), exemplify as follows:

Broadly, corpus linguistics may be performed in two ways: quantitative and qualitative. The quantitative approach usually looks for the largest corpus possible … from as wide a range of sources as possible. These data are then analyzed computationally and the output comprises sets of figures that tell the discourse analyst about the frequency of occurrence of words, phrases, collocations or structures. These statistics are then used to produce dictionaries, grammars, and so on. But for the discourse analyst, statistical facts raise the question *Why?*, and the answers can only be found by looking at the contexts of the texts in the corpus. Discourse analysts, therefore, work with corpora in a qualitative way.

In this way, corpus researchers in the latter tradition use statistics to formulate and check hypotheses and research questions to be explored more closely in a qualitative way (for example, McCarthy, 1998; 2002; 2003; Koester, 2001; Tao and McCarthy, 2001; Farr and O'Keeffe, 2002; O'Keeffe, 2003; O'Keeffe and Farr, 2003). At the other end of the continuum, linguists focus strongly on frequencies, patterns, recurrence (for example, Biber, 1990; 1993; Hunston, 1995; Sinclair, 1997; Biber *et al.*, 1998; Fox, 1998; Hunston and Francis, 1998; Biber *et al.*, 1999; Kennedy, 2002). This does not mean to suggest that one approach excludes the other, simply that one takes precedence over the other resulting from differences in research interest and objectives. This befits the premise that 'neither the quantitative data of a corpus alone nor the one-off analysis of conversational fragments is sufficient, and that much extra insight can be gained by working from the former to the latter and vice-versa, keeping both in constant dialectal relationship' (McCarthy and Handford, 2004).

The following analytical sections of this chapter will use POTTI in both ways as a tool for describing the nature of oral behaviour and participation in the context. In this sense, the spoken word is a primary and necessary data source for reflecting on how we conduct reflection in LTE, thereby completing the reflective loop (Schön, 1983; 1991). The underlying assumption is that such research leads to deeper understandings, which will ultimately promote continuous professional development. Freeman (2001a: 7), in his discussions on the current state of teacher training, emphasizes the need to draw on the past to forecast the present. This, he argues, can be most effectively done through reflection on practices that have been appropriately documented. Wallace (1998: 4), rationalizes further:

1. It is a way of accelerating and enhancing our expertise, and it turns problems into positive versus negative experiences
2. It allows us to identify areas for self-development and at the same time raises awareness of professional strengths
3. It results in increased effectiveness
4. It promotes a healthy spirit of inquiry and research.

The discussion so far has brought us through snapshots of some of the theoretical issues and approaches that can be used to envelop spoken language analyses, which, in this case, can aid in LTE professional development and reflection. The remainder of this chapter is devoted to the primary exploration of one such spoken language corpus.

The genre of POTTI: a qualitative analysis

Amidst conflicting findings in relation to teacher and trainee preferences for prescriptive versus collaborative supervision (Perlberg and Theodor, 1975; Copeland and Atkinson, 1978; Copeland, 1980; 1982, Bax, 1997) there remains one constant, affective factors are highly significant and feedback is better received when it is 'tempered by mutual respect, a warm and pleasant manner, a lucid and organized presentation of one's point of view, and a recognition of strengths as well as weaknesses' (see also Goldhammer *et al.*, 1980; Gower, 1988; Hoover *et al.*, 1988; Holland, 1989; Gore, 1991; Wallace, 1991: 116; Wajnryb, 1992; Woodward, 1992; Maynard and Furlong, 1995; Randall and Thornton, 2001). Notions of nurturing, care-giving, sponsoring, encouraging, counselling, and befriending among others have all been cited as central to the process (Anderson and Lucasse-Shannon, 1995: 32).

One aspect that seems to remain constant throughout the literature is the importance afforded to effective oral communication and the provision of psychological and interpersonal support for trainees (Hoover, O'Shea and Carroll, 1988; Elliot and Calderhead, 1995; Roberts, 1998; Koerner *et al.*, 2002). A number of prerequisite conditions and dispositions have been deemed conducive to establishing and maintaining an effective and affective feedback environment. These have manifested themselves within a number of proposed frameworks over the last number of years, many of which have their roots in theories of client-centred counselling. One which is adapted in this section is Heron's division between effective authoritative and facilitative interventions (Randall and Thornton, 2001). Added to these are the not so successful strategies, or what Heron calls degenerative interventions, otherwise know as immature or neurotic defences (Boote, 2003). There is often a fine line between when a strategy is effective in a confrontational way and when it breaks down in degeneration. An analysis of the spoken data shows the full range to be present in POTTI, where they seem to be the combined result of the cooperative interactive efforts of both parties. This section may at times also draw on concepts from the field of discourse analysis, most notably pragmatic frameworks such as politeness theory (Goffman, 1967; Brown and Levinson, 1978) and speech act theory (Austin, 1962; Searle, 1969). Before beginning the analysis, some details of the context and the participants may help the reader's interpretation through the remainder of this chapter.

The POTTI corpus is 81,944 words and consists of 14 feedback sessions. The recorded feedback takes place in the physical context of the university-based office of the relevant trainer. Only the relevant trainer and trainee are present in each session. This location, in which recording takes place, is that used in all feedback sessions in normal situations and is not therefore artificial in that sense. Feedback usually takes place at any time up to three days after the TP lesson, although there is a general tendency to do feedback the following day. Each session lasts between twenty-five and forty-five minutes, with an average of thirty minutes per session. The sessions recorded in POTTI take place in Weeks 6, 7 and 8 of the first semester of a two semester MA in the ELT programme.

TP started in Week 4, so each trainee had participated in a minimum of two feedback sessions before the recordings commenced. Two trainers and seven trainees are recorded. Both trainers are female. Fionnuala (all names are pseudonyms) is older, with considerable teaching experience, and had been employed on a part-time basis by UL for seven years at the time of the recordings. Edwina is a newly employed trainer/academic, with just three years' training experience at the time. Four of the trainee participants are female and three are male. All but one of the males are Irish. Participants are aged between twenty and thirty-five years of age, and only one of the males had any considerable teaching experience before starting the programme. All trainees hold primary degrees from a range of academic disciplines. This short description of the speakers and the location of the data should contextualize the analysis below, which begins with a qualitative exploration before moving to a more corpus-based investigation. The degree to which one might generalize from the following analysis is difficult to speculate and, while I feel relatively confident that the quantitative results might be reflective of other contexts similar to that of POTTI, this is probably much less true for the specific samples that follow in the next section. However, in many ways the issue of generalization is at odds with the type of approach espoused here, which aims to promote local explorations in local contexts for local solutions to local problems. If others should see similarities or findings that they find relevant, then this is an additional benefit rather than the intended aim in the present chapter.

Authoritative interventions

In Heron's model, authoritative interventions can take any of a number of strategies, all of which can be identified in POTTI.

Prescriptive interventions

The most obvious way of being authoritative is by being prescriptive. This is where the advisor proposes, recommends and suggests that the trainee carries out certain things in TP or refrains from doing so. Prescription can range from being highly directive to highly consultative. The trainer can employ a hierarchical stance in relation to the trainee, use direct speech acts, be on-record, and use few hedging devices; or, prescription can be much more consultative, with trainer and trainee building the advice together. This is evidenced in the following extract, where we see the trainer going to great lengths to coconstruct the advice through elicitation; see the movement from questions on lines 3, 12, 15, which, because of their limited success in prompting the required responses, are followed by more directive techniques from line 17 onwards, where the trainer takes more authoritative control of the interaction. The trainee, eager to participate and offer her contribution, initially provides extended responses to the trainer's questions, acknowledges the trainer's switch to more prescription on line 17 through the use of 'right' in line 19, and afterwards also continues to contribute in a way that shows agreement or tries to preempt the trainer's comments (for example, line 22), as well as deferring to the trainer's insights through her response tokens on lines 27 (right), 33, 47, 50 (yeah), and 36, 42, 52 (mmhm). They finally reach the desired directive 'the instructions need to be ah a lot clearer' (line 54), some 40 turns after the initial question is asked by the trainer (the transcription symbols are illustrated in an Appendix, p. 208).

Extract 1

1 <$Tr> +for those students em <$E> pause five seconds </$E> now when you
2 wanted them to do the the instruct= to do this exercise here what did you ask
3 them to do?
4 <$Tee> Em 'look at exercise B' <$E> laughing </$E> I said 'fill in the gap
5 exercise' I never told them that the words were in the bottom.
6 <$Tr> Yeah.
7 <$Tee> The box at the bottom.
8 <$Tr> Yeah mmhm.
9 <$Tee> And I don't think they understood that until I said 'oh by the way'+
10 <$Tr> Yeah.
11 <$Tee> +'forgot to tell you there's a box at the bottom with the words in it'.
12 <$Tr> Yeah now what other instruction would you need ah?
13 <$Tee> I should have told them that there were four words that wouldn't have
14 been used that would not necessarily fit into the.
15 <$Tr> Do you need to tell them that they are four?
16 <$Tee> Maybe some words just.
17 <$Tr> Y= y= you see you want them what you're trying to do is get them to
18 work a bit harder so+
19 <$Tee> Right.
20 <$Tr> +maybe there are a few words or there are some words that are not in that
21 aren't relevant or that you don't have to.
22 <$Tee> Put in yeah.
23 <$Tr> Put in.
24 <$Tee> And I should have told them that th= with some of them that you can
25 have different different <$G2> mind you that was there anyway starter
26 advertiser.
27 <$Tr> Well you see they can't have different words because this is the only
28 one+

29 <$Tee> Right.
30 <$Tr> +because they have to choose from a a limited+
31 <$Tee> Oh but I mean and to start <$G?>.
32 <$Tr> +number yeah.
33 <$Tee> Either would do.
34 <$Tr> Oh well they would they know that+
35 <$Tee> Yeah.
36 <$Tr> +that's quite clear from the the slash between them so I wouldn't explain
37 that but you do need to explain that they are to choose from this and that+
38 <$Tee> Mmhm.
39 <$Tr> +everything is not+
40 <$Tee> Instructions.
41 <$Tr> +and that they can only use each word once so that's awful because if you
42 ta= there are other exercises not here where there's here I think there's only one
43 definite word for each space+
44 <$Tee> Mmhm.
45 <$Tr> +but sometimes in gap you'd need to look at gap fill exercises and see
46 can one word+
47 <$Tee> Fit into two places+
48 <$Tr> +go into two places.
49 <$Tee> Yeah.
50 <$Tr> So you have to look at the whole thing and see yeah that if I put it up here
51 then I really need it for down+
52 <$Tee> Yeah.
53 <$Tr> +here.
54 <$Tee> Mmhm.
55 <$Tr> So they have to your instructions need to carry this sort of information if
56 it's relevant so you need the instructions need to be ah a lot clearer.

Informative interventions

A second type of authoritative intervention is the provision of information. This is done to provide instruction and is very much in the mode of teaching the trainee in the feedback session. It is done in a number of ways. Firstly, the trainer can provide technical advice on the language content of the lesson, which may not have been dealt with very well in the TP lesson. Some examples from POTTI include the trainee's inability to explain differences between the following pairs of lexical items: injury/wound, rob/steal, bill/cheque. In addition, the trainer often tackles the more sensitive and face-threatening issue of the trainee's personal use of language. The following extract illustrates how the trainer corrects the trainee's pronunciation of certain words. The face-threat is heightened by the fact that the trainee is a native speaker of English, and this type of informative intervention therefore has the potential to carry the perlocutionary force of a criticism. Hence, we see much consultation (for example, lines 5, 6), hedging (for example, line 1 'a difficult area'), and other solidarity and self-disclosure strategies (for example, lines 11, 12 'all of us would…') employed by the trainer. In fact it is bordering at times on a degenerative intervention in what Randall and Thornton call 'pussyfooting' (2001: 84). It takes 45 turns for the trainer to inform the trainee that she is incorrectly pronouncing the word 'boil'. We see traces of avoidance, for example, line 5, and displacement (Boote, 2003: 266) during the entire discussion on the pronunciation of 'pen' and 'pin', which the trainer had already established was not a problematic issue for this particular trainee. Pragmatic forces are clearly at play.

Extract 2

1   <$Tr> … now one area that I want you to try a difficult area to
    work on+
2   <$Tee> My voice is it? I noticed.
3   <$Tr> The sounds you know the pronunciation of the T H
    sounds+
4   <$Tee> Mmhm.
5   <$Tr> +ah don't don't do you ever use them correctly? You're
    from Cork are
6   you?
7   <$Tee> Killarney.
8   <$Tr> Killarney.
9
10 (five turns later)
11
12 <$Tr> The the T H you because we do dental most Irish
    speaker= I mean all of

13 us would do dental Ts where it should be+
14 <$Tee> Mm.
15 <$Tr> +and we don't+
16 <$Tee> Right mmhm.
17 <$Tr> +but if you're teaching on a at an international level if you're teaching it
18 is a sound that you need to actually have.
19 <$Tee> Mmhm.
20 <$Tr> The th= you know that at least you're aware that this is if you're giving
21 specific classes that this is how you+
22 <$Tee> Yeah.
23 <$Tr> +this is how they ah this should be pronounced and there was one other
24 sound that I+
25
26 (five turns later)
27
28 <$Tr> Now this word is 'aw' boil right whereas you pronounce it 'bile' 'bile'+
29 <$Tee> Right.
30 <$Tr> +now if you pronounce it 'bile' I+
31 <$Tee> Like B I L E.
32 <$Tr> +you're prono= yeah+
33 <$Tee> Mmhm.
34 <$Tr> Now they because when it comes to teaching pronunciation later on and
35 if you take the words.
36 <$Tee> Pen and pin <$E> reading </$E>.
37
38 (six turns later)
39
40 <$Tr> You mightn't no Cork Cork Cork speakers do you know they tend to say
41 'hand me the pin'+
42 <$Tee> Oh right.
43 <$Tr> +an they're talking about this+
44 <$Tee> Mmhm.
45 <$Tr> +which is a pen but it's just be aware of it.
46 <$Tee> Okay.

Personal interpretation is identified by Randall and Thornton (2001, p. 111) as being another type of informative intervention and is pervasive in all of the tapescripts in POTTI. Its obvious nature does not merit specific attention. However, the use of metaphor as an informative strategy is often present. In one instance, when the trainer is advising on physical movement and positioning in the classroom, she uses football and goalkeeping as a comparative.

Confrontational interventions

We saw earlier that the trainer criticism on issues of pronunciation of certain words was met by a preferred response from the trainee, who supports and reinforces the negative assessment. Therefore, the episode falls within the illocutionary and perlocutionary realm of informational. It is accepted and resolved and the episode does not degenerate to any extend. There are other occasions, such as that illustrated below, when the trainer's critical assessment becomes much more confrontational and borders on degeneration. This happens when the assessment, although acknowledged by all trainees as being one of the anticipated happenings in a feedback session, meets with a dispreferred response of disagreement (Pomerantz, 1984a). In this extract, the trainer questions the personality traits of the trainee, who had been particularly harsh and pedantic with her students (see also Farr, 2005).

Extract 3

1   <$Tr> … the one area that I want to talk to you about Joanna is because I say
2   the content of the lesson wasn't what I focussed in on yesterday at all wh= what
3   focussed in on yesterday was your approach to the students themselves now
4   wh= what sort of a person do you consider yourself in terms of are you+
5   <$Tee> A teacher.
6   <$Tr> +are you a friendly person or are you an aloof person or+
7   <$Tee> Oh no I'm friendly and+
8   <$Tr> Mmhm+
9   <$Tee> +I try and get on listening to them.
10 <$Tr> Now you see I didn't get any of this I my only meeting with you has been
11 in TP+

12 <$Tee> Mmhm mmhm.
13 <$Tr> +sessions when you're very friendly and you contribute and you make
14 very sensible contributions and things like that and yesterday when I went into
15 the classroom I found somebody who was like I suppose the best thing is like an
16 old style muinteoir+
17 <$Tee> Me?
18 <$Tr> Yes.
19 <$Tee> Okay.
20 <$Tr> Now th= please don't take this+
21 <$Tee> Oh no <$OTee> that's fine that's okay </$OTee>.
22 <$Tr> <$OTee> This is what came </$OTee> across to me now you started by
23 when you looked at the video how many times did you ask them to keep quiet?
24 <$Tee> Three or four.
25 <$Tr> You asked them about six+
26 <$Tee> Did I? Right.

This extract opens with a blatant and unhedged divergence of opinion by the trainee in line 7. The trainer attempts to diffuse the potential conflict through distancing and displacement to a completely different context in lines 10 and 13, 14. The reference is to a TP preparation session where the trainer has been the tutor. This acts as an immediate side-step by the trainer and allows her to introduce a series of compliments before returning to the criticism. The exclamatory trainee question in line 17 affirms that the conflictual stance remains unchanged, and even her 'okay' response in line 19 is not convincing to the trainer, as evidenced in line 20 where the trainer offers an apology. Despite the trainee's apparent pacification in line 21 the trainer, sensing the mood, feels it necessary to depersonalize the situation and make reference to the video evidence in line 23. She has judged the situation to be irreconcilable on the basis of personal interpretation and introspection. The introduction of external evidence firmly re-establishes the trainer's position of authority and allows her to make the categorical statement in line 25. Phillips (1999: 195) refers to this concept as 'neutrality', Pomerantz (1984b) terms it 'evidence' and 'evidentiality', and other pragmaticians have included it under the broader term 'reference' (for example, Yule, 1996).

Throughout the data, the introduction of external authority, (mainly in the form of documented theory and reference to other trainers' advice), and objective video evidence is used to settle difficult moments such as this one and usually does so effectively and efficiently, as it gives added weight and authority to the trainer putting her out of the reach of argumentation, dispute or contradiction. It protects her negative face (Brown and Levinson, 1978) and achieves the desired outcome and resolves the issue, finally ensuring the preferred agreement in line 26.

Facilitative interventions

In addition to the use of the type of authoritative interventions just discussed, Heron also acknowledges what he calls facilitative interventions. Facilitative strategies from POTTI are illustrated and discussed in this section. Some new illustrations are provided but reference to some of the extracts already presented in the previous section will also be used to exemplify.

Supportive interventions

A typical supportive strategy in POTTI is validation, which takes the forms of praising, complimenting, boosting and so on. The following table provides an example of the type of lexis employed for validation purposes. The items in the following table have been chosen on the basis of a qualitative examination of the discourse combined with their appearance on some of the POTTI frequency and/or keyword lists. The

Table 9.1   Validating words in POTTI

Word	Occurrences
Good	139
Nice	41
Interesting	34
Very well	27
Best	14
Pleased	10
Great	6
Effective	4
Excellent	4

negative meanings of some of these words have been excluded in the statistics presented (for example, *not great*, *not good*, and so on).

Clearly, there is a lot of praise and encouragement going on through the validation of the actions of the trainees, through the use of words such as *good*, *interesting*, and so on. This is important for building confidence.

Apologizing is another supportive strategy used by both parties in POTTI. It indicates mutual respect and deference. Extract (4) is a good example of both parties engaging in the act of apologizing, with both parties granting each other's request for forgiveness, before moving on to a different topic.

Extract 4

```
1   <$Tr> ...I was sorry for having interrupted you because+
2   <$Tee> Oh no.
3   <$Tr> +I that just made you more nervous.
4   <$Tee> I couldn't hear you with the the class was so big and I
    couldn't hear what
5   you were saying and+
6   <$Tr> Yeah.
7   <$Tee> +oh God I didn't know what you meant so.
8   <$Tr> Yeah.
9   <$Tee> I'm sorry for not arranging them the way you <$G3> I
    didn't have a clue
10  what you were saying <$E> laughing </$E>.
11  <$Tr> No no no that that's okay em so wh= you ha= you've had
    a look at the
12  video.
```

Catalytic interventions

Facilitation can also take the form of promoting critical thinking, probing, questioning and elicitation. This type of intervention is evident in the type of consultative direction already illustrated in Extract 1 above.

Cathartic interventions

Anxiety and defensiveness can be dealt with through open discussion of emotional states instead of avoiding or suppressing them. The POTTI data shows trainees talking about personal issues, especially in relation to how nervous they felt during the lesson, their lack confidence, career choice, difficulty in personal circumstances, and often reciprocal trainer disclosure coincides. The following extract provides one example:

Extract 5

1   <$Tee> ....I got rattled again and now I am kind of shaking
    when they ask me a
2   question I'm going no <$E>laughing<\$E> so I'm not in the
    best of form with
3   confidence of them asking me+
4   <$Tr> No I thought you were very confident in the classroom I
    thought your
5   personality came across very nicely in the classroom and you
    struck me as being
6   somebody who was confident+
7   <$Tee> Yeah
8   <$Tr> +in the classroom.
9   <$Tee> Yeah that is what I wanted well I don't tend to feel as
    nervous but
10 when they ask me to explain something it's like 'oh my god no'
    like and my
11 mind goes blank ....

Participation and interactivity in POTTI

This section uses the corpus in a much more quantitative way to
examine degrees of participation and interactivity in the discourse
(Wordsmith Tools was used for the analysis). Phillips (1999: 91), using
just one pre-service feedback session of approximately twenty minutes,
found a trainer/trainee split of 64 per cent/36 per cent participation,
measured by the number of words uttered by each party as a percentage
of the total number of words uttered. The results from POTTI, based on
all 14 sessions, are almost identical with trainer talk (2 trainees)
accounting for 63.57 per cent, and trainee talk (7 trainees) being at
36.43 per cent. On average, trainers speak almost twice as much as
trainees. The precise breakdown per session is included in Table 9.2
below.

This table shows that in all cases the trainer speaks more than the
trainee. Session 3 shows the most even distribution of talk between
both parties with just over two percentage points difference, while 14
is the session that contains most deviation from the average with the
trainer speaking three and a half times as much as the trainee. Very
interestingly, these two sessions are conducted by different trainers.
However, the individualized nature of each session and the tailoring

Table 9.2   Speaker participation in POTTI

Feedback session	Trainer	Trainee	Trainer words	Trainee words	Total words	% Trainer talk	% Trainee talk
1	Edwina	Lorna	1,879	954	2,833	66.33	33.67
2	Fionnuala	Roseanna	3,447	1,798	5,245	65.72	34.28
3	Fionnuala	Jim	4,748	4,552	9,300	51.06	48.94
4	Edwina	Petra	2,726	1,808	4,534	60.12	39.88
5	Fionnuala	Peter	5,050	2,173	7,223	69.92	30.08
6	Edwina	Michael	4,462	3,884	8,346	53.46	46.54
7	Fionnuala	Joanne	3,492	1,951	5,443	64.16	35.84
8	Edwina	Jim	5,365	3,281	8,646	62.05	37.95
9	Edwina	Roseanna	4,422	1,829	6,251	70.74	29.26
10	Edwina	Joanne	3,082	1,619	4,701	65.56	34.44
11	Fionnuala	Lorna	2,930	1,143	4,073	71.94	28.06
12	Fionnuala	Michael	2,408	1,332	3,740	64.39	35.61
13	Fionnuala	Petra	4,035	2,352	6,387	63.18	36.82
14	Edwina	Peter	4,045	1,177	5,222	77.46	22.54
Total			52,091	29,853	81,944	63.57	36.43

ability of the trainer is evidenced by the fact that these statistics show no notable trends for one trainer or another to consistently speak more in their feedback sessions, with both trainers reaching into the 50 and 70 percentage bracket on occasion. On the other hand, there is a notable trend among the female trainees to speak approximately the same amount in sessions with both trainers. None of the four female trainees differ by more than 5.6 percentage points in the number of words they utter in each of their two sessions, and Joanne differs least with just a 1.4 per cent difference between her session 7 with Fionnuala, and her session 10 with Edwina.

The three males, on the other hand, show an average of almost 10 per cent difference between their two sessions with different trainers, although there is no trend evident in relation to which trainer they prefer to speak more with. This raises a question in relation to the influence of gender on accommodation in POTTI, but one which cannot adequately be explored or resolved using the data distribution design employed.

Measures of interactivity are also useful for describing the participatory nature of different registers. Based on research by Biber (1988;

1995), Csomay (2002) uses a classification system of number of turns per 1000 words of discourse and suggests that fewer than 10 turns per 1000 words is interactively low and more than 25 turns per 1000 words is highly interactive. Poos and Simpson (2002), similarly based on previous work by Biber, propose a three-tier system of discourse modes: monologic, interactive, and mixed. The POTTI data, using such measures is pitched on the highly interactive end of the scale. It contains, in 81,944 words, 5,776 turns, giving 70.45 turns per 1000 words, almost three times in excess of the required 25 suggested by Csomay as an indictor of high interactivity, although some of these turns consist of minimal responses and acknowledgement tokens (see Farr, 2003), which may skew the interactivity statistics slightly. Nonetheless, I would argue that such responses are also valuable indicators of engaged listenership, and I therefore include them in my measures of interactivity.

However, looking at interactivity in this way leads to a perhaps more insightful investigation of the length of utterance in POTTI. The average utterance length for the entire corpus is 14.19 words. The average utterance length per trainer is 18.03 words, in line with the above average amount of talk they engage in, and per trainee it is 10.37 words. Table 9.3 illustrates utterance lengths per speaker in the data, computed as mean paragraph length by the software.

Table 9.3   Utterance length by participant in POTTI

Feedback session	Trainer	Trainee	Trainer utterance length (mean)	Trainee utterance length (mean)
1	Edwina	Lorna	23.49	12.08
2	Fionnuala	Roseanna	13.57	6.75
3	Fionnuala	Jim	15.52	15.22
4	Edwina	Petra	13.56	9.48
5	Fionnuala	Peter	22.48	8.48
6	Edwina	Michael	13.24	11.59
7	Fionnuala	Joanne	13.86	7.76
8	Edwina	Jim	19.28	11.97
9	Edwina	Roseanna	21.06	8.88
10	Edwina	Joanne	23.71	12.74
11	Fionnuala	Lorna	25.93	10.16
12	Fionnuala	Michael	16.49	9.79
13	Fionnuala	Petra	19.13	11.70
14	Edwina	Peter	27.52	8.17

The data in this table again show a consistently longer average length of utterance by trainers vis á vis trainees, although only very marginally in session 3, in line with its closeness in number of words uttered by each of the participants as seen in Table 9.2. There are no trends obvious from this data to show consistency among individual trainers or trainees, except that some trainees, such as Michael, have average turns shorter than those uttered by others such as Lorna.

Conclusion

The centrality of action research and reflective practice in language teaching and LTE has been forefronted by authors such as Michael Wallace and Julian Edge. These and other proponents hold strong convictions that some 'of the most effective ways of solving professional problems, and of continuing to improve and develop as a teacher, teacher trainer, or manager in ELT is through reflection on our professional practice' (Wallace, 1998: 1).

Through this formal framework, actions and experiences are recorded and shared so that we can better understand the processes in which we are involved, and ultimately make a difference to the quality of these actions and experiences. The intention should ideally be to learn and not justify (Edge, 2001: 6). 'Action research is teacher development made explicit' (Edge and Hancioglu, 2001: 7). Clearly, there is a need for collection procedures and analysis to be systematic, formalized and properly documented if this process is to be considered valid.

We are operating in educational systems where external validation and transparency are more important than ever in light of a more general decreased confidence in the professions resulting from the various professional, vocational, and public improprieties of our time. Notions of self-examination, scrutiny, and preservation are now paramount, and Schön (1991) even suggests that many professions now require formal evidence of professional reflection and development for continued eligibility for membership. Myers and Clark, (2002: 50) conclude that continued professional development is crucial for individuals and their organizations, should be continuous and lifelong (Randall and Thornton, 2001: 55), and should happen at the 'meta' level so that any resultant modifications in practice are more than superficial. Additionally, such research allows for the localization of solutions based on local problems, an approach which has been advocated in teacher training (Gill, 1997).

The collection and transcription of spoken language corpora is an example of a perfect facility with ongoing ease of access and inbuilt transparency. This chapter has illustrated the use of a corpus to examine qualitatively the types of interventions used in TP feedback and to investigate quantitatively participation frameworks. However, the same or other corpora could be used in a number of different and complementary ways to complete the picture of our professional practice. Additionally, the insider's view, or what anthropologists call the 'emic perspective' (Patton, 1990: 241; see also Gall, Borg and Gall, 1996; Phillips, 1999; Lazaraton, 2003), can be obtained through elicitations from the actors (for example, through questionnaires, notes, think-aloud protocols and so on), or more directly by employing a participative researcher research paradigm (Freeman, 1996; Heron, 1996; Morrow and Schocker, 1993). Both were employed in the larger POTTI research project but present limitations prevent elaboration here. All of these actions, measures and reports provide the destabilization necessary (arguably) for the prevention of potential complacency in our LTE professional practices.

Appendix

Transcription symbols in POTTI

<$Tr>	Trainer
<$Tee>	Trainee
<$E>	Exatralinguistic information
+	Interruption
=	Incomplete word
<$G2>	Guessed word with 2 syllables
<$G?>	Guessed word with unknown number of syllables
<$O>	Overlapped utterance

Bibliography

Anderson, E.M. and Lucasse-Shannon, A. (1995) 'Toward a conceptualization of mentoring', in T. Kerry and A. Shelton-Mayes (eds), *Issues in Mentoring* (London/ New York: Routledge in association with The Open University) 25–34.

Austin, J. (1962) *How To Do Things With Words* (Oxford: Oxford University Press).

Bailey, F., Hawkins, M., Irujo, S., Larsen-Freeman, D., Rintell, E. and Willett, J. (1998) 'Language teacher educators collaborative conversations', *TESOL Quarterly*, 32, 3: 536–46.

Bailey, K.M., Bergthold, B., Braunstein, B., Jagodzinski-Fleischman, N., Holbrook, M.P., Tuman, J., Waissbluth, X. and Zambo, L.J. (1996) 'The language learner's autobiography: Examining the "apprenticeship of observation"', in D. Freeman and J.C. Richards (eds), *Teacher Learning in Language Teaching* (Cambridge: Cambridge University Press) 11–29.

Bakhtin, M.M. (1981) *The Dialogic Imagination. Four Essays by M. M. Bakhtin* (Austin: University of Texas Press).

Bakhtin, M.M. (1986) 'The problem of speech genres', in C. Emerson and M. Holquist (eds), *Speech Genres and Other Late Essays* (Austin: University of Texas Press) 60–102.

Bax, S. (1997) 'Roles for a teacher educator in context-sensitive teacher education', *English Language Teaching Journal*, 51, 3: 232–41.

Bax, S., and Cullen, R. (2003) 'Generating and evaluating reflection through teaching practice', in J. Gollin, G. Ferguson and H. Trappes-Lomax (eds), *Proceedings of Symposium for Language Teacher Educators, Edinburgh, 2000, 2001, 2002* (Edinburgh: IALS, CD Publication).

Beyer, L.E. (1991) 'Teacher education, reflective inquiry and moral action', in B.R. Tabachnick and K.M. Zeichner (eds), *Issues and Practices in Inquiry-Oriented Teacher Education* (New York: Falmer Press) 113–29.

Biber, D. (1988) *Variation across Speech and Writing* (New York: Cambridge University Press).

Biber, D. (1990) 'Methodological issues regarding corpus-based analyses of linguistic variation', *Literary and Linguistic Computing*, 5, 4: 257–69.

Biber, D. (1993) 'Representativeness in corpus design', *Literary and Linguistic Computing*, 8, 4: 243–57.

Biber, D. (1995) *Dimensions of Register Variation* (New York: Cambridge University Press).

Biber, D., Conrad, S. and Reppen, R. (1998) *Corpus Linguistics: Investigating Language Structure and Use* (Cambridge: Cambridge University Press).

Biber, D., Johansson, S., Leech, G., Conrad, S. and Finegan, E. (1999) *Longman Grammar of Spoken and Written English* (London/New York: Longman).

Boote, D.N. (2001) 'An "indoctrination dilemma" in teacher education?', *Journal of Educational Thought*, 35, 1: 61–82.

Boote, D.N. (2003) 'Teacher educators as belief and attitude therapists: exploring psychodynamic implications of an emerging role', *Teachers and Teaching: Theory and Practice*, 9, 3: 257–77.

Breen, M. (1989) 'The evaluation cycle for language learning tasks', in R.K. Johnson (ed.), *The Second Language Curriculum* (Cambridge: Cambridge University Press) 187–206.

Brown, P. and Levinson, S. (1978) 'Universals in language usage: politeness phenomena', in E.N. Goody (ed.), *Questions and Politeness* (Cambridge: Cambridge University Press) 56–289.

Burke, K. (1969) *A Grammar of Motives* (Berkeley: University of California Press).

Burns, A. (1996) 'Starting all over again: from teaching adults to teaching beginners', in D. Freeman and J.C. Richards (eds), *Teacher Learning in Language Teaching* (Cambridge: Cambridge University Press) 154–77.

Byrnes, H. (2000) 'Shaping the discourse of a practice: the role of linguistics and psychology in language teaching and learning', *Modern Language Journal*, 84, 4: 472–84.

Candlin, C.N. and Maley, Y. (1997) 'Intertextuality and interdiscursitivity in the discourse of alternative dispute resolution', in B.-L. Gunnarsson, P. Linell and B. Nordberg (eds), *The Construction of Professional Discourse* (London/New York: Longman) 201–21.

Carter, K. and Doyle, W. (1996) 'Personal narrative and life history in learning to teach', in J. Sikula (ed.), *The Handbook of Research on Teacher Education*, 2nd edn (New York: Macmillan) 120–42.

Copeland, W.D. (1980) 'Affective dispositions of teachers in training toward examples of supervisory behavior', *Journal of Educational Research*, 74, 1: 37–42.

Copeland, W.D. (1982) 'Student teachers' preference for supervisory approach', *Journal of Teacher Education*, 33, 2: 32–6.

Copeland, W.D. and Atkinson, D.R. (1978) 'Student teachers' perceptions of directive and non-directive supervisor behavior', *Journal of Educational Research*, 71: 123–6.

Coxhead, A. (2000) 'A new academic word list', *TESOL Quarterly*, 34, 2: 213–38.

Crookes, G. (1997) 'What influences what and how second and foreign language teachers teach?', *Modern Language Journal*, 81, i: 67–79.

Csomay, E. (2002) 'Variation in academic lectures: interactivity and level of instruction', in R. Reppen, S. Fitzmaurice and D. Biber (eds), *Using Corpora to Explore Linguistic Variation* (Amsterdam: John Benjamins) 203–24.

Day, R.R. (1991) 'Models and the knowledge base of second language teacher education', in E. Sadtono (ed.), *Issues in Language Teacher Education* (Singapore: Seameo Regional Language Centre) 38–48.

Duff, T. (1988) 'The preparation and development of teacher trainers', in T. Duff (ed.), *Explorations in Teacher Training. Problems and Issues* (London: Longman) 110–17.

Edge, J. (2001) 'Search and re-search', *English Teaching Professional*, 20: 5–7.

Edge, J. and Hancioglu, D. (2001) 'TDTR – teacher development and classroom research', *IATEFL Issues*, 162: 7.

Edge, J. and Richards, K. (1998) 'Why *best practice* is not good enough', *TESOL Quarterly*, 32, 3: 569–76.

Elbaz, F. (1981) 'The teacher's "practical knowledge": report of a case study', *Curriculum Inquiry*, 11, 1: 43–71.

Elbaz, F. (1991) 'Research on teacher's knowledge: the evolution of a discourse', *Journal of Curriculum Studies*, 23, 1: 1–19.

Elliot, B. and Calderhead, J. (1995) 'Mentoring for teacher development: possibilities and caveats', in T. Kerry and A. Shelton-Mayes (eds), *Issues in Mentoring* (London/New York: Routledge in association with the Open University) 35–58.

Fairclough, N. (1992) *Discourse and Social Change* (Cambridge: Polity Press).

Fairclough, N. (1995) *Critical Discourse Analysis: The Critical Study of Language* (London/New York: Longman).

Fang, Z. (1996) 'A review of research on teacher beliefs and practices', *Educational Research*, 38, 1: 48–65.

Farr, F. (2005) 'Relational strategies in the discourse of professional performance review in an Irish academic environment: the case of language teacher education', in K. Schneider and A. Barron (eds), *Variational Pragmatics: The Case of English in Ireland* (Berlin: Mouton de Gruyter) 203–34.

Farr, F. (2003) 'Engaged listenership in spoken academic discourse: the case of student–tutor meetings', *Journal of English for Academic Purposes*, 2, 1: 67–85.

Farr, F. and O'Keeffe, A. (2002) 'Would as a hedging device in an Irish context: an intra-varietal comparison of institutionalized spoken interaction', in R. Reppen, S. Fitzmaurice and D. Biber (eds), *Using Corpora to Explore Linguistic Variation* (Amsterdam: John Benjamins) 25–48.

Fox, G. (1998) 'Using corpus data in the classroom', in B. Tomlinson (ed.), *Materials Development in Language Teaching* (Cambridge: Cambridge University Press) 25–43.

Freeman, D. (1996) '"To take them at their word": language data in the study of teachers' knowledge', *Harvard Educational Review*, 66, 4: 732–61.

Freeman, D. (2001a) 'Rethinking the tools of the trade: teacher learning and trainer learning', *IATEFL Teacher Trainers and Educators SIG Newsletter*, 1: 7–8.

Freeman, D. (2001b) 'Second language teacher education', in R. Carter and D. Nunan (eds), *Cambridge Guide to Teaching English to Speakers of Other Languages* (Cambridge: Cambridge University Press) 72–9.

Freeman, D. and Johnson, K.E. (1998) 'Reconceptualizing the knowledge-base of language teacher education', *TESOL Quarterly*, 32, 3: 397–417.

Gall, M.D., Borg, W.R. and Gall, J.P. (eds) (1996) *Educational Research: An Introduction* (New York: Longman).

Gee, J.P. (1989) 'Literacy, discourse, and linguistics: introduction', *Journal of Education*, 171, 1: 5–17.

Gill, S. (1997) 'Local problems, local solutions', in L. McGrath (ed.), *Learning to Train: Perspectives on the Development of Language Teacher Trainers* (Hemel Hampstead: Prentice Hall) 215–24.

Goffman, E. (1967) *Interaction Ritual. Essays on Face-to-Face Behaviour* (New York: Anchor/Doubleday).

Goldhammer, R., Anderson, R.H. and Krajewski, R.J. (1980) *Clinical Supervision: Special Methods for the Supervision of Teachers* (USA: Holt, Rinehart and Winston).

Golombek, P.R. (1998) 'A study of language teachers' personal practical knowledge', *TESOL Quarterly*, 32, 3: 447–64.

Gore, J.M. (1991) 'Practising what we preach: action research and the supervision of teachers', in B.R. Tobachnick and K.M. Zeichner (eds), *Issues and Practices in Inquiry-Oriented Teacher Education* (New York: Falmer Press) 253–72.

Gower, R. (1988) 'Are trainees human?', in T. Duff (ed.), *Explorations in Teacher Training. Problems and Issues* (London: Longman) 20–6.

Heron, J. (1996) *Co-operative Inquiry. Research into the Human Condition* (London: Sage).

Holland, P.E. (1989) 'Implicit assumptions about the supervisory conference: a review and analysis of literature', *Journal of Curriculum and Supervision*, 4, 4: 362–79.

Holliday, A. (1999) 'Small cultures', *Applied Linguistics*, 20, 2: 237–64.

Holmes, J. and Meyerhoff, M. (1999) 'The community of practice: theories and methodologies in language and gender research', *Language in Society*, 28, 2: 173–83.

Hoover, N.L., O'Shea, L.J. and Carroll, R.G. (1988) 'The supervision-intern relationship and effective interpersonal communication skills', *Journal of Teacher Education*, 39, 2: 17–21.

Hunston, S. (1995) 'Grammar in teacher education: the role of a corpus', *Language Awareness*, 4, 1: 15–31.

Hunston, S. and Francis, G. (1998) 'Verbs observed: a corpus-driven pedagogic grammar', *Applied Linguistics*, 19, 1: 45–72.

Hyland, K. (2002) 'Genre: language, context and literacy', *Annual Review of Applied Linguistics*, 22: 113–35.

Jaworski, A. and Coupland, N. (1999) 'Introduction: perspectives on discourse analysis', in A. Jaworski and N. Coupland (eds), *The Discourse Reader* (London: Routledge) 1–44.

Johns, A. and Swales, J. (2002) 'Literacy and disciplinary practices: opening and closing perspectives', *Journal of English for Academic Purposes*, 1, 1: 13–28.

Johnson, K.E. (1996) 'The role of theory in L2 teacher education', *TESOL Quarterly*, 30, 4: 765–71.

Kennedy, C. (1997) 'Training trainers as change agents', in I. McGrath (ed.), *Learning to Train: Perspectives on the Development of Language Teacher Trainers* (Hemel Hampstead: Prentice Hall) 127–39.

Kennedy, G. (2002) 'Variation in the distribution of modal verbs in the British National Corpus', in R. Reppen, S. Fitzmaurice and D. Biber (eds), *Using Corpora to Explore Linguistic Variation* (Amsterdam: John Benjamins) 73–90.

Kinginger, C. (1997) 'A discourse approach to the study of language educators' coherence systems', *Modern Language Journal*, 81, i: 6–14.

Koerner, M., O'Connell-Rust, F. and Baumgarter, F. (2002) 'Exploring roles in student teaching placements', *Teacher Education Quarterly*, 29, 2: 35–58.

Koester, A. (2001) *Interpersonal Markers in Workplace Genres: Pursuing Transactional and Relational Goals in Office Talk,* Unpublished PhD Thesis (Nottingham: University of Nottingham).

Korthagen, F. and Russell, T. (1995) 'Teachers who teach teachers: some final considerations', in T. Russell and F. Korthagen (eds), *Teachers Who Teach Teachers* (London/Washington: Falmer Press) 187–92.

Kramsch, C. (1998) *Language and Culture* (Oxford: Oxford University Press).

Kramsch, C. (2000) 'Second language acquisition, applied linguistics, and the teaching of foreign languages', *Modern Language Journal*, 84, 3: 311–26.

Kress, G. (1990) 'Two kinds of power: Gunter Kress on genre', *English Magazine*, 24: 4–7.

Labov, W. (1972) 'The study of language in its social context', in J.B. Pride and J. Holmes (eds), *Sociolinguistics* (Middlesex: Penguin) 180–202.

Lantolf, J.P. (2000) 'A century of language teaching and research: looking back and looking ahead', *Modern Language Journal*, 84, 4: 467–71.

Lantolf, J.P. (2001) 'A century of language teaching and research: looking back and looking ahead, part 2', *Modern Language Journal*, 85, 1: 1–4.

Lantolf, J.P. and Appel, G. (1994) 'Theoretical framework: an introduction to Vygotskian approaches to second language research', in J.P. Lantolf and G. Appel (eds), *Vygotskian Approaches to Second Language Research* (New Jersey: Ablex) 1–32.

Lave, J. and Wenger, E. (1991) *Situated Learning. Legitimate Peripheral Participation* (Cambridge: Cambridge University Press).

Lazaraton, A. (2003) 'Evaluative criteria for qualitative research in applied linguistics: whose criteria and whose research', *Modern Language Journal*, 87, 1: 1–12.

Lieberman, A. (1986) 'Collaborative research: working with, not working on....' *Educational Leadership*, 43: 28–32.

Lortie, D.C. (1975) *School-teacher: A Sociological Study* (Chicago/London: University of Chicago Press).

Mann, S.G. (2003) 'An evaluation of tutor-led feedback in the context of initial teacher training in EFL', in J. Gollin, G. Ferguson, and H. Trappes-Lomax (eds), *Proceedings of Symposium for Language Teacher Educators, Edinburgh, 2000, 2001, 2002* (Edinburgh: IALS, CD Publication).

Maynard, T. and Furlong, J. (1995) 'Learning to teach and models of mentoring', in T. Kerry and A. Shelton-Mayes (eds), *Issues in Mentoring* (London/New York: Routledge in association with The Open University) 10–24.

McCarthy, M.J. (1998) *Spoken Language and Applied Linguistics* (Cambridge: Cambridge University Press).

McCarthy, M.J. (2001) *Issues in Applied Linguistics* (Cambridge: Cambridge University Press).

McCarthy, M.J. (2002) 'Good listenership made plain: British and American non-minimal response tokens in everyday conversation', in R. Reppen, S.M. Fitzmaurice and D. Biber (eds), *Using corpora to explore linguistic variation* (Amsterdam: John Benjamins) 49–72.

McCarthy, M.J. (2003) 'Talking back: "small" interactional response tokens in everyday conversation', *Research in Language and Social Interaction*, 36: 33–63.

McCarthy, M.J. and Carter, R. (1995) 'Spoken grammar: what is it and how can we teach it?', *English Language Teaching Journal*, 49, 3: 207–18.

McCarthy, M.J. and Handford, M. (2004) '"Invisible to us": a preliminary corpus-based study of spoken business English', in U. Connor, and T. Upton (eds), *Discourse in the Professions: Perspectives from Corpus Linguistics* (Amsterdam: John Benjamins) 107–201.

McCarthy, M.J., Matthiessen, C. and Slade, D. (2002) 'Discourse analysis', in N. Schmitt, (ed.), *An Introduction to Applied Linguistics* (London: Arnold) 55–73.

Mercer, N. (1995) *The Guided Construction of Knowledge. Talk Amongst Teachers and Learners* (Philadelphia: Multilingual Matters).

Morrow, K. and Schocker, M. (1993) 'Process evaluation in an INSET course', *English Language Teaching Journal*, 47, 1: 47–55.

Myers, M. and Clark, S. (2002) 'CPD, lifelong learning and going meta', in J. Edge (ed.), *Continuing Professional Development. Some of our Perspectives* (Kent: IATEFL) 50–62.

Nystrand, M. (1992) 'Social interactionism versus social constructionism: Bakhtin, Rommetveit, and the semiotics of written text', in A. Heen-Wold (ed.), *The Dialogic Alternative. Towards a Theory of Language and Mind* (Oslo: Scandinavian University Press) 157–74.

O'Keeffe, A. (2003) *Strangers on the Line: A Corpus-based Lexico-grammatical Analysis of Radio Phone-in* Unpublished PhD Thesis (University of Limerick).

O'Keeffe, A. and Farr, F. (2003) 'Using language corpora in language teacher education: pedagogic, linguistic and cultural insights', *TESOL Quarterly*, 37, 3: 389–418.

Oxford, R. (1997) 'Constructivism: shape-shifting, substance, and teacher education applications', *Journal of Education*, 72, 1: 35–66.

Patton, M.Q. (1990) *Qualitative Evaluation and Research Methods* (London: Sage).

Pennington, M.C. (1995) 'The teacher change cycle', *TESOL Quarterly*, 29, 4: 705–31.

Perlberg, A. and Theodor, E. (1975) 'Patterns and styles in the supervision of teachers', *British Journal of Teacher Education*, 1: 203–11.

Phillips, D. (1999) *The Feedback Session within the Context of Teacher Training and Development: An Analysis of Discourse, Role and Function* Unpublished PhD Thesis (University of London).

Pomerantz, A. (1984a) 'Agreeing and disagreeing with assessments: some features of preferred/dispreferred turn shapes', in J. Maxwell, J. Atkinson and D. Heritage (eds), *Structures of Social Action. Studies in Conversation Analysis* (Cambridge: Cambridge University Press) 57–101.

Pomerantz, A. (1984b) 'Giving a source or basis: the practice in conversation of telling "How I know"', *Journal of Pragmatics*, 8: 607–25.

Poos, D. and Simpson, R. (2002) 'Cross-disciplinary comparisons of hedging: some findings from the Michigan Corpus of Academic Spoken English', in R. Reppen, S. Fitzmaurice and D. Biber (eds), *Using Corpora to Explore Linguistic Variation* (Amsterdam: John Benjamins) 3–24.

Randall, M. and Thornton, B. (2001) *Advising and Supporting Teachers* (Cambridge: Cambridge University Press).

Roberts, J. (1998) *Language Teacher Education* (New York: Arnold).

Rommetveit, R. (1985) 'Language acquisition as increasing linguistic structuring of experience and symbolic behaviour control', in J.V. Wertsch (ed.), *Culture, Communication and Cognition. Vygotskian Perspectives* (New York: Cambridge University Press) 183–204.

Rossner, R. (1988) 'Selecting teacher educators – establishing criteria', in T. Duff (ed.), *Explorations in Teacher Training. Problems and Issues* (London: Longman) 101–09.

Schön, D.A. (1983) *The Reflective Practitioner: How Professionals Think in Action* (Aldershot: Avebury).

Schön, D.A. (1991) *The Reflective Practitioner: How Professionals Think in Action* (Aldershot: Arena).

Searle, J.R. (1969) *Speech Acts. An Essay in the Philosophy of Language* (Cambridge: Cambridge University Press).

Shavelson, R.J. and Stern, P. (1981) 'Research on teachers' pedagogical thoughts, judgements, decisions, and behavior', *Review of Educational Research*, 51, 4: 455–98.

Sinclair, J.M. (1997) 'Corpus evidence in language description', in A. Wichmann, S. Fligelstone, T. McEnery and G. Knowles (eds), *Teaching and Language Corpora* (New York: Longman) 27–39.

Smyth, J. (1987) *Educating Teachers: Changing the Nature of Pedagogical Knowledge* (New York: Falmer Press).

Swales, J. (1990) *Genre Analysis* (Cambridge: Cambridge University Press).

Swales, J. (1998) *Other Floors, Other Voices: A Textography of a Small University Building.* (Mahwah, NJ: Erlbaum).

Tanner, R. and Green, C. (1998) *Tasks for Teacher Education. A Reflective Approach* (Harlow: Longman).

Tao, H. and McCarthy, M. (2001) 'Understanding non-restrictive *which*-clauses in spoken English, which is not an easy thing', *Language Sciences*, 23: 651–77.

Tognini-Bonelli, E. (2001) *Corpus Linguistics at Work* (Amsterdam: John Benjamins).

VanPatten, B. (1997) 'How language teaching is constructed', *Modern Language Journal*, 81, i: 1–5.

Vygotsky, L.S. (1978) *Mind in Society. The Development of Higher Psychological Processes* (Cambridge, MA: Harvard University Press).

Wajnryb, R. (1992) 'Learning to teach – the place of self-evaluation', *TESL Reporter*, 19, 4: 63–8.

Wallace, M. (1991) *Training Foreign Language Teachers* (Cambridge: Cambridge University Press).

Wallace, M. (1998) *Action Research for Language Teachers* (Cambridge: Cambridge University Press).

Wallace, M. (2003) 'Teaching practice: from experience to expertise', in J. Gollin, G. Ferguson, and H. Trappes-Lomax (eds), *Proceedings of Symposium for Language Teacher Educators, Edinburgh, 2000, 2001, 2002* (Edinburgh: IALS, CD Publication).

Warford, M.K. and Reeves, J. (2003) 'Falling into it: novice TESOL teacher thinking', *Teachers and Teaching: Theory and Practice*, 9, 1: 47–65.

Wenger, E. (1998) *Communities of Practice. Learning, Meaning, and Identity* (Cambridge: Cambridge University Press).

Wertsch, J.V. (1998) *Mind as Action* (Oxford: Oxford University Press).

Widdowson, H.G. (1993) 'Innovation in teacher development', *Annual Review of Applied Linguistics*, 13: 260–75.

Wideen, M., Mayer-Smith, J. and Moon, B. (1998) 'A critical analysis of the research on learning to teach: making the case for an ecological perspective in inquiry', *Review of Educational Research*, 68, 2: 130–78.

Woodward, T. (1992) *Ways of Training* (London: Longman).

Yule, G. (1996) *Pragmatics* (Oxford: Oxford University Press).

10
Analyzing Classroom Discourse: a Variable Approach

Steve Walsh

Introduction

In this chapter, the second language classroom is characterized by the ways in which teachers and learners jointly construct meanings through the 'talk' that they produce. Understanding and language acquisition do not simply 'happen'; they are negotiated in the give-and-take of classroom interaction. In order to gain an understanding of classroom discourse, a variable approach is proposed, which views any lesson as a series of complex, dynamic and inter-related micro-contexts. There are three reasons for adopting a variable stance. Firstly, all L2 classroom discourse is goal-oriented and related to teachers' unfolding pedagogic goals; secondly, the prime responsibility for establishing and shaping the interaction lies with the teacher; thirdly, pedagogic goals and language use are inextricably linked.

By considering the relationship between pedagogic actions and the language used to achieve those actions, a more realistic perspective of classroom discourse can be attained. A variable view of classroom discourse recognizes that interaction patterns change according to the different agendas and social relationships of the participants and according to teachers' linguistic and pedagogic goals. This view contrasts starkly with the more traditional description which utilizes a single, simple exchange structure: IR(F), where teacher Initiates, learner Responds and teacher offers Feedback. It is suggested here that a variable approach offers the potential for greater understanding of the finer variations that make up the different contexts, or *modes*, (Walsh, 2003) under which L2 classrooms operate.

Why study classroom discourse?

Classroom discourse has been the focus of attention in educational literature for more than 40 years. During that time, the study of interaction in the second language classroom (L2 classroom) has provided valuable insights into the complex relationship between interaction and learning. Why is there still a need to study interaction in the classroom and how much scope is there for new insights? A number of reasons can be identified.

According to van Lier (1996: 5), 'interaction is the most important element in the curriculum', a position echoed by Ellis (2000: 209), 'learning arises not *through* interaction, but *in* interaction' (emphasis in original). Given the centrality of interaction to the curriculum and to language learning, a fuller understanding needs to be gained of its precise function. Further, in light of the lack of empirical evidence for negotiation for meaning in *learner–learner* interaction (Foster, 1993; 1998; Ellis, 2000), there is increasingly a realization that the *teacher* has an important role to play in shaping learner contributions (Jarvis and Robinson, 1997). At least two key theories of class-based SLA have been modified in recent years to acknowledge the role of the teacher in constructing understanding and knowledge. Long's Interaction Hypothesis (1983; 1996), for example, has been adjusted to take account of the importance of negotiation for meaning in the feedback learners receive on their contributions from the teacher. Swain too, in her latest version of the Output Hypothesis (1995), adopts a socio-cultural perspective which highlights the importance of teacher-learner dialogues in promoting acquisition. The point is that even in the most student-centred class, the teacher is instrumental to managing the interaction (Johnson, 1995); there is, then, a need for both teachers and researchers to acquire 'microscopic understanding' (van Lier, 2000a) of the interactional organization of the L2 classroom.

Second, 'good teaching' is concerned with more than good planning (Richards, 1998). As van Lier (1991) has commented, teaching has two essential ingredients: planning and improvising. The interactive decisions taken by teachers – their improvisations – are at least as important as the planning which occurs before teaching. Under this view of teaching, decisions are taken in relation to the pedagogic goals of the teacher, the goals of the learners and the opportunities or constraints imposed by the context. Good decisions are those that are appropriate to the moment, not ones that 'follow the plan'. Teachers may restrict or facilitate learning opportunities in their moment-by-moment decision-making (Walsh, 2002). Their ability to make the 'right decision' entails an understanding of interactional choices: choices which influence the flow of the discourse and which largely determine the extent to which opportunities for learning are created.

Third, there is as yet no widely available metalanguage that can be used by teachers and researchers to describe the micro-contexts in which L2 classroom interaction takes place (Seedhouse, 1996; Kumaravadivelu, 1999). Understanding of interactional processes must begin with description (van Lier, 2000a); understanding is coconstructed by participants as they engage in dialogue about their professional world (Lantolf, 2000). Description and dialogue, both of which are central to promoting interactional awareness, require an appropriate metalanguage, a language that can be used by teachers to enhance understanding of their local context. Presently, teachers' understanding of that context is partial and impoverished owing to the lack of an appropriate metalanguage. Terms such as 'high' or 'low TTT' (teacher talking time), and 'communicative' or 'uncommunicative' are commonly used but do little to foster awareness of the 'interactional architecture' (Seedhouse, 1996: 97) of the L2 classroom. Access to a more sophisticated, widely available metalanguage and opportunities for dialogue are central to professional development (Edge, 2001). Expertise and understanding emerge through the insights and voices of L2 teachers (Richards, 1998); these voices need a language that allows concerns to be raised, questions to be asked and reflections to be discussed.

What are the features of L2 classroom discourse?

The communication patterns found in language classrooms are special, different from those found in content-based subjects like history, geography, science. Communication is unique because the linguistic forms used are often the aim of a lesson and the means of achieving those aims. Meaning and message are one and the same thing, 'the vehicle and object of instruction' (Long, 1983: 9); language is both the focus of activity, the central objective of the lesson, as well as the instrument for achieving it (Willis, 1992). This situation is, in many respects, atypical, most unlike, for example, the one prevailing in a history or geography lesson, where all attention is on the message, not on the language used. As Thornbury (2000: 28) puts it:

language classrooms are **language** classrooms [original emphasis], and for the teacher to monopolise control of the discourse – through, for example, asking only display questions – while possibly appropriate to the culture of geography or maths classes, would seem to deny language learners access to what they most need – opportunities for real language use.

One consequence of this observation is that any attempt to analyze communication in the L2 classroom must take account, first of all, of its uniqueness and, secondly, of its complexity. As Cazden points out (1986: 432), classroom communication is a 'problematic medium'. The process of communication in an EFL/ESL class – a multinational, multi-lingual and multi-cultural setting – is further complicated by the fact that misunderstandings, which almost certainly impair teaching and learning, are potentially more frequent. This is due to differences in the backgrounds, expectations and perceptions of language learners, together with the status they attach to the teacher, who may be the only native-speaker present. Clashes of expectations are by no means uncommon in the EFL context and present the teacher with enormous interactional difficulties (Shamin, 1996). An understanding of the dynamics of classroom discourse is therefore essential for teachers to establish and maintain good communicative practices (Johnson, 1995). The first step in gaining such an understanding is familiarization with the features of L2 classroom discourse. Recent surveys of interaction in classes that adopt a predominantly CLT (communicative language teaching) methodology identify a number of broad characteristics. For example, Lightbown and Spada (1993: 72–3) have commented that features such as the limited amount of error correction, the emphasis on communication over accuracy, and learners' exposure to a wide range of discourse types distinguish the communicative classroom from more 'traditional' learning modes.

Perhaps surprisingly, there is now a growing body of evidence to suggest that peer interaction is not as effective as was once thought in promoting acquisition (Dornyei and Malderez, 1997; Foster, 1998). Rampton clearly questions the value of learner–learner interaction (1999: 333):

> some of the data we have looked at ... provides grounds for doubting any assumption that peer group rituals automatically push acquisition forwards.

Observations like the previous one are borne out in other studies (see, for example, Mitchell and Martin, 1997), indicating that the role of the teacher in shaping classroom interaction may need to be reconsidered, as does the very notion of whole class teaching. Simply handing over to learners is apparently an inadequate means of promoting SLA; there is both an expectation and responsibility that the teacher is there to *teach* the second language, not simply to organize practice activities.

In the remainder of this section, as a first step to understanding communication in the second language classroom, the *characteristics* of L2 classroom discourse are presented, largely from the teacher's perspective, under four key areas: control of patterns of communication, questioning, repair, modifying speech to learners.

Control of the patterns of communication

The features of the second language classroom discourse, its 'text' (Breen, 1998: 121), are easy to identify and present a very clear structure, where teachers control both the topic of conversation and turn-taking. Students take their cues from the teacher through whom they direct most of their responses. Owing to their special status, teachers control most of the patterns of communication which take place in the L2 classroom. They do this primarily through the ways in which they restrict or allow learners' interaction (Ellis, 1998), take control of the topic (Slimani, 1989), and facilitate or hinder learning opportunities (Walsh, 2002). Put simply, even in the most decentralized L2 classroom, it is the teacher who 'orchestrates the interaction' (Breen, 1998, p. 119). The underlying structure of second language lessons is typically IR(E/F), involving teacher initiation (I), learner response [R] and an optional evaluation or feedback (E/F) by the teacher (Sinclair and Coulthard, 1975). (Henceforth, this is referred to as the IRF sequence). For every one move made by the learner, a teacher makes two, leading Chaudron (1988), to the conclusion that teacher talk represents approximately two-thirds of classroom speech.

Questioning

Typically, classroom discourse is dominated by question and answer routines, with teachers asking most of the questions, one of the principal ways in which teachers control classroom discourse. According to Chaudron (1988), most of the studies on teachers' questioning behaviour have examined the ways in which questions facilitate the production of target language forms or correct content-related responses. Many of the question types selected and used by language teachers are of the closed variety and produce only short responses from students (van Lier, 1988a). Other studies have focused on the extent to which questions produce responses that are 'communicative', arguing that referential questions are more likely to produce 'natural' responses than display questions (Long and Sato, 1983; Brock, 1986; Nunan, 1987).

More recent studies (Banbrook and Skehan, 1990; Seedhouse, 1996) query the value of the typical distinction between *display* and *referential* questions. Traditionally, display questions, to which the teacher already knows the answer (for example, *'what's the past tense of go?*) are seen as being different from referential questions, where the answer is not known in advance (for example, *when does this lesson end?)* and typically produce shorter, simpler responses from learners. While accepting that the purpose of all questions is to elicit responses, the display/referential distinction is, arguably, a useful one of which teachers should be aware (Thompson, 1997; Cullen, 1998). According to a teacher's pedagogic goal, different question types are more or less appropriate: the extent to which a question produces a communicative response is less important than the extent to which a question serves its purpose at a particular point in a lesson. In short, the use of appropriate questioning strategies requires an understanding of the *function* of a question in relation to what is being taught (Thompson, 1997; Nunn, 1999).

Repair

According to van Lier, 'apart from questioning, the activity which most characterizes language classrooms is correction of errors' (1988b: 276). He goes on to suggest that there are essentially two conflicting views of repair: one that error correction should be avoided completely, the other that consistent error correction is necessary. One of the reasons for such polarity is the importance of maintaining face in the classroom. While repair between native and non-native adults outside the classroom might be deemed inappropriate, since it would result in a loss of face, there is absolutely no reason why errors should not be corrected in the L2 formal context. Indeed, as Seedhouse confirms, this is what learners want (1997: 571):

> learners appear to have grasped better than teachers and methodologists that, within the interactional organisation of the L2 classroom, making linguistic errors and having them corrected directly and overtly is not an embarrassing matter.

For many teachers, repair, as other practices which prevail in language classrooms, is a ritual, something they 'do to learners' without really questioning their actions. This is not intended as a criticism, merely an observation. The consequences of such ritualistic behaviour, however, are far-reaching, since for many practitioners, the feedback move, where correction of errors typically occurs, is crucial to learning (Willis, 1992; Jarvis and Robinson, 1997). Taking this a little further, error correction may be direct or indirect, overt or covert; in short, teachers are open to many options – their split-second decisions in the rapid flow of a lesson may have consequences for the learning opportunities they present to their learners. Although feedback is understandably perceived by most learners as evaluative (Allwright and Bailey, 1991), other researchers have posited a variable approach to feedback. Kasper (1986: 39), for example, notes that specific repair strategies are preferred or dispreferred according to the teacher's goal, contrasting 'language centred' with 'content centred' repair. Van Lier concludes that repair is 'closely related to the context of what is being done' (1988a: 211), the implication being that repair, as other aspects of classroom discourse, either is, or should be, related to pedagogic goals.

Modifying speech to learners

Lynch (1996: 57–8) suggests three reasons for the interest in language modification by teachers for learners, first, because there is a link between comprehension and progress in L2; second, teacher language has a strong influence on learner language; third, owing to the fact that learners frequently have difficulties understanding their teachers.

He identified a number of ways in which teachers modify their inter-action, including the use of confirmation checks to make sure that the teacher understands the learner, and comprehension checks to ensure that learners understand the teacher. Other modification strategies identified by Lynch include repetition, reformulation, completion and backtracking.

According to Chaudron (1988), teachers modify four aspects of their speech: vocabulary, by avoiding idioms and using more common words; grammar, by using shorter, simpler utterances and by using the present tense; pronunciation, by speaking more slowly and more clearly and using standard forms; and non-verbal language such as the increased use of gestures and facial expressions.

Similarly, Tardif (1994) identified five modification strategies, includ-ing self-repetition, where teachers simply repeat an utterance; linguistic modelling, where teachers provide an exact word or statement to be modelled by students; providing information needed to complete an activity or task; expansion, elaborating a student response; and making extended use of questions is made to ensure participation, check understanding, facilitate comprehension.

Tardif's work supports the earlier findings of Long and Sato (1983), who conclude that expansion and question strategies are the most frequently used in teachers' discourse modifications. More recent studies have focused on the relevance of scaffolded instruction to learning (see, for example, Roehler *et al.*, 1996).

How can classroom discourse be investigated?

The case for describing classroom interaction has already been made in the preceding sections. In the words of Kumaravadivelu (1999: 454):

> [the] classroom is the crucible where the prime elements of education ... all mix together to produce exclusive and at times explosive environments that might help or hinder the creation and utilization of learning opportunities. What actually happens there largely determines the degree to which desired learning outcomes are realized. The task of systematically observing, analyzing and understanding classroom aims and events therefore becomes central to any serious educational enterprise.

In the remainder of this section, a review is presented of the most relevant contributions to the significant research body that now exists on the study of L2 classroom interaction. Three approaches to analyzing classroom discourse are first critiqued – interaction analysis, discourse analysis, conversation analysis – before proposing a variable and dynamic approach.

Interaction analysis (IA) approaches

Proponents of the 'scientific method' (Cohen *et al.*, 2000: 15–19) would argue that one of the most reliable, quantitative approaches to analyzing classroom interaction comprises a series of observational instruments, or coding systems, which are used to record what the observer deems to be happening in the L2 classroom. From these recordings and the ensuing statistical treatment, classroom profiles can be established, which, it is argued, provide an objective and 'scientific' analysis of classroom discourse. With their roots firmly planted in behavioural psychology, 'which emphasizes objective analysis of observable behaviour' (Kumaravadivelu, 1999: 455), a huge range of observation instruments has proliferated since the 1960s and 1970s. In 1988, Chaudron calculated that there were approximately 25 systems available for analyzing interaction in the L2 classroom.

The main features of observation instruments are that they use some system of ticking boxes, making marks, recording what the observer sees, often at regular time intervals. In addition, they are considered to be 'reliable', enabling ease of comparison between observers and generalizability of results, but are also criticized for being essentially behaviourist, assuming a stimulus/response progression to classroom discourse. One field in which observation instruments have been used successfully is teacher education, where they have been useful in developing competencies and raising awareness. Indeed, some writers (for example, Edwards and Westgate, 1994) suggest that observation instruments might be better suited to teacher education than research.

A review of the many different instruments which are now available is beyond the scope of this chapter. (For comprehensive reviews, the reader is referred to Malamah-Thomas, 1987; Allwright, 1988; Chaudron, 1988; Warjnryb, 1992). It is now generally recognized that system-based interactional approaches to L2 classroom discourse can only provide a partial picture of reality, based as they are only on what is observable or measurable (Nunan, 1989; Wallace, 1998). Their main limitations are now summarized.

First, the patterns of interaction that occur have to be matched to the categories provided; the results are pre-determined and cannot account for events that do not match the descriptive categories. No allowance is made for overlap; the categories for observation are discrete and there is an underlying assumption that classroom discourse proceeds in a sequential manner (T -> S -> T -> S and so on). In fact, this is simply not the case: overlaps, interruptions, back-channelling, false starts, repetitions, hesitations are as common in language classrooms as they are in naturally occurring conversation (Edwards and Westgate, 1994).

Second, observation instruments are based on the assumption that one move occurs at once, obliging the observer to make snap decisions about how to categorize utterances as they occur. Inevitably, inaccuracies and reductions will ensue and the complexities of classroom interaction will be lost forever (Wallace, 1998: 112).

Third, the observer is always considered as an outsider 'looking in on' events as they occur (Long, 1983). Consequently, any coding system assumes the centrality of the observer rather than the participants – the observer's interpretation of events excludes that of the participants. One serious criticism of coding systems put forward by Chaudron (1988) is that observers may fail to agree on how to record what they see. This has clear implications for the validity and reliability dimensions of research, in addition to indicating problems when coding systems are used in classroom observation as a 'multi-faceted tool for learning' (Warjnryb, 1992: 1).

Finally, coding systems make the assumption that research findings 'are evident "beneath" or "within" the words exchanged' (Edwards and Westgate, 1994: 60). Put simply, recording patterns of L2 interaction in 'real-time' fails to take adequate account of the classroom context and of the inter-relationship between strands of utterances. In short, there is a question as to whether recording and coding of classroom language adequately represents 'what is happening'. Seedhouse makes the important point that coding systems fail to take account of context and 'evaluate all varieties of L2 classroom interaction from a single perspective and according to a single set of criteria' (1996: 42). In the multi-layered, ever-changing, complex language classroom context, this is clearly a severe deficiency and perhaps as strong an argument as any for selecting alternative means of recording and describing the interaction patterns of L2 classrooms.

Discourse analysis (DA) approaches

Levinson (1983: 286) proposes that there are two major approaches to the study of naturally occurring interaction: discourse analysis and conversation analysis. Seedhouse (1996: 27) suggests that 'the overwhelming majority of previous approaches to L2 classroom interaction have implicitly or explicitly adopted what is fundamentally a discourse analysis approach.'

Perhaps the earliest and most well-known proponents of a discourse analysis (DA) approach to classroom interaction are Sinclair and Coulthard (1975) who, following a structural-functional linguistic route to analysis, compiled a list of 22 speech acts representing the verbal behaviours of both teachers and students participating in primary classroom communication. The outcome is the development of a descriptive system incorporating a discourse hierarchy:

LESSON
TRANSACTION
EXCHANGE
MOVE
ACT

The act is therefore the smallest discourse unit, while lesson is the largest; acts are described in terms of their discourse function, as in the two examples of speech acts below (* indicates a pause of 1 second or more):

Act	*Function*	*Realization*
Evaluation	evaluates	Ah that won't help then will it
Cue	evokes bid	what is the situation * at the beginning of the story *

(based on Sinclair and Coulthard, 1975)

It is now widely accepted that most classroom communication is characterized by an IRF or IRE structure, where **I** corresponds to teacher Initiation, **R** to student **R**esponse and **F** / **E** to optional teacher Feedback or teacher Evaluation. This exchange comprises two teacher moves for every student move and typifies much of the communication to be found in both content-based and L2 classrooms (Sinclair and Coulthard, 1975; Edwards and Westgate, 1994). Example:

1	T:	two things to establish for the writer at the beginning of the story one
2		situation situation what is the situation* at the beginning of the story
3		* anybody what's the situation Douglas * have you read the story
4		Douglas
5	S:	no sir
6	T:	ah that won't help then will it who's read the story what is the
7		situation at the beginning * Michael * is it Michael

(Walsh, 1987)

In extract 1, the initial teacher move (**I**) (lines 1–4) is followed by a single student move (**R**) (line 5) and followed immediately by the teacher feedback move (**F**) in lines 6–7. More recent interpretations of this structure (Jarvis and Robinson, 1997; Seedhouse, 1997) suggest that there may be instances in which the second teacher move should be viewed as a type of repair rather than an evaluation.

One of the main limitations of the Sinclair and Coulthard system is that it was derived from data recorded in traditional primary school classrooms during the 1960s which demonstrated clear status and power relations between teacher and learners. In the contemporary L2 classroom, where there is far more equality and partnership in the teaching-learning process, it is doubtful whether the framework would adequately describe the structure of classroom communication (Walsh, 1987). There is evidence (Griffin and Mehan, 1981; Mayher, 1990) that the more formal, ritualized interactions between teacher and learners are not as prevalent today as they were in the 1960s; today, there is far more learner-initiated communication, more equal turn-taking and less reliance on teacher-fronted and lockstep modes of learning.

While DA approaches (such as the Sinclair/Coulthard model) are certainly valuable in portraying the features of classroom discourse, they also have a number of limitations. First, the approach is both descriptive and prescriptive: it tries to categorize naturally occurring patterns of interaction and account for them by reference to a discourse hierarchy. Second, DA takes as its starting point structural-functional linguistics: classroom data are analyzed according to their function. For example, *'what time does this lesson end?'* could be interpreted as a request for information, an admonishment, a prompt or cue. The DA model has been criticized for its *multifunctionality* (Stubbs, 1983) because it is almost impossible to say precisely what function is being performed by a teacher (or learner) act at any point in a lesson. Classification of classroom discourse in purely structural-functional terms is consequently problematic. Thirdly, no attempt is made to take account of the more subtle forces at work such as role relations, context and sociolinguistic norms which have to be obeyed. In short, a DA treatment fails to adequately account for the dynamic nature of classroom interaction and the fact that it is socially constructed by its participants.

While DA approaches to describing classroom discourse certainly have their place and have done much to further our understanding of the interactional processes at work, they are perhaps too static to account fully for the complexity of classroom interaction. Using other approaches (see below) which operate on much longer stretches of discourse, allows a different picture to be presented; one which, arguably, more faithfully represents 'reality' by allowing data to speak for themselves. In the next section, the discussion is advanced under a review of Conversation Analysis approaches to investigating classroom discourse.

Conversation analysis (CA) approaches

In the tradition of ethnomethodology (Garfinkel, 1967), conversation analysis (CA) approaches to classroom interaction have a number of features which set them apart from the more quantitative, static and product-oriented techniques described in the preceding two sections. The origins of current CA methodologies stem from the interest in the function of language as a means for social interaction (Sacks *et al.*, 1974). Its underlying philosophy is that social contexts are not static but are constantly being formed by the participants through their use of language and the ways in which turn-taking, openings and closures, sequencing of acts, and so on are locally managed. Interaction is examined in relation to meaning and context; the way in which actions are sequenced is central to the process. In the words of Heritage (1997: 162):

> In fact, CA embodies a theory which argues that sequences of actions are a major part of what we mean by context, that the meaning of an action is heavily shaped by the sequence of previous actions from which it emerges, and that social context is a dynamically created thing that is expressed in and through the sequential organisation of interaction.

According to this view, interaction is *context-shaped* and *context-renewing*; that is, one contribution is dependent on a previous one and subsequent contributions create a new context for later actions. Context is 'both a project and a product of the participants' actions' (Heritage, 1997: 163).

Although the original focus of CA was naturally occurring conversation, it is perhaps in specific institutional settings, where the goals and actions of participants are clearly determined, that the value of CA approaches can be most vividly realized. An institutional discourse CA methodology takes as its starting-point the centrality of talk to many work tasks: quite simply, the majority of work-related tasks are completed through what is essentially conversation, or 'talk-in-interaction' (Drew and Heritage, 1992: 3); many interactions (for example, doctor–patient interviews, court-room examinations of a witness, classrooms) are completed through the exchange of talk between specialist and non-specialist.

The purpose of a CA methodology in an institutional setting is to account for the ways in which context is created for and by the participants in relation to the goal-oriented activity in which they are engaged. All institutions have an over-riding goal or purpose which constrains both the actions and interactional contributions of the participants according to the business in hand, giving each institution a unique interactional 'fingerprint' (Heritage and Greatbatch, 1991:

95–6). Thus, the interactional patterning (or 'fingerprint') that is typical of, for example, a travel agent will be different from that of, say, a dentist's surgery. By examining specific features in the institutional interaction, an understanding can be gained of the ways in which context is both constructed and sustained; features which can be usefully examined include turn-taking organization, turn design, sequence organization, lexical choice and asymmetry of roles (Heritage, 1997).

The discussion turns now to a consideration of how such an approach might be applied to the second language classroom, an institutional setting in its own right, with asymmetrical roles, goal-oriented activities and a context which is constantly being created for and by participants through the classroom interaction. While the discourse of L2 classrooms does not and should not be interpreted as having any resemblance to conversation, there are nonetheless good reasons for using a CA methodology (Edwards and Westgate, 1994: 116):

> The point is not that classroom talk 'should' resemble conversation, since most of the time for practical purposes it cannot, but that institutionalised talk ... shows a heightened use of procedures which have their 'base' in ordinary conversation and are more clearly understood through comparison with it.

The relevance of a CA approach to the L2 classroom context is not difficult to perceive. CA attempts to account for the practices at work which enable participants in a conversation to make sense of the interaction and contribute to it. There are clear parallels: classroom talk is made up of many participants; it involves turn-taking, -ceding, -holding and -gaining; there have to be smooth transitions and clearly defined expectations if meanings are to be made explicit. Possibly the most significant role of CA is to **interpret** from the data rather than **impose** pre-determined categories.

The main reasons for using a CA approach to analyze L2 classroom interaction are briefly discussed. In the first instance, there is no preconceived set of descriptive categories at the outset. Thus, the approach is strictly empirical. Both Levinson (1983) and Seedhouse (1996) make the important point that CA forces the researcher to focus on the interaction patterns emerging *from* the data, rather than relying on any preconceived notions which language teachers may bring *to* the data. The observer is regarded as a 'player' in the construction of the classroom discourse, trying to view the experience through the eyes of the participants.

Second, a CA approach sees the context as being *dynamic*. In contrast to discourse analysis approaches, where context is regarded as static and fixed categories of talk are imposed, CA approaches consider the ways in which the context is mutually constructed by the participants. A dynamic position on context allows for variability; contexts are not fixed entities which operate across a lesson, but dynamic and changing processes which vary from one stage of a lesson to another (Cullen, 1998). A CA methodology is better equipped to take variations in linguistic and pedagogic purpose into account since one contribution is dependent on another.

Third, the behaviour and discourse of the participants are considered as being *goal-oriented*, in that they are striving towards some overall objective related to the institution. In a language classroom, for example, the discourse is influenced by the fact that all participants are focusing on some pre-determined aim, learning a second language. Different participants, depending on their own agenda may have different individual objectives; nonetheless, the discourse which is jointly constructed is dependent on both the goals and the related expectations of the participants.

In spite of the considerable flexibility offered by CA approaches to analyzing classroom discourse, there are a number of limitations to the approach. First, there is no attempt to impose any kind of 'order' on the apparent chaos of classroom interaction. Snatches of discourse and their ensuing commentaries may appear to have been selected randomly with no attempt to evaluate their significance to the discourse as a whole. Because there are no pre-conceived categories, the selection of data may appear contrived or idealized in order to illustrate a particular point with little attempt to relate them to the exchange as a whole.

Second, CA approaches are largely unable to generalize findings owing to the fact that they consider classrooms in isolation and make no attempt to extend their findings to other settings. While this may be true of many qualitative research tools, it is particularly applicable to CA methodology owing to the centrality of context. That is not to say that context-specific data are not valid or worthwhile; merely that they cannot be extended to other contexts.

This section has considered the major attributes and features of a CA methodology and its suitability for describing and evaluating L2 classroom interaction. The main strengths of the methodology lie in its ability to take account of the constantly changing classroom context and of the role of participants in constructing that context, while its main weakness is the fact that it is in some ways more impressionistic than other methods.

A variable approach to investigating L2 classroom interaction

According to Drew and Heritage (1992), much of the research on L2 classroom interaction to date has adopted an approach whereby context is viewed as something static, fixed and concrete. The majority of studies have had one of two central goals, attempting to account for either the nature of verbal exchanges or the relationship between SLA and interaction (Wu, 1998). Whatever their focus, most studies have referred to **the** L2 classroom context (singular), implying that there exists such an entity and that it has fixed and describable features which are common to all L2 contexts. There are a number of possible explanations for this uni-directional and static view.

In the first instance, there has been an over-riding concern to compare L2 classroom interaction with 'real' communication, whereby 'authentic' features of 'genuine' communication occurring in the 'real' world are somehow imported into the L2 classroom setting (Nunan, 1987; Cullen, 1998). By following this line of enquiry, many researchers have failed to acknowledge that the classroom is as much a 'real' context as any other situation in which people come together and interact. As van Lier says (1988a: 267):

> The classroom is in principle and in potential just as communicative or uncommunicative as any other speech setting, no more, no less. Nor should the 'real world' stop at the classroom door; the classroom is part of the real world, just as much as the airport, the interviewing room, the chemical laboratory, the beach and so on.

Blanket interpretations of L2 classroom discourse as either 'communicative' or 'uncommunicative' (Nunan, 1987; Kumaravadivelu, 1993), adopting an invariant view of context, have failed to take account of the relationship between language use and pedagogic purpose (van Lier, 1988a; Seedhouse, 1996). When language use and pedagogic purpose are considered *together*, different contexts emerge, making it possible to analyze the ensuing discourse more fairly and more objectively. Under this variable view of contexts (plural), learner and teacher patterns of verbal behaviour can be seen as more or less *appropriate*, depending on a particular pedagogic aim. So, for example, teachers' language should not be regarded as 'uncommunicative' if their pedagogic goal is to provide a detailed grammar explanation.

Second, previous studies have had a tendency to focus heavily on IRF routines. Following the earlier work of Sinclair and Coulthard (1975) and Bellack *et al.* (1966), many studies of L2 classroom interaction have focused on the three-part exchange which so often typifies the language of the classroom. More recent studies, considering longer stretches of discourse, suggest quite different interactional organizations (van Lier, 1996; Jarvis and Robinson, 1997). The Jarvis and Robinson study, for example, identified *focus*, *build*, *summarize* patterns of interaction which can facilitate learner participation in the discourse. Breen (1998: 115) adopts a similar perspective, considering the ways in which learners learn 'to navigate the opportunities and constraints provided by classroom discourse' through social and pedagogic patterns of interaction. By focusing on longer stretches of discourse, more complex, complete relationships emerge between interactions which are jointly constructed.

Third, in a quest to pursue 'rigorous' modes of scientific enquiry usually reserved for 'hard' disciplines such as physics and chemistry, there has been a tendency to use reductionist research tools which have ignored the important details of interaction in the L2 classroom; a position summarized by van Lier (1988a: iv):

> Research into second language classrooms is to date ... still very much concerned with the aim of finding cause-effect relationships between certain actions and their outcomes. ... At the risk of over-simplification, research can be divided into a type which wants to obtain proof and a type which wants to understand. So far, research into foreign language classrooms leans overwhelmingly towards the former type of research.

Van Lier's more recent call (2000b) is for ecologically framed modes of investigation, which focus on the shifting environment of the L2 classroom and offer an understanding of the interactional processes at work. The work of van Lier (ibid.) adds to the growing calls for more flexible approaches to understanding classroom interaction and their dissemination among teachers, teacher-educators and researchers. A number of writers have proposed that classroom interaction should be investigated from a multi-layered perspective; a perspective where participants play a crucial role in constructing the interaction and under which different varieties of communication can be identified as the lesson unveils according to particular pedagogic purposes (see, for example, Tsui, 1987; 1994; Hasan, 1988; van Lier 1988a; 1996; 2000b; Seedhouse, 1994; 1996; 1997; Lantolf, 2000; McCarthy and Walsh, 2003; Walsh, 2003).

If we accept the complex and dynamic nature of classroom discourse and the need to understand interaction more fully, and, in particular, the ways in which it mediates language and learning, it is apparent that more flexible tools are needed to investigate these phenomena. Assigning data to 'tick boxes', allocating classroom actions and language to checklists, or applying hierarchical discourse structures to complex interactions are no longer adequate means of accounting for 'what really happens' when a teacher and a group of learners come together to learn a second language. While variable approaches may not have all the answers, they do acknowledge the goal-oriented nature of the discourse, the fact that roles are asymmetrical, and that teaching objectives and the language used to achieve them are inextricably linked.

In the next section, there follows a brief summary of some of the more recent studies offering a variable approach to classroom contexts.

Johnson (1995)

Johnson's study makes extensive use of classroom transcripts to illustrate the relationship between pedagogic purpose and patterns of interaction, identifying both academic and social task structures within her data. While she does not present a tightly bound theoretical framework, she nonetheless explores extracts of classroom transcripts according to teachers' use of language. In addition, Johnson, like Kumaravadivelu (1999, see below), considers the influence of teachers' and learners' cultural, educational and linguistic backgrounds on socially constructed interactions. Like other writers (see above), Johnson makes the link between pedagogic purpose and language use to illustrate how teachers' use of language may control subsequent patterns of communication (p. 145):

> the patterns of classroom communication depend largely on how teachers use language to control the structure and content of classroom events.

Jarvis and Robinson (1997)

Adopting a Vygotskyan perspective on language and learning, this study draws on previous work in educational psychology and discourse analysis and presents 'a framework for the analysis of verbal interaction between teacher and pupils in primary-level EFL lessons' (p. 212). Considering the pedagogic functions of language in a state primary setting, the researchers identified a *focus-build-summarize* structure to classroom interaction, based on six pedagogic functions:

1   Show acceptance of pupils' utterances;
2   Model language;
3   Give clues;
4   Develop, elaborate, build up the discourse;
5   Clarify understanding, task, purpose, principles;
6   Disconfirm, reject, rebuke.

The study examined teachers' 'responsive use of children's answers' (p. 214); that is, the 'feedback' moves as a means of assessing the extent to which meanings were aligned or formulated (Nofsinger, 1991). This process, resulting in cognitive change, is based on the Vygotskyan principle of appropriation (Vygotsky, 1978; 1999; Leont'ev, 1981) whereby children 'appropriate' new meanings through two-way interaction with a more experienced interlocutor. According to Mercer (1994), appropriation can be compared to a process of paraphrase and recapping within the learner's pedagogic framework. One of the main findings of Jarvis and Robinson's study is that teachers can facilitate or hinder learning opportunities by using language which is or is not pedagogically appropriate (p. 227):

> We would, however, like to suggest that the elaboration of the *Focus, Build, Summarize* pattern may be a step toward the identification of an interactive discourse means by which a teacher can support his/her pupils' learning.

Seedhouse (1997)

Seedhouse's 1997 study examines one specific context out of a total of six he had identified earlier (Seedhouse, 1996: 124–31). The six contexts identified in the earlier study are form and accuracy, where the focus is on linguistic form and accuracy and the pedagogic purpose of the teacher is to elicit from learners a string of forms for evaluation; classroom as speech community, where the aim is to maximize interaction and exploit the learning potential of the classroom context; task-oriented context, where learners communicate with each other to complete a specific task using largely transactional language; real-world target speech community, where the teacher aims to bring the outside world into the classroom and involve learners in some simulated 'real-life' task; text-based context, where the main focus is on a text and the interaction and language acquisition that derive from that text; finally, procedural context, where the teacher's aim is to 'set something up', instruct or establish a procedure for work in progress.

Seedhouse's 1997 study looks at the relationship between pedagogy and interaction with regard to repair. How do teachers organize repair? Specifically, what strategies do they use when correcting oral errors and what strategies do learners expect them to use? His finding, 'that teachers perform a great deal of interactional work to avoid performing direct and overt negative evaluation of learner linguistic errors' (1997: 563) indicates not only that teachers tend to avoid overt error correction, but, perhaps more significantly, that their choice of language and pedagogic purpose are in opposition. That is, although the teacher's intention is to correct errors (pedagogic purpose), their choice of language militates against this. While learners accept that error correction is an essential part of the language learning process, teachers seem to shy away from overt correction because they believe it is in some way 'face-threatening'. The stance adopted by teachers is largely influenced by what would constitute an appropriate course of action outside the classroom where overt correction might be considered less acceptable. Yet in the language classroom, learners expect and indeed want to be corrected. A teacher's decision to correct errors in a less 'threatening' manner by carefully selecting language that avoids loss of face may actually prevent repair from occurring (p. 574):

> But the relationship between pedagogy and interaction is complex and reflexive ... Clearly, pedagogical recommendations would work best in harmony with the interactional organisation of the L2 class-room, rather than in opposition to it. For teachers to implement pedagogical intentions effectively, then, it is important to develop an understanding of the interactional organisation of the L2 class-room.

Kumaravadivelu (1999)

Kumaravadivelu conceptualizes a framework for what he terms Critical Classroom Discourse Analysis (CCDA) (p. 453), a framework for 'understanding what actually transpires in the L2 classroom' (ibid.). The framework reflects the sociolinguistic, socio-cultural and sociopolitical dimensions of classroom discourse.

CCDA is socially constructed, politically motivated and historically determined; the L2 classroom is viewed as a constituent of a larger society which includes many forms of power, domination and resistance (p. 472). Understanding the interaction that occurs requires an awareness of the voices, fears, anxieties and cultural backgrounds which result in the commonly found mismatches between 'intentions and interpretations of classroom aims and events' (p. 473). In the words of Kramsch (1993: 238), cited in Kumaravadivelu (p. 470):

> From the clash between the familiar meanings of the native culture and the unexpected meanings of the target culture, meanings that were taken for granted are suddenly questioned, challenged, problematized.

Understanding classroom interaction, under the perspective advanced by Kumaravadivelu calls for far more than an understanding of the roles of input and acquisition in SLA; far more, too, than an awareness of conversational conventions manifested in turn-taking routines. Under CCDA, understanding the interaction of the second language classroom requires an awareness of 'discourse participants' complex and competing expectations and beliefs, identities and voices, and fears and anxieties' (1999: 472). In its 'transformative function', the researcher advocates a reflective role for CCDA in which teachers learn to understand their classroom environment by equipping themselves with the knowledge and skills necessary to conduct CCDA for themselves (ibid.). The research tool which is posited for conducting CCDA is critical ethnography (McLaren, 1995), which offers a rich, multilayered analysis of data from multiple sources and multiple perspectives.

Walsh (2003)

In the framework put forward by Walsh, four classroom *modes* are identified and characterized. A mode is defined as 'an L2 classroom micro-context which has a clearly defined pedagogic goal and distinctive interactional features determined largely by a teacher's use of language' (2003:125). The definition is intended to portray the relationship between the actions and words, behaviour and discourse which are the very essence of classroom interaction. It is used to embrace the idea that interaction and classroom activity are inextricably linked, and to acknowledge that as the focus of a lesson changes, interaction patterns and pedagogic goals change too. A modes analysis recognizes that understanding and meaning are jointly constructed, but that the prime responsibility for their construction lies with the teacher.

The four modes identified are described briefly (Walsh, 2003: 126–30). In *managerial mode*, the main pedagogic goal is to transmit information and organize learning. This mode is characterized by a single, extended teacher turn and the absence of learner turns; under *materials mode*, the main pedagogic goal is to provide language practice around a piece of material, or to check and display learning. This mode is characterized by display questions, form-focused feedback, direct repair and the use of scaffolding; in *skills and systems mode*, on the other hand, the pedagogic goal is to enable learners to produce correct forms and manipulate the target language. The features of this mode include direct repair, teacher echo, clarification requests, extended teacher turns; finally, under *classroom context mode*, the main pedagogic goal is to promote oral fluency. Typical features include minimal repair, referential questions, extended learner turns, content feedback and clarification requests.

While each of the studies presented above is included by way of exemplification, they do share a number of features, common to all variable approaches to classroom interaction. A critical summary of those shared features is now proposed.

All the studies summarized here recognize that the L2 classroom setting is made up of a series of contexts which are linked to the social, political, cultural and historical beliefs of the participants. Contexts are created by teachers and learners as they engage in face-to-face interaction according to their pedagogic goals at a given moment. Classroom interaction is therefore socially constructed by and for the participants, leading some writers to suggest that we should think of learning:

> as a process of becoming a member of a certain community [necessitating] the ability to communicate in the language of this community and act according to its particular norms. (Sfard, 1997a: 6)

A variable approach to the study of L2 classroom contexts, by focusing more on participation, enables greater understanding of 'language socialization' (Pavlenko and Lantolf, 2000: 156).

An understanding of the relationship between classroom communication and educational goals, the ways in which language use can facilitate learning (Jarvis and Robinson, 1997; Walsh, 2002) has implications for teacher education since it replaces 'broad brush' views of interaction with fine-grained paradigms which permit greater understanding of the interactional and learning processes at work;

In the studies reviewed above (see pages xxx), there is an absence of an agreed metalanguage for describing and accounting for L2 classroom micro-contexts. Seedhouse proposes six 'contexts' (1996: 124); Jarvis and Robinson, six 'pedagogic functions' (1997: 212); van Lier, four 'types of interaction' (1988a: 156); Walsh, four 'modes' (2003). This lack of an agreed metalanguage makes the processes of comparison and generalization practically impossible, as the constructs used have different meanings depending on the context. Description and understanding of L2 classroom interaction is unlikely to be advanced until an appropriate nomenclature is identified and utilized by teachers and researchers alike.

Conclusions

In this chapter, the case for a variable approach to analyzing classroom interaction has been proposed. The paper depicts the L2 classroom as a complex, dynamic and fluid blend of micro-contexts, created, sustained and managed by interactants in their pursuance of goals. A variable approach acknowledges that interaction patterns vary according to the different agendas and social relations of the participants, but primarily according to teachers' pedagogic goals. By studying the ways in which meanings are coconstructed in the interaction and by recognizing that the L2 classroom context is not static or invariant, it is argued that a more representative, fine-grained analysis of the discourse is possible.

The key to understanding interactional processes is in describing them. At present, L2 classroom research is only beginning to offer descriptions that are both plausible and usable in extending awareness. There is still much more work to be done, especially in identifying ways of enabling teachers to access the interactional processes of their classes, and of making description and understanding part of their day-to-day teaching.

Bibliography

Allwright, R.L. (1988) *Observation in the Language Classroom* (Harlow: Longman).
Allwright, R. and Bailey, K. (1991) *Focus on the Language Classroom: an Introduction to Classroom Research for Language Teachers* (Cambridge: Cambridge University Press).
Banbrook, L. and Skehan, P. (1990) 'Classrooms and Display Questions', in C. Brumfit and R. Mitchell (eds), *Research in the Language Classroom* (London: Modern English Publications and the British Council).
Bellack, A., Kliebard, H., Hyman, R. and Smith, F. (1966) *The Language of the Classroom* (New York: Teachers College Press).
Breen, M.P. (1998) 'Navigating the discourse: on what is learned in the language classroom', in W.A. Renandya and G.M. Jacobs (eds), *Learners and Language Learning*, Anthology Series 39 (Singapore: SEAMO Regional Language Centre).
Brock, C. (1986) 'The effects of referential questions on ESL classroom discourse', *TESOL Quarterly*, 20: 47–59.

Cazden, C.B. (1986) 'Classroom discourse', in M.C. Wittrock (ed.), *Handbook of Research on Teaching* (New York: MacMillan).

Chaudron, C. (1988) *Second Language Classrooms: Research on Teaching and Learning* (New York: Cambridge University Press).

Cohen, L., Manion, L. and Morrison, K. (2000) *Research Methods in Education*, 5th edn (London: Routledge Falmer).

Cullen, R. (1998) 'Teacher talk and the classroom context', *English Language Teaching Journal*, 52, 3: 179–87.

Dornyei, Z. and Malderez, A. (1997) 'Group dynamics and foreign language teaching', *System*, 25, 1: 65–81.

Drew, P. and Heritage, J. (eds) (1992) *Talk at Work: Interaction in Institutional Settings* (Cambridge: Cambridge University Press).

Edge, J. (2001) *Action Research* (Alexandria, VA: TESOL Inc.).

Edwards, A. and Westgate, D. (1994) *Investigating Classroom Talk* (London: Falmer).

Ellis, R. (1998) 'Discourse control and the acquisition-rich classroom', in W.A. Renandya and G.M. Jacobs (eds), *Learners and Language Learning*, Anthology Series 39 (Singapore: SEAMO Regional Language Centre).

Ellis, R. (2000) 'Task-based research and language pedagogy', *Language Teaching Research*, 49, 3: 193–220.

Foster, P. (1993) 'Discoursal outcomes of small group work in an EFL classroom: a look at the interaction of non-native speakers', *Thames Valley University Working Papers in English Language Teaching*, 2: 1–32.

Foster, P. (1998) 'A classroom perspective on the negotiation of meaning', *Applied Linguistics*, 19, 1: 1–23.

Garfinkel, H. (1967) *Studies in Ethnomethodology* (Englewood Cliffs, NJ: Prentice Hall).

Griffin, P. and Mehan, H. (1981) 'Sense and ritual in classroom discourse', in F. Coulmas (ed.), *Conversational Routine* (The Hague: Mouton).

Hasan, A.S. (1988) Variation in Spoken Discourse in and Beyond the English Foreign Language Classroom: A Comparative Study, Unpublished PhD Thesis (University of Aston).

Heritage, J. (1997) 'Conversational analysis and institutional talk: analysing data', in D. Silverman (ed.), *Qualitative Research: Theory, Method and Practice* (London: Sage).

Heritage, J. and Greatbatch, D. (1991) 'On the institutional character of institutional talk: the case of news interviews', in D. Boden and D.H. Zimmerman (eds), *Talk and Social Structure: Studies in Ethnomethodology and Conversation Analysis* (Berkeley: University of California Press).

Jarvis, J. and Robinson, M. (1997) 'Analysing educational discourse: an exploratory study of teacher response and support to pupils' learning', *Applied Linguistics*, 18, 2: 212–28.

Johnson, K.E. (1995) *Understanding Communication in Second Language Classrooms* (Cambridge: Cambridge University Press).

Kasper, G. (1986) 'Repair in foreign language teaching', in G. Kasper (ed.), *Learning, Teaching and Communication in the Language Classroom* (Aarhus: Aarhus University Press).

Kramsch, C. (1993) *Context and Culture in Language Teaching* (Oxford: Oxford University Press).

Kumaravadivelu, B. (1993) 'Maximising learning potential in the communicative classroom', *English Language Teaching Journal*, 47, 1: 12–21.

Kumaravadivelu, B. (1999) 'Critical classroom discourse analysis', *TESOL Quarterly*, 33: 453–84.

Lantolf, J.P. (2000) *Sociocultural Theory and Second Language Learning* (Oxford: Oxford University Press).

Leont'ev, A.N. (1981) *Problems of the Development of the Mind* (Moscow: Progress).

Levinson, S. (1983) *Pragmatics* (Cambridge: Cambridge University Press).

Levinson, S. (1993) *Pragmatics* (Cambridge: Cambridge University Press).

Lightbown, P. and Spada, N. (1993) *How Languages are Learned* (Oxford: Oxford University Press).

Long, M.H. (1983) 'Native speaker/non-native speaker conversation and the negotiation of meaning', *Applied Linguistics*, 4: 126–41.

Long, M.H. (1996) 'The role of the linguistic environment in second language acquisition', in W.C. Ritchie and T.K. Bhatia (eds), *Handbook of Second Language Acquisition* (San Diego: Academic Press).

Long, M.H. and Sato, C.J. (1983) 'Classroom foreigner talk discourse: forms and functions of teachers' questions', in H.W. Seliger and M.H. Long (eds), *Classroom Oriented Research in Second Language Acquisition* (Rowley, MA: Newbury House).

Lynch, T. (1996) *Communication in the Language Classroom* (Oxford: Oxford University Press).

Malamah-Thomas, A. (1987) *Classroom Interaction* (Oxford: Oxford University Press).

Mayher, J. (1990) *Uncommon Sense* (Portsmouth: Boynton Cook).

McCarthy, M. and Walsh, S. (2003) 'Discourse', in D. Nunan (ed.), *Practical English Language Teaching* (San Francisco: McGraw-Hill).

McLaren, P. (1995) 'Collisions with otherness: "travelling" theory, postcolonial criticism, and the politics of ethnographic practice – the mission of the wounded ethnographer', in P. McLaren and J. Giarelli (eds), *Critical Theory and Educational Research* (Albany, NY: SUNY Press).

Mercer, N. (1994) 'Neo-Vygotskian theory and vlassroom education', in B. Stierer and J. Maybin (eds), *Language, Literacy and Learning in Educational Practice* (Clevedon, Avon: Multilingual Matters/Open University).

Mitchell, R. and Martin, C. (1997) 'Rote learning, creativity and "understanding" in classroom foreign language teaching', *Language Teaching Research*, 1, 1: 1–27.

Nofsinger, R.E. (1991) *Everyday Conversation* (Newbury Park: Sage).

Nunan, D. (1987) 'Communicative language teaching: making it work', *English Language Teaching Journal*, 41, 2: 136–45.

Nunan, D. (1989) *Understanding Language Classrooms* (London: Prentice Hall).

Nunn, R. (1999) 'The purpose of language teachers' questions', *IRAL*, 37, 1: 23–42.

Pavlenko, A. and Lantolf, J.P. (2000) 'Second language learning as participation and the (re)construction of selves', in J.P. Lantolf (ed.), *Sociocultural Theory and Second Language Learning* (Oxford: Oxford University Press).

Rampton, B. (1999) 'Dichotomies, difference and ritual in second language learning and teaching', *Applied Linguistics*, 20, 3: 316–40.

Richards, J.C. (ed.), (1998) *Teaching in Action* (Alexandria, Virginia: TESOL).

Roehler, L., Hallenback, M., McLellan, M. and Svoboda, N. (1996) 'Teaching skills through learning conversations in whole language classrooms', in E. McIntyre and M. Pressley (eds), *Balanced Instruction: Strategies and Skills in Whole Language* (Norwood MA: Christopher Gordan).

Sacks, H., Schegloff, E. and Jefferson, G. (1974) 'A simplest systematics for the organisation of turn-taking in conversation', *Language*, 50: 696–735.

Seedhouse, P. (1994) 'Linking pedagogical purposes to linguistic patterns of interaction: the analysis of communication in the language classroom', *IRAL*, 32, 4: 303–20.

Seedhouse, P. (1996) *Learning Talk: a Study of the Interactional Organisation of the L2 Classroom from a CA Institutional Discourse Perspective*, Unpublished PhD Thesis (University of York).

Seedhouse, P. (1997) 'The case of the missing "no": the relationship between pedagogy and interaction', *Language Learning*, 47, 3: 547–83.

Sfard, A. (1997a) 'Commentary: on metaphorical roots of conceptual growth', in L. English (ed.), *Mathematical Reasoning: Analogies, Metaphors, and Images* (London: Erlbaum) 339–71.

Sfard, A. (1997b) 'On Two Metaphors for Learning and the Dangers of Choosing Just One', *Educational Reseacher*, 27, 2: 4–13.

Shamim, F. (1996) 'In or out of the action zone: location as a feature of interaction in large ESL classes in Pakistan', in K.M. Bailey and D. Nunan (eds), *Voices from the Language Classroom* (Cambridge: Cambridge University Press).

Sinclair, J. and Coulthard, M. (1975) *Towards an Analysis of Discourse* (Oxford: Oxford University Press).

Slimani, A. (1989) 'The role of topicalisation in classroom language learning', *System*, 17: 223–34.

Stubbs, M. (1983) *Discourse Analysis: the Sociolinguistic Analysis of Natural Language* (Oxford: Blackwell).

Swain, M. (1995) 'Three functions of output in second language learning', in G. Cook and B. Seidelhofer (eds), *Principle and Practice in Applied Linguistics: Studies in Honour of H.G. Widdowson* (Oxford: Oxford University Press).

Tardif, C. (1994) 'Classroom teacher talk in early immersion', *Canadian Modern Language Review*, 50, 3: 466–81.

Thompson, G. (1997) 'Training teachers to ask questions', *English Language Teaching Journal*, 51, 2: 99–105.

Thornbury, S. (2000) 'A dogma for EFL', *IATEFL Issues*, 153: 24–8.

Tsui, A.B.M. (1987) 'An analysis of different types of interaction in ESL classroom discourse', *IRAL*, 25, 4: 336–53.

Tsui, A.B.M. (1994) *English Conversation* (London: Oxford University Press).

van Lier, L. (1988a) *The Classroom and the Language Learner* (London: Longman).

van Lier, L. (1988b) 'What's Wrong with Classroom Talk?', *Prospect*, 3, 3: 267–83.

van Lier, L. (1991) 'Inside the classroom: learning processes and teaching procedures', *Applied Language Learning*, 2, 1: 48–64.

van Lier, L. (1996) *Interaction in the Language Curriculum: Awareness, Autonomy and Authenticity* (New York: Longman).

van Lier, L. (2000a) 'The ecology of the language classroom: towards a new unity of theory, research and practice', *IATEFL Teachers Develop Teachers Research 4 Conference Proceedings* (Whitstable: IATEFL).

van Lier, L. (2000b) 'From input to affordance: social-interactive learning from an ecological perspective', in J.P. Lantolf (ed.), *Sociocultural Theory and Second Language Learning* (Oxford: Oxford University Press).

Vygotsky, L.S. (1978) *Mind in Society: the Development of Higher Psychological Processes* (Cambridge: Harvard University Press).

Vygotsky, L.S. (1999) *Collected Works*, Vol. 6, R. Rieber and M. Hall (eds) (New York: Plenum Press).

Wallace, M. (1998) *Action Research for Language Teachers* (Cambridge: Cambridge University Press).

Walsh, S. (1987) *Classroom Discourse: 'Towards an Analysis of Discourse' Revisited* Unpublished MA dissertation (University of Leeds).

Walsh, S. (2000) 'Construction or obstruction: teacher talk and learner involvement in the EFL classroom', *Language Teaching Research*, 6, 1: 3–24.

Walsh, S. (2003) 'Developing interactional awareness in the second language classroom', *Language Awareness*, 12, 2: 124–42.

Warjnryb, R. (1992) *Classroom Observation Tasks* (Cambridge: Cambridge University Press).

Willis, J. (1992) 'Inner and outer: spoken discourse in the language classroom', in M. Coulthard (ed.), *Advances in Spoken Discourse Analysis* (London: Routledge).

Wu, B. (1998) 'Towards an understanding of the dynamic process of L2 classroom interaction', *System*, 26: 525–40.

Part IV
Assessing Speaking

11
Pronunciation and the Assessment of Spoken Language

John M. Levis

Introduction

The ACTFL Guidelines for foreign language proficiency, the dominant measure for assessing foreign language proficiency in the United States, describe ten different levels of proficiency.[1] Although they are extensive and detailed, the guidelines are strikingly random in describing how pronunciation contributes to speaking proficiency. Four of the levels (Advanced Mid, Advanced Low, Intermediate High, and Novice Mid) do not mention pronunciation, while three others (Intermediate Mid and Low, Novice High) suggest that pronunciation may be important as evidence of L1 influence, and thus, it appears, lower levels of proficiency. Another level, Advanced High, mentions only 'precise vocabulary and intonation' (Breiner-Sanders *et al.*, 2000: 15). Only at the top level, Superior, and the bottom, Novice Low, do descriptors suggest a significant contribution for pronunciation. Superior speakers are able to use suprasegmentals to support coherent discourse, while Novice Low speakers may be unintelligible due to poor pronunciation. The overall effect of this haphazard collection of descriptors suggests that pronunciation is relatively unimportant in determining speaking proficiency. Evidence of L1 influence (common in almost all adult learners) automatically places speakers below the advanced level, and being intelligible does not appear to be closely related to pronunciation. Yet any experienced teacher knows that L2 speakers can be both very advanced in most elements of speaking ability and still be unintelligible due to pronunciation errors.

De-emphasizing pronunciation in rating guidelines does not mean that assessors will treat it as unimportant. Instead, it almost ensures that pronunciation will become a stealth factor in ratings and a source of unsystematic variation in the test. As one assessment expert puts it, we all, both those used to analyzing language and those not, 'make note of features related to pronunciation when we listen to someone speak, and it would be foolish to deny this' (Sari Luoma, personal communication). Unlike the ACTFL guidelines, most standardized tests of speaking proficiency recognize the importance of pronunciation, although the variety of ways they address it indicates that is difficult to include it but not give it too much influence.

Assessing pronunciation in speaking tests requires a distinction between linguistic features, communicative effects, and identifying markers. Few tests are specific about linguistic features that are involved in pronunciation. The Test of Spoken English (TSE) and its institutional counterpart, the SPEAK, originally had a feature called pronunciation based on 'consistent phonemic errors and foreign stress and intonation patterns' (Celce-Murcia *et al.*, 1996: 347). The speaking portions of the Cambridge Certificate of Proficiency in English (CPE) and related tests still use pronunciation as a rated category, with specific mention made of stress, rhythm, intonation and individual sounds. The CPE, however, defines pronunciation's role ultimately by its effects upon communication. It 'refers to the candidate's ability to produce comprehensible utterances to fulfil the task requirements' (ffrench, 2003: 470). In fact, almost all tests appeal to presumed effects of inadequate pronunciation, usually through a term such as intelligibility, defined by McNamara (1996) as 'the communicative effect of pronunciation features' (p. 220). The TOEFL Academic Speaking Test (TAST) includes intelligibility as part of a larger category called 'Delivery', which includes other features such as pace (speed/fluency).

Other tests refer not to communicative effects but to identifying features of L2 pronunciation. The current TSE refers to *accent*, an identifying feature that does not necessarily have anything to do with understanding. Accent is measured by the amount of listener effort required (John Miles, personal communication), an effect also mentioned by the IELTS exam, which measures pronunciation partly by 'the amount of strain caused to the listener' (UCLES, 2003: 31). Accent is also part of the descriptors used by CPE examiners, although an examinee with a foreign accent may still be awarded the highest score on the CPE (ffrench, 2003), a clear contrast to the ACTFL guidelines.

How diagnostic assessment can inform proficiency assessment

Although pronunciation is usually assessed globally in standardized exams, looking at detailed assessments of pronunciation can make certain issues relating to standardized assessment clearer. To do this, I will briefly discuss a course I teach on the teaching of speaking, listening and pronunciation. As is common in most US based MA programmes, my students are a combination of less and more experienced teachers. Some come with a small amount of formal training but extensive foreign teaching experience, while others begin their programme with little or no formal experience in English language teaching. Invariably, whatever their strengths and weaknesses, they feel strongly about two things: that teaching pronunciation is important, and that they have no idea of how to teach it. In these feelings, MA candidates are not different from many trained teachers. The teaching of pronunciation is not addressed in a large number of training programmes at any level, and many teachers have never adequately learned how to teach it (Murphy, 1997; Burgess and Spencer, 2000).

If these MA candidates have little sense of how to teach pronunciation, they have less sense of how to assess it. To learn, they do an individual tutoring project in which they assess one learner's speech, decide on targets for tutoring, prepare materials, and teach the learner over a period of several weeks. The assessment component is necessarily extensive because of the need to train the teachers to identify a range of features involved in pronouncing English. But the intensive assessment of a single learner and the subsequent teaching based on that assessment illustrate two key issues that are important to including pronunciation as a factor in oral language assessment: being able to talk about pronunciation beyond global impressions and distinguishing between accuracy and importance.

The first thing that teachers must learn is to give more than global impressions of pronunciation. They need to become aware of relevant phonological categories and be able to name important errors. This knowledge is not a given for any teacher, experienced or inexperienced. While most teachers are aware of some consonant and vowel errors, few are able, without training, to speak knowledgeably of other phonological categories. This appears to be true of most native English speaking teachers, regardless of location. Macdonald (2003) reports that in Australia 'many [experienced] teachers tend to avoid dealing with pronunciation because they lack confidence, skills and knowledge,' (paragraph 1 in the electronic text) confirming earlier findings for North America and the United Kingdom (Murphy, 1997; Burgess and Spencer, 2000).

In my experience, being able to diagnose pronunciation in detail makes the teachers more fit to assess standardized tests, which is important since teachers are the primary source of raters. Beyond their understanding of what is involved in pronunciation, being able to pinpoint phonological deviations makes them more skilled in giving pronunciation its proper place in assessment. Pronunciation is always an issue in oral language assessment, since one cannot speak without pronouncing. By giving teachers the tools to assess pronunciation, I find that they are less likely to believe that pronunciation is the magic key to oral communication.

The second issue highlighted is the relative importance of accuracy. Looking at a learner's speech under a microscope, so to speak, makes it unmistakably clear that all errors are not created equal. Many deviations simply do not affect understanding, while others, either due to frequency or how they muddle a message, take on a greater importance. Teachers who can listen for and identify details of pronunciation are less likely to believe all deviations are important.

The rest of this chapter will discuss these and other key issues in more detail, and will refer to parts of standardized speaking tests as needed. The first section will discuss issues surrounding accuracy, followed by intelligibility/comprehensibility, then listener factors, and finally, fluency and speech rate. Accent overlaps with both accuracy and intelligibility and will be discussed as needed in those sections.

Why pronunciation accuracy should not be assessed

At some level, all attempts to incorporate pronunciation into spoken language assessment must address the issue of accuracy. If pronunciation either facilitates or impairs understanding in a significant way, it must involve the speaker's accuracy or lack thereof in producing an expected phonetic representation. Such a phonetic string for English includes, at the very least, vowel and consonant sounds, rhythmic patterns of words and phrases, and intonation at various points in the tone unit.

Pronunciation accuracy is potentially a very attractive criterion for spoken language assessment. More than many other features of spoken language, pronunciation is quantifiable. Count the number of errors, one might reason, and adjust the score on the oral test accordingly. Fulcher (2000: 486) describes a somewhat extreme version of this practice, quite in line with the assumption that pronunciation accuracy is directly related to oral proficiency.

> in the United States the College Boards test in English as a Foreign Language used throughout the 1920s and 1930s included a 15-min. oral interview as part of the test battery. However, the language sample was graded for pronunciation [only], as this was considered more reliable than any other criteria that might have been used.

Today, such a practice would elicit disbelief and perhaps horror. Speaking is clearly more than pronunciation, and good pronunciation alone cannot make up for lack of skill in communicating. The reason this kind of assessment no longer happens, of course, at least for any reputable test, is that its assumptions are rightly seen as flawed. The flaws suggest some of the difficulties in using pronunciation accuracy for oral assessment:

- Accuracy is always a relative term;
- Accuracy assumes a standard against which errors can be measured;
- Pronunciation accuracy may be quantifiable, but the effect of deviation is not.

Although accuracy implies the ability to match a phonological target, accuracy in pronunciation is always a relative term since targets are highly variable. Sounds constantly vary within well-defined parameters, changing because of the influence of nearby sounds, speech register, and speaker dialect. In phonological terms, this can be seen in the distinction between phonemes and allophones. Speakers of a language have certain sound categories which make a difference in meaning (phonemes, for example, /p/ vs /b/). Each of these categories, however, is pronounced slightly differently depending on where the sound occurs in a word (for example, *p*ill vs a*pp*le), the sounds it occurs next to (for example, *p*ill vs *sp*ill), and dialect (for example, Ba*p*tist pronounced Ba*b*tist). While many allophonic variants are well known (for example, aspirated vs unaspirated voiceless stops), the extent of the variation that actually occurs is not often recognized (Shockey, 2002).

However, in applied contexts, such as speech synthesis and speech recognition, variability of speech sounds is a central problem. Speech synthesis, in which machines pronounce written text (for instance, simple systems such as automated telephone systems for refilling prescriptions, and more complicated systems such as those that read texts aloud for the visually impaired), rarely sound like natural speech because vowel and consonant phonemes have many small phonetic variations that are not interchangeable. A more successful application of technology, speech recognition, has led to dictation programs for word-processing, among other applications. While these programs are fairly successful, it does not take much effort to demonstrate their limitations. The recognition programs must be trained to be used by one speaker, and even then, the recognition process does not have the flexibility of a human listener (Derwing *et al.*, 2000). Instead, such attempts to recognize speech are regularly tripped up by phonetic variation, changes in speaking speed, and volume differences.

This assumption of a norm is a second reason why pronunciation accuracy is problematic. Assessing accuracy based on prestige NS variety norms institutionalizes dialect discrimination. Usually RP and GA accents are considered the prestige varieties, even though few NSs in the United Kingdom or North America speak with prestige accents. In other inner circle countries, RP and GA are not norms at all. This means that most NSs do not conform to such models. This fact alone should give us pause in attempting to use accuracy as a standard for assessment. Why use a standard that most NSs do not match?

The situation becomes more complicated in outer circle countries such as India or Singapore, where despite lip-service to prestige varieties, local norms for pronunciation are more important. These local norms, at least at the acrolect level, deserve to be considered equal in status to any inner circle variety. Because they are part of a positive social identity, they are unlikely to change (nor should they) in the direction of becoming more like prestigious inner circle varieties.

Perhaps the most serious problem in appealing to accuracy is that there can be no measure of how much inaccuracy is too much. For NS interlocutors, speakers of regional dialects may deviate greatly from the prestige norm, but rarely do differences in pronunciation cause misunderstanding. Similarly for NNSs, it is clear that errors are not directly related to understanding. Many L2 learners communicate quite successfully despite having a large number of obvious, even stigmatizing pronunciation errors that loudly announce the influence of their L1. In contrast, other speakers may have few identifiable errors, yet these errors severely impair their communication. An example of such a learner was a post-graduate student I once taught. His ability to copy and internalize prosodic patterns (especially word stress and nuclear stress) was unusually good, as was his accuracy with most segmentals. He was consistently inaccurate on several sounds, however. One error in particular involved a substitution of [aj] for [e], so that *bed* sounded like *bide*; *let*, *light*; and *said*, *side*. This one error often made it almost impossible to comprehend his message. Even when I became familiar with the error, I often did not recognize it as an error until I realized I did not understand.

This example suggests that deviations are more severe if they are unexpected. This error was always unexpected, and it was consistently difficult to come up with a possible interpretation. In contrast, the use of [s] or [t] for [θ], leading to *Sank you* for *Thank you*, and *I tink so* for *I think so* involve substitutions that are perceptually close to the intended sound. These substitutions also have the advantage of being familiar to English speakers, and thus rarely cause misunderstanding.

Some writers also argue that deviations that carry a high functional load in the language will be perceived as more serious (Brown, 1988). Thus saying [ɪ], as in *beat*, when the goal is to say [ɨ], as in *bit*, is likely to be a more serious error simply because the error involves a pair of sounds that have many possible minimal pairs in English. An extension of this idea of functional load is that certain categories of errors are more likely to affect understanding. Indeed, much of the research on pronunciation for the past 15 years has been an attempt to define what types of errors are more serious, and thus, to focus teaching practices on what actually will make a difference. For example, misplaced word stress can have the potential to cause decoding problems (Murphy, 2003). While this is true when L2 learners speak to native speaker listeners, it can also occur between L1 varieties of English that otherwise have a high degree of mutual intelligibility.

The differential effects of errors on understanding seem largely based on the expectations that interlocutors bring. While errors involving suprasegmentals can be particularly difficult for NS listeners, there is persuasive evidence that errors in segmentals may be more problematic in NNS–NNS communication (Jenkins, 2000). This occurs because of the L1 phonological perceptions that NNSs bring to interaction in English. One example of the tendency to focus on segmental information involved a picture description task between Japanese and Swiss German interlocutors. Both had the same set of six pictures, and the Swiss student's task was to identify the picture described by the Japanese student. The Swiss student 'had problems in completing the task successfully because the speaker had told him that in her picture there were "three [led] cars". This breakdown in communication occurred even though only one of the pictures contained any cars, these cars were red, and there was no evidence to suggest that they were for hire' (Jenkins, 2000: 81). Because of a production problem, where [r] sounded like [l], and a perception problem, because of the Swiss German listener hearing final stops as being voiceless (making him hear the [d] as [t]), communication broke down, with the Swiss German interlocutor trying to find a picture with a 'let' (rented) car. The misunderstanding was created mostly by bottom-up processing difficulties based on segmental errors, factors that are not usually given much importance in pronunciation teaching. For assessment, the difficulty in consistently specifying which errors are serious and which factors make the errors more serious means that accuracy is likely an unuseable criterion.

The additive effect of errors may also cause a speaker to be misunderstood, even if none of the errors are in themselves serious. This is 'the straw that broke the camel's back' approach to accuracy. Prator and Robinett (1985) espouse this position when they say that unintelligibility is '*the cumulative effect of many little departures from the phonetic norms of the language*' (p. xxii, emphasis in original). This position suggests that pronunciation errors have a cumulative effect on the listener, and that when the attention required to process the speech signal becomes too great, the listener loses the ability, or the desire, to understand. This explanation also shows the impossibility of a quantifiable standard of pronunciation accuracy. Since unintelligibility depends on listener-internal factors, not just on number of errors, any attempt to quantify an appropriate level of accuracy will have little relationship to whether speakers can actually make themselves understood.

Pronunciation accuracy cannot be an adequate criterion for assessment of speech. How many pronunciation errors are too much? It is impossible to know since pronunciation is only one part of a spoken message and interlocutors have many clues to meaning available beyond phonetic form. Which errors are most likely to affect understanding? Despite numerous studies, answers are only beginning to be suggested. Inaccuracy becomes important only when a speaker cannot be understood. This is a question of intelligibility, or comprehensibility, both commonly used terms in assessment.

Intelligibility and comprehensibility: the key to pronunciation assessment

In assessing pronunciation's role in spoken language, one of the most commonly used criteria is intelligibility. Although intelligibility includes a variety of speaking related features, it is often closely tied to pronunciation (McNamara, 1996). In a non-technical sense, intelligibility refers to whether a listener is able to understand a speaker. Munro and Derwing (1999) say that 'intelligibility can be broadly defined as the extent to which a speaker's message is actually understood by a listener' but then add that 'there is no universally accepted way of assessing it' (p. 289). Intelligibility in this broad sense is not usually distinguished from closely related terms such as comprehensibility. Intuitively, intelligibility is a powerful concept. If a speaker's message is accessible in content, yet presented in a way that impairs recognition (such as with inadequate pronunciation), a listener is likely to have greater difficulty understanding. The intuitive appeal of intelligibility, however, masks a number of difficulties with using it for assessment. Judgements of understanding are particularly subject to contamination, especially from social attitudes about language that have little to do with understanding. Judgements can also be contaminated by unclear definitions as to what constitutes intelligible speech.

Attitude related terms abound in describing pronunciation. One such term is accentedness. Munro and Derwing (1999) show that judgements of accent are independent of ability to understand a speaker's message. Speech can be strongly accented and socially stigmatized while still being fully understandable. In assessment, such a divide between understanding and acceptability invites error. Accent judgements also do not distinguish between native and nonnative speech. Accent judgements for NS speech are really judgements of social acceptability and are based on notions of a standard language ideal (Milroy and Milroy, 1999). Acceptability emphasizes the norms associated with standard forms, and by extension, the norms associated with social power. Standard accents in both the United Kingdom and North America are marked more by a lack of regional and stigmatized forms than by the presence of prestige forms. Mugglestone (1995), in her treatment of accent as a social symbol in the United Kingdom, shows how regional accents went from being accepted at the end of the 18th century to being largely unacceptable 100 years later. Similarly strong reactions to regional and social accents occur in the United States, though the social factors that evoke the reactions are historically distinct (Lippi-Green, 1997). Notions of acceptability can create an atmosphere in which otherwise understandable non-prestige pronunciations influence assessment of speaking skills, through real or imagined irritation, the flip side of acceptability. Irritation comes from 'the form of the message intruding upon the interlocutor's perception of the communication' (Ludwig, 1982: 275) or 'the communicative effect on the listener that may distract from the message' (Fayer and Krasinski 1987: 315). Thus, social attitudes may cause raters to be more critical than understanding alone warrants.

These various definitions also indicate that listener difficulties can come from different sources. Understanding can be impaired because a listener has difficulty decoding an utterance, because the utterance meaning is not clear, or because the utterance is not easily interpretable. Gallego (1990), following Smith and Nelson (1985), called these three types of difficulty, intelligibility, comprehensibility, and interpretability. Intelligibility, the first level of difficulty, is primarily an issue of decoding. A word or utterance is 'unintelligible when the listener is unable to make it ours, and thus to repeat it' (Gallego, 1990: 221).

The second level of difficulty, comprehensibility, refers to difficulty with semantic content. Speech becomes 'incomprehensible when the listener can repeat it ... but is unable to understand its meaning in the context (Gallego, 1990: 221). In other words, a listener can find a speaker both intelligible and incomprehensible at the same time. L2 pronunciation may be implicated in both kinds of difficulty.

Smith and Nelson's third level of difficulty, interpretability, occurs when 'the listener recognizes [the surface meaning] but is unable to understand the speaker's intentions behind it' (Gallego, 1990: 221). While this is a serious communicative problem, it is also the hardest to assess. Listeners might believe that they understand the intent of utterances, yet be wrong. Such difficulties abound in everyday communication. Albrechtsen *et al.* (1980) say that listeners 'can only guess whether the interpretation they give an interlanguage text is in fact the interpretation intended by the interlanguage user (p. 367). Current research also implicitly recognizes this problem. While intelligibility and comprehensibility continue to be used, interpretability has fallen by the wayside.

The broad definition of intelligibility given at the beginning of this section is really describing comprehensibility, in Smith and Nelson's terms. Careful research and assessment now distinguish between decoding and more global misunderstanding. Comprehensibility is measured via comprehension questions or other types of comprehension tests (Tyler, 1992; Williams, 1992; Hahn, 1999). Since comprehension questions are neither a precise measure nor easy to administer, a different measure, called perceived comprehensibility (Munro and Derwing, 1999) has been developed. Munro and Derwing, who have used this measure extensively, measure it on a 9-point Likert Scale (similar to traditional language attitude studies). However, while perceived comprehensibility is straightforward to rate, and is most similar to how pronunciation is assessed in speaking tests, it is not a measure of what is actually understood. It is instead a measure of how comfortable a speaker is to listen to. For assessment, it is subject to the same sociolinguistic biases of other measures. As a general principle, whenever a speaker's intended message and a listener's expectations do not match, comprehensibility will be affected. The effect will be greater if there is noise in the environment. Difficulties with content can, of course, affect comprehensibility, but if content is restricted, as in most assessments of oral proficiency, pronunciation is thought to be the primary cause of misunderstandings. Thus comprehensibility is a function of three things: a speaker, a listener, and an environment. In assessment, the environment should be standardized. Listeners are usually trained raters with specified topics, which limits listener expectations to a few likely answers for which schemata are available. That leaves the speaker, with the assumption being that lack of understanding on the listener's part is due to the speaker's lack of spoken language ability. A flexible two-sided model of communication is, however, far from irrelevant in assessment, since several common speaking tests require interaction, and almost all spoken assessment requires both listening and speaking.

Speaking assessment takes place within a speaker–hearer framework. The hearer may be in the same room as the speaker or remote. In addition, both speaker and hearer may be native or nonnative speakers. These parameters help to understand the range of issues that are involved in assessing comprehensibility (Figure 11.1). Quadrant A, in which both speaker and listener are native speakers, reflects normal L1 communication and is usually assumed to be the standard against which successful communication is measured. Quadrant B, with native speakers and nonnative listeners, is a classic configuration for language teaching, especially in ESL contexts. Quadrant C, with NNS speakers and NS listeners, is the traditional configuration for intelligibility studies. Quadrant D, with NNS speakers and NNS listeners, reflects an increasingly common communicative setting where NSs are not involved. This is the quadrant of English as an international language. Each of these quadrants has implications for the role of pronunciation in speaking assessment.

		LISTENER	
		Native speaker	Nonnative speaker
SPEAKER	Native speaker	(A) NS–NS	(B) NS–NNS
	Nonnative speaker	(C) NNS–NS	(D) NNS–NNS

Figure 11.1   A framework for understanding comprehensibility

Quadrant A: NS listeners/NS speakers

Quadrant A is the domain of psycholinguistic studies of speech processing, as well as dialect attitude and comprehensibility studies. Its importance for assessment lies first in what it reveals about how NS listeners process (and expect to process) speech, and second, in what it shows about our willingness to judge accented speech negatively. In regard to processing, a large body of research emphasizes the facilitating role of prosody. Cutler *et al.* (1997), in an extensive review of research on speech processing, say that 'the prosodic structure of a heard utterance forms part of the memory representation which listeners form of the input' (p. 143). This means that NS listeners expect speech to have the right suprasegmentals, the part of pronunciation that NNSs are least likely to have mastered, and the part of pronunciation usually thought to be most worth teaching. The review shows that not all prosodic elements are equally important. Rhythmic structure and sentence accent both appear to be particularly important in facilitating processing, while lexical stress is less so. The authors report that rhythmic structures help listeners to segment continuous speech, and that the position of major syntactic boundaries is also signalled prosodically. Recall is better when the expected prosody is used, even for nonsense sentences. Sentence accent (nuclear or tonic stress) also is important in signalling information structure. When new information is accented and given information is deaccented, processing is facilitated. When new information is deaccented, however, listeners experience significant difficulties with understanding messages. Overall, these findings indicate that NS assessors are likely to react to prosodic information in NNS speech, and that any assessment rubrics must take this into account.

Cutler *et al.* also report on the effects of noise on processing (see also Munro, 1998). In general, any noise affects our ability to process speech. This is especially true with nuclear stress. When the environment promotes good sound quality, normal hearing listeners are more accurate than hearing impaired listeners in processing accented information regardless of information structure. Hearing impaired listeners show the greatest difficulty when nuclear stress is placed on unexpected, that is, given information. When sound quality is poor, both hearers with normal and impaired hearing listeners struggle with interpreting nuclear stress accurately.

Quadrant B: NNS listeners/NS speakers

Quadrant B, with NNS listeners and NS speakers, focuses on the listener's ability to process NS speech. Language teachers can enumerate the kinds of difficulties faced by NNS learners of English, such as the inability accurately to hear unstressed syllables and words, identifying the words involved in fast-speech adjustments such as palatalization, and difficulty in identifying and interpreting prominent words. Most of these micro-listening skills are related directly to the pronunciation of English in natural discourse. This quadrant has two implications for speaking assessment. First, in interview type tests, the speech of the interviewer can affect success on the test. Brown and Lumley (1997) say that interviewers may over-enunciate, slow down, or even use intonation with sarcastic intent, all of which may affect examinees. This can happen if the interviewer is inconsistent in the use of careful or casual speech. The type of speech a test-taker is familiar with can also affect success. Matsura *et al.* (1999), in a study of Japanese learner reactions to American and Irish English teachers, found that Japanese learners believed that familiar accents were more comprehensible even though both varieties were equally intelligible (easy to write down). Those learners who had an Irish English speaking teacher found Irish English more comfortable, although they still preferred the prestige variety (American). In another study of reactions to nonnative accents in ESL assessment, Major *et al.* (2002) examined the listening comprehension section of the Test of English as a Foreign language (TOEFL). Chinese, Spanish and Japanese speaking learners listened to English lectures with four accents: Standard American English, Chinese, Japanese, and Spanish. The listeners appeared to be disadvantaged by the use of NNS accents, even when they shared the same L1 as the speaker on the tape.

A second implication of Quadrant B is the effect of reductions and phonetic adjustments in conversational speech. These pronunciation-related features of Inner Circle Englishes have always been important in assessments of listening, but they are also important in any assessment that emphasizes the ability to use conversational speech. A learner who does not use these features may be downgraded for not having smooth, fluent speech, no matter how clearly they are able to communicate. This is especially important for assessment of outer-circle Englishes, which usually do not have these features, yet show no difficulty in being able to communicate in English. Thus, while receptive knowledge of these features may be necessary, as in listening assessment, it is not clear that productive use is necessary for comprehensibility (Jenkins, 2000).

Quadrant C: NS listeners/NNS speakers

Quadrant C, with NNS speakers and NS listeners, is the traditional domain of intelligibility research. Here, NSs are charged with judging the clarity of NNS speech. Even though there can be no firm criteria for measuring relative intelligibility based on numbers of deviations, the core assumption of most of this research is that NSs know whether speech is or is not understandable. In studies that have examined the comprehensibility of NNS speech, incorrect pronunciation is consistently implicated as the major factor in impaired understanding, although it must be admitted, definitions of pronunciation are often quite loose. Gallego (1990), for example, examined NNS graduate teaching assistants in the United States and found that approximately 3 out of 5 problems with comprehensibility were directly related to pronunciation, three times the frequency of the next most common area, vocabulary choice. Other studies have been more careful on definitions and have still found that certain elements of pronunciation are particularly important. Hahn (1999) used three versions of the same spoken lecture read by a Korean graduate student to test whether sentence accent placement impaired NS listeners' understanding. One text was read by a Korean graduate student with normal sentence accent placement, one with sentence accent on the wrong words, and one with no identifiable sentence focus. She found that comprehension was significantly better for expected placement than for either of the other conditions. The no sentence accent condition was rated as more comprehensible (but less pleasant) than the version with misplaced sentence accents.

The assumption that NSs know whether speech is understandable suffers from the same difficulty that NS listeners have with nonstandard dialects: Is speech judged on whether it is understandable or whether it is not acceptable? Accented speech is likely to be graded down whether or not the accent is nonstandard or nonnative. In research my students have undertaken, it is clear that NS listeners react to both types of accents similarly. Consistently, accented speech is rated as coming from speakers who are less intelligent, less hard working, less attractive, and so on. These sociolinguistic judgements cannot help but be present when assessing NNS speech. It is essential therefore that they be minimized through explicit mention of their irrelevance to intelligibility.

Quadrant D: NNS listeners/NNS speakers

Quadrant D, with NNS speakers and listeners, reflects the reality of the spread and influence of English. As long ago as 1982, Smith and Bisazza said that

> A speaker's comprehensibility in a language is usually based solely on the judgement of native speakers of that language. We are convinced that this criterion is no longer appropriate for speakers of English as an international language. (p. 259)

Jenkins (2000) argues that NNS–NNS interaction sheds light on critical distinctions that pronunciation teachers should address. She says that instruction should de-emphasize the suprasegmental features that seem so important in NS–NS interaction (for example, rhythm and weak forms), and instead should emphasize segmentals and sentence accent because these are the main causes of incomprehensibility in NNS–NNS interaction. What does this research have to offer speaking assessment?

First, Jenkins offers convincing evidence of how NNSs adjust their pronunciation to fit their interlocutor; that is, they converge on assumed norms. This leads to somewhat paradoxical results. When a NNS is speaking with another NNS of the same L1, the norm is their shared way of speaking the L2. This means that their interaction will be more error-filled in regards to pronunciation, but it is likely to be more successful communicatively. When a NNS is speaking with another NNS of a different L1, the norm is their perceptions of more native-like speech. In other words, their pronunciation will have fewer errors, but they may not have as much success in communicating with one another because pronunciation errors are likely to impair communication.

In assessments that use paired interaction, such as the Cambridge Oral Proficiency Exams (Jenkins, 1997), NNS pairs who share an L1 are likely to be judged as having worse pronunciation than they would otherwise have, but may be seen as being more successful communicatively. On the other hand, NNS pairs who do not share an L1 will likely be rated higher on pronunciation but not on communication. Either way, the format of the test may be a disadvantage. Criteria that stress intelligibility or lack of an obtrusive accent will work against same L1 pairs, while criteria that stress communicative effectiveness will work against different L1 pairs. Keeping track of these dynamics can be especially challenging for interviewers.

Listener factors

Whether speech is understandable depends not only on the speaker's ability but also on the listener. Just as parents may understand their own young children when no one else is able to, foreign accents may not cause much difficulty for listeners who are familiar with such accents, while listeners who are not used to them may find a speaker incomprehensible. In speaking assessment, this means that the listener is a particularly important variable in whether a speaker's pronunciation can be understood, and thus, what kind of mark the test taker receives. Thus Fayer and Krasinski (1987) say, 'Intelligibility is hearer-based; it is a judgement made by the listener' (p. 313). Listeners are usually the same people assessing the test taker, although they may also be other test takers, as happens in interview formats (such as the Cambridge Speaking papers) where two test-takers are expected to interact. The listener's role in assessment raises three important issues for pronunciation: the effect of familiarity, whether raters should be language professionals or naive, person-in-the-street types, and the language background of the examiners.

It is usually assumed that listeners who are familiar with an accent will be more lenient toward the speaker. This is the upshot of Gass and Varonis (1984). English-speaking listeners who are used to listening to Chinese, Korean or Indian speakers of English, for example, are more likely to have their ears tuned to common phonetic deviations from those they would expect from speakers of their own variety of English. This in turn leads to, we assume, greater intelligibility.

However, even if raters find familiar accents more intelligible (in the sense of being easier to decode), this does not guarantee that they will rate them higher. The well-documented tendency of NS listeners to downgrade NNS speech simply because of noticeable accents has frequently been commented on (Barnwell, 1989; Munro and Derwing, 1999). It may even be that familiar accents will be critiqued more harshly because of social attitudes. Brooks (2002) studied NS reactions to accented speech. NS listeners were asked to judge fully grammatical recordings from three groups: NSs of American English, Spanish-accented English, and Other-accented English (L1= Mandarin, Malay, Arabic, Tamil). The recordings were randomly presented to NS listeners who rated the speakers using attitudinal descriptors (for example, friendly/unfriendly) on a 7-point Likert Scale. While all accented speech was rated more negatively than NS speech, Spanish-accented English was consistently rated the most negatively. Brooks interpreted this as being a result of both the familiarity of Spanish-accented English to US listeners and the generally negative social attitudes toward Latino immigrants in the US. Jenkins (1997) says that this tendency to downgrade accented speech which is otherwise intelligible is a danger that may lead raters 'to mark down in other more flexible global categories such as Task Achievement or Interactive Communication' (p. 8).

Listener factors are particularly important in the qualification and training of raters. Speaking assessment is usually done by highly trained raters who are experienced language teachers or researchers. Speaking is a multifaceted skill, and non-expert raters cannot be expected to separate out and understand details from the whole speech event. Just as we would not expect a non-expert to be able to judge a dog show or a gymnastics competition, so non-expert raters cannot reliably judge speaking proficiency. Or so the argument goes. Where it breaks down is the assumption of expertise. People who are not language teachers or researchers are not, as a result, non-experts in language. They use language for multiple purposes each day, make decisions about how to communicate particular messages, and judge the spoken language of others, just as language 'experts' do. As one writer says, 'assessing communicative effectiveness is not an esoteric skill requiring arduous special training and licensing; it is one of the normal component of linguistic and social adulthood' (cited in Barnwell, 1989: 155). Non-experts in language are different from experts in that they, by and large, cannot explain and analyze why they make the decisions and judgements they do. To some language experts, the unanalyzed intuitions of the non-experts make them particularly good raters of speaking proficiency, especially as regards pronunciation. Tench (1997) describes this position most transparently. 'If intelligibility is under investigation ... let native speakers without linguistic training and professional involvement with foreign language teaching evaluate; that is the real test of intelligibility – by the so-called "man-in-the-street"'(p. 35).

Naive raters, the 'man-in-the-street' intuitive experts, may have an advantage over experts who are too heavily involved with language teaching to really understand how a NNS will be actually understood outside the classroom. Teachers are likely to be too familiar with L1 influenced pronunciation and, like parents who understand their own toddlers, may be unreliable judges because of their familiarity with NNS speech. Brown (1995) reflects this view when she charges that teachers may actually have lost the ability to listen to NNS language as a naive listener would. Thus, the use of naive NS raters in performance testing may make the performance testing of speaking ability more valid. Since the examinees will have to interact with average people who have no special expertise, using naive raters simply reflects this fact. Barnwell (1989) even argues that 'the role of the ACTFL interviewer/rater is to act as a kind of surrogate for native speakers' (p. 154). How tenable is this line of reasoning? Are naive raters' judgements of intelligibility likely to be more valid than trained experts? Although 'the involvement of ... non-teachers and non-native speakers is not the norm in language testing' (Brown, 1995: 2), several studies give a tentative answer to these questions. They all seem to show that while the use of naive raters may improve face validity in performance testing, the improvement comes at a loss in reliability.

Barnwell (1989) examined whether untrained NSs of Spanish could reliably use the ACTFL scale to judge the speech of four L2 learners of Spanish by looking at whether their judgements of proficiency correlate with trained raters. Barnwell tested the 'man-in-the-street' assumption that being a native speaker was sufficient expertise for such assessment. The study found that the naive raters all ranked the four candidates the same way, but that there was little interrater reliability in their ratings. This suggests that, even if using naive NS raters is more valid (an open question), it is in no way more reliable.

Yule and Hoffman (1993) found much the same thing. They used small groups of undergraduate students to rate the speaking proficiency of international graduate teaching assistants (ITA) in a US university setting. They found that the naive raters were not reliable when working alone, but when scores were calculated according to the majority scores of the group, their ratings were highly consistent with those of trained ESL raters and ESL programme administrators. They say that 'in small groups, undergraduate observers can reach decisions which are overwhelmingly in agreement with ... ESL professionals (p. 326). The advantage of using these undergraduate students was not their reliability, however. In the politically charged atmosphere of ITA training, 'the clear advantage ... is that it provides the ESL professionals with a powerful validation of their verdicts (p. 326). In other words, the face validity of using students to judge the teachers' English provides an extra shield to protect ESL professionals from political fall-out.

Another area in which non-experts in language have been studied is in relation to occupation specific language tests. Brown and Lumley (1997) say that raters who are experts in industry and those who are language experts rate performance differently. Brown (1995) studied the differences between the ratings of these two groups. Overall, she found no significant difference between industry representatives and language teacher ratings. However, in subscores, the two groups were quite different. Teachers were harsher toward grammar, vocabulary and fluency errors, while industry representatives were harsher toward problems with pronunciation and comprehension. Brown suggests that the main advantage of industry raters in a performance test is again validity. Industry raters have a better sense of whether the examinee has performed adequately, although they may not be very good at describing why in terms of language. McNamara (1996) also looked at industry and teacher ratings. He found that teachers were harsher raters for most language related categories, while industry raters were harsher toward pronunciation errors.

In related findings, Elder (1993) found that raters who were subject specialists systematically differed from ESL teachers. Subject specialists were consistent in judging the quality of subject specific language, while they were inconsistent in judging decontextualized language. ESL teachers, on the other hand, were consistent with judging language but showed large amounts of variation on evaluating successful task completion. This indicates that naive raters can be better raters for certain areas, but that they are usually unreliable in judging language. To judge language reliably, they would need training, which then would change their value as 'naive' raters (Lumley and McNamara, 1995).

Fluency and assessment

Pronunciation is part of another common construct, fluency, found in most assessments of spoken language. Like intelligibility, fluency appears to have a psychological reality. Barnwell (1989) says that non-expert raters used fluency to describe the speech of L2 speakers, even though they were unable to specify exactly what they meant by the term. Fluency, according to Koponen and Riggenbach (2000), can be difficult to differentiate from pronunciation, suggesting that both categories overlap to some extent. For example, fluency is closely tied to spoken phrasing, a pronunciation feature known as tone units or thought groups. Fluency in language is similar to fluency in other areas, in which it is a measure of ability to perform a motor activity. For language, this means ease and speed in speaking, with an ability to smoothly use grammar and vocabulary (cited in Koponen and Riggenbach, 2000). While pronunciation is clearly part of fluency, this definition includes more than pronunciation.

Fluency, like intelligibility, is often ill-defined. Fluency scales have always been hard to operationalize, and even when they are specified, it is not certain that the parts add up to the whole (Fulcher, 1996). Like a former US Supreme Court Justice's quote about pornography, most people think they know fluency when they see (or hear) it, despite not being able to define it. This difficulty occurs partly because fluency has two related but different meanings.

The first definition of fluency focuses on smooth transmission. Lennon (2000) calls this 'the rapid, smooth, accurate, lucid, and efficient translation of thought ... into language' in real time (p. 26). Implicit in Lennon's definition are both positive and negative qualities. Positively, fluency includes smoothness, clarity, and rapidity of expression. Fluency may also be associated with use of intonation (Wennerstrom, 2000). When the positive qualities are present, they are often not noticeable, and like pronunciation, fluency is judged by its errors: misplaced or overly frequent pauses and hesitations, searching for words, and too many false starts.

A second definition of fluency is akin to overall spoken proficiency, and remains influential in the rating scales of most standardized tests. One description (Koponen and Riggenbach, 2000: 9) of this says that

> nonnative speakers who have reached a high level of proficiency and can speak 'smoothly,' without the noticeable effort evident in hesitations and a 'groping for words,' are often considered fluent in the language.

This global sense of fluency includes more than smooth, even delivery, and involves at the very least an ability to access the grammatical system of the language to communicate without unusual effort. Even though few current assessment instruments would agree that the full range of skills in this quote are necessary for fluent speech, most researchers feel that fluent speech is unlikely without a high degree of proficiency in the foreign language. Two underlying features seem to reflect fluency's relationship to overall speaking proficiency: automaticity and the ability to plan ahead while monitoring the developing communication for clues.

Automaticity describes the extent to which elements of speech do not have to be consciously considered while communicating. More proficient speakers usually have greater automaticity than less proficient speakers. Two types of automaticity seem to be involved in fluent speech. The first type involves the sound and word level, and the second the phrase level.

Lack of automaticity at the sound or word level is where fluency overlaps significantly with pronunciation. Speakers who must pay attention to articulation or the word stress will be less fluent than those who do not need to pay attention to pronunciation. Speakers who are not consistently able to put words together into a coherent message, even with good word-level pronunciation, will also be seen as having pronunciation errors, since the rhythm and melody of their speech will be impaired. Although this type of automaticity problem is common with less proficient learners, it is not the only place that it occurs. Some learners who have studied and used English extensively may find the need later to work on pronunciation, due to difficulties with intelligibility. This is common with advanced users with professional needs for using English, such as post-graduate teaching assistants in North American classrooms or medical professionals. If their English at the sound and word level is relatively automatic, albeit inadequate for their professional speaking needs, bringing articulation under conscious control is then likely to affect their fluency.

Lack of automaticity at the phrase level is less likely to be heard as a pronunciation difficulty. Lennon (2000) says that 'fluent discourse is characterized by an optimal mix between highly automatized chunks of language ... and phases where the speaker is composing more creatively' (p. 32). A fluent speaker, then, is one who has access to a stock of verbal idioms, phrases that do not need to be consistently reconstructed. Around these preset frames of language, fluent speakers construct the messages needed for their current interactions. Both automaticity at the sound/word level and the automatized chunks of language at the phrase level contribute to what Segalowitz (2000) calls 'cognitive fluency' which underlies 'performance fluency'; that is, fluid, smooth and accurate speech.

Fluent speakers also have the ability to plan ahead as they speak, juggling the encoding of new intentions while finishing the current utterance. Pawley and Syder (2000) say that 'even though spontaneous [fluent] speakers often do not know exactly what they are going to say when they start a multi-clause construction,' they avoid breakdowns by having a general sense of what they want to communicate (p. 170). This 'look-ahead facility' (Lennon, 2000: 33) can only operate efficiently when other elements of spoken language are sufficiently automatized and speakers can formulate the elements required to form meaningful sentences. The key difference between fluent and non-fluent speakers is the ability to formulate utterances smoothly under time pressure.

These descriptions of fluency appear to assume monologue, or at least extended speaking types of speech rather than interactive speech. Many assessments of speaking also fit this assumption as well. Tests such as the Test of Spoken English®, TOEFL Academic Speaking Test®, and Ordinate Corporation's SET-10®, which deliver cues via audio or telephone, ask for responses to a non-present voice. However, there is evidence that interaction can greatly alter how fluency is perceived. Lennon (2000) implicitly recognizes the effect of context or speaking goals in arguing for a difference between fluency (ostensibly based on an objective measure) and perceived fluency, or the impression of a listener that a speaker is speaking smoothly. Fiksdal (1990; 2000), examining adviser–student interviews, found that standard measures of dysfluency (such as false starts, changes in tempo, and short pauses) did not necessarily affect perceptions of fluency. Many of the interviews she looked at included large numbers of these features, but what affected judgements of fluency were the presence of rapport strategies and backchannelling (Fulcher, 1996). Speech was seen as fluent if the interaction was appropriate and rewarding. Fiksdal says that 'such dysfluencies as tempo changes, false starts, and micropauses are not remarked on by the speakers unless the face system is affected' (2000: 129). These findings affect how fluency should be operationalized for interview type tests. When an examinee and interviewer have to interact, interviewers should be careful to build common ground to give those being assessed the best chance of success. When two examinees have to interact, both may be at a disadvantage if fluency is assessed by traditional means.

While fluency in monologue may be measureable by using markers of dysfluency, interaction clearly requires a different strategy. One writer (Lehtonen (1978), in Koponen and Riggenbach, 2000: 14) says that

> to be fluent in the right way one has to know how to hesitate, how to be silent, how to self-correct, how to interrupt and how to complete one's expression, and how to do all this fluently, in a way that is expected by the linguistic community and that represents normal, acceptable and relaxed linguistic behavior

Fluency is also related to another understudied feature that is sometimes seen as part of pronunciation; speech rate. Fluent speech is often thought of in terms of rapidity (Lennon, 2000) or speed (Koponen and Riggenbach, 2000). Yet it may be possible for speakers to speak too fast, or at least appear to. This is especially true for examinees who are very fluent. When I used to train raters for the SPEAK test, the institutional form of the Test of Spoken English, examinees from India or other outer circle countries were consistently heard as either completely understandable or completely incomprehensible. A common critique given by those raters who struggled to understand was that the speakers spoke too fast and were thus impossible to understand. The perception of rate was likely due to an unfamiliar speech rhythm, or to the lack of observeable silence (Pawley and Syder, 2000).

How fast do native speakers of English speak? Pawley and Syder (2000: 172) report that the average rate of speech is 'around 4.5 to 5 syllables per second' although they do not say whether this is for read or spontaneous speech. It also seems fast relative to one of the only studies of speech rate. Munro and Derwing (1994) found that native English speakers spoke significantly more quickly when reading than speaking spontaneously (4.13 vs 3.47 syllables/second), and quicker than Mandarin speakers of English, who showed no difference in speech rate between spontaneous speech and reading (2.35 vs 2.42 syllables/second). The relatively slow rate of the nonnative speakers suggest that rating fluency based on speed rather than continuity of speech may unfairly use 'idealised native speaker norms' (Leung and Teasdale, 1997: 314) as a basis for judging speaking ability.

Conclusion

Pronunciation is central to speech, and any assessment of spoken language must address its role. After its time in the wilderness, when it was marginalized as communicative language teaching grew in importance, pronunciation has become the subject of innovative research, reflecting interest in its central role in oral communication. Its role is complex rather than simple, which should encourage rather than discourage interest in how it contributes to communicative success. Rather than being irrelevant because of the spread of English away from the centres of traditional influence, pronunciation is more and more seen as a key to international intelligibility (Jenkins, 2000). One thing is certain – its importance will not go away. As long as L2 learners need to speak and listen, and speech needs to be assessed, teachers and researchers will have to deal with pronunciation. Teacher training programmes tried neglect, and a generation of teachers grew up with inadequate skills in teaching pronunciation. Students suffered, as did assessment. Today's teachers deserve to understand how to teach pronunciation. Students' communicative needs demand it, and by addressing pronunciation openly, standardized assessment will benefit.

Note

1 ACTFL stands for the *American Council on the Teaching of Foreign Languages*. See http://www.actfl.org for more information on the goals and scope of the Council.

Bibliography

Albrechtsen, D., Henrichsen, B. and Færch, C. (1980) 'Native speaker reactions to learners' spoken interlanguage', *Language Learning*, 30: 365–96.

Barnwell, D. (1989) '"Naïve" native speakers and judgements of oral proficiency in Spanish', *Language Testing*, 6: 152–63.

Breiner-Sanders, K., Lowe, P. Jr, Miles, J. and Swender, E. (2000) 'ACTFL proficiency guidelines – Speaking Revised 1999', *Foreign Language Annals*, 33: 13–18.

Brooks, S. (2002) *Attitudes of Native English Speakers Toward Spanish-accented English*, Master's thesis (Iowa State University).

Brown, A. (1988) 'Functional load and the teaching of pronunciation', *TESOL Quarterly*, 22: 593–606.

Brown, A. (1995) 'The effect of rater variables in the development of an occupation-specific language performance test', *Language Testing*, 12: 1–15.

Brown, A. and Lumley, T. (1997) 'Interviewer variability in specific-purpose language performance tests', in A. Huhta, V. Kohonen, L. Kurkir-Suonio and S. Luoma (eds), *Current developments and alternatives in language assessment* (Finland: University of Jyväskylä) 137–50.

Burgess, J. and Spencer, S. (2000) 'Phonology and pronunciation in integrated language teaching and teacher education', *System*, 28: 191–215.

Celce-Murcia, M., Brinton, D. and Goodwin, J. (1996) *Teaching pronunciation: a reference for teachers of English to speakers of other languages* (New York: Cambridge University Press).

Cutler, A., Dahan, D. and van Donselaar, W. (1997) 'Prosody in the comprehension of spoken language: a review', *Language and Speech*, 40: 141–201.

Derwing, T., Munro, M. and Carbonaro, M. (2000) 'Does popular speech recognition software work with ESL speech?', *TESOL Quarterly*, 34: 592–602.

Elder, C. (1993) 'How do subject specialists construe language proficiency?', *Language Testing*, 10: 235–54.

Fayer, J. and Krasinski, E. (1987) 'Native and nonnative judgements of intelligibility and irritation', *Language Learning*, 37: 313–26.

ffrench, A. (2003) 'The change process at the paper level. Paper 5, Speaking', in C. Weir and M. Milanovic (eds), *Continuity and Innovation: Revising the Cambridge Proficiency in English Examination 1913–2002* (Cambridge: Cambridge University Press) 367–471.

Fiksdal, S. (1990) *The Right Time and Pace* (Norwood, NJ: Ablex).

Fiksdal, S. (2000) 'Fluency as a function of time and rapport', in H. Riggenbach (ed.), *Perspectives on Fluency* (Ann Arbor: University of Michigan Press) 128–40.

Fulcher, G. (1996) 'Does thick description lead to smart tests? A data-based approach to rating scale construction', *Language Testing*, 13: 208–38.

Fulcher, G. (2000) 'The "communicative" legacy in language testing', *System*, 20: 483–97.

Gallego, J. (1990) 'The intelligibility of three nonnative English-speaking teaching assistants: an analysis of student reported communication breakdown', *Issues in Applied Linguistics*, 1: 219–37.

Gass, S. and Varonis, E. (1984) 'The effect of familiarity on the comprehensibility of nonnative speech', *Language Learning*, 34: 65–89.

Hahn, L. (1999) *Native speakers' reactions to non-native stress in English discourse* (Ann Arbor: University Microfilms International) UMI 9944870.

Jenkins, J. (1997) 'Testing pronunciation in communicative exams', *Speak Out*, 20: 7–11.

Jenkins, J. (2000) *The Phonology of English as an International Language* (Oxford: Oxford University Press).

Koponen, M. and Riggenbach, H. (2000) 'Overview: varying perspectives on fluency', in H. Riggenbach (ed.), *Perspectives on Fluency* (Ann Arbor: University of Michigan Press) 5–24.

Lehtonen, J. (1978) 'On the problems of measuring fluency', in M. Leiwo and A. Rasanen (eds) *AFinLA Yearbook 1978*, Publications de I'Association Finlandaise de Linguistique Appliquée (AFinLA) 23 (Jyväskylä: AFinLA) 53–68.

Lennon, P. (2000) 'The lexical element in spoken second language fluency', in H. Riggenbach (ed.), *Perspectives on Fluency* (Ann Arbor: University of Michigan Press) 25–42.

Leung, C. and Teasdale, A. (1997) 'What do teachers mean by speaking and listening? A contextualised study of assessment in multilingual classrooms in the English National Curriculum', in A. Huhta, V. Kohonen, L. Kurkir-Suonio and S. Luoma (eds), *Current Developments and Alternatives in Language Assessment* (Finland: University of Jyväskylä) 291–324.

Lippi-Green, R. (1997) *English with an Accent: Language, Ideology and Discrimination in the United States* (New York: Routledge).

Ludwig, J. (1982) 'Native-speaker judgements of second-language learners' efforts at communication: a review', *Modern Language Journal*, 66: 274–83.

Lumley, T. and McNamara, T. (1995) 'Rater characteristics and rater bias: implications for training', *Language Testing*, 12: 54–71.

Macdonald, S. (2003) 'Pronunciation – views and practices of reluctant teachers', *Prospect*, 17 (3) http://www.nceltr.mq.edu.au/prospect/17/pros17_3.html

Major, R., Fitzmaurice, S., Bunta, F. and Balasubramanian, C. (2002) 'The effects of nonnative accents on listening comprehension: implications for ESL assessment', *TESOL Quarterly*, 36: 145–71.

Matsuura, H., Chiba, R. and Fujieda, M. (1999) 'Intelligibility and comprehensibility of American and Irish Englishes in Japan', *World Englishes*, 18 (1): 49–62.

McNamara, T. (1996) *Measuring Second Language Performance* (London: Longman).

Milroy, J. and Milroy, L. (1999) *Authority in Language: Investigating Standard English*, 3rd edn (London: Routledge).

Mugglestone, L. (1995) *'Talking Proper' – The Rise of Accent as Social Symbol* (Oxford: Clarendon Press).

Munro, M. (1998) 'The effects of noise on the intelligibility of foreign-accented speech', *Studies in Second Language Acquisition*, 20: 139–54.

Munro, M. and Derwing, T. (1994) 'Evaluations of foreign accent in extemporaneous and read material', *Language Testing*, 44: 253–65.

Munro, M. and Derwing, T. (1999) 'Foreign accent, comprehensibility and intelligibility in the speech of second language learners', *Language Learning*, 49, supp. 1: 285–310.

Murphy, J. (1997) 'Phonology courses offered by MATESOL programs in the US', *TESOL Quarterly*, 31: 741–64.

Murphy, J. (2003) 'Attending to word-stress while learning new vocabulary', *English for Specific Purposes*, 23: 67–82.

Pawley, A. and Syder, F. (2000) 'The one-clause-at-a-time-hypothesis', in H. Riggenbach (ed.), *Perspectives on Fluency* (Ann Arbor: University of Michigan Press) 163–99.

Prator, C. and Robinett, B.W. (1985) *Manual of American English Pronunciation* (New York: Holt, Rinehart & Winston).

Segalowitz, N. (2000) 'Automaticity and attentional skill in fluent performance', in H. Riggenbach (ed.), *Perspectives on Fluency* (Ann Arbor: University of Michigan Press) 200–19.

Shockey, L. (2002) *Sound Patterns of Spoken English* (Oxford: Blackwell).

Smith, L. and Bisazza, J. (1982) 'The comprehensibility of three varieties of English for college students in seven countries', *Language Learning*, 32: 259–69.

Smith, L. and Nelson, C. (1985) 'International intelligibility of English: directions and resources', *World Englishes*, 4: 333–42.

Tench, P. (1997) 'Towards a design of a pronunciation test', *Speak Out*, 20: 29–43.

Tyler, A. (1992) 'Discourse structure and the perception of incoherence in international teaching assistants' spoken discourse', *TESOL Quarterly*, 26: 713–29.

UCLES (2003) *IELTS Handbook 2003*. http: www.ielts.org/handbook.htm

Wennerstrom, A. (2000) 'The role of intonation in second language fluency', in H. Riggenbach (ed.), *Perspectives on Fluency* (Ann Arbor: University of Michigan Press) 102–27.

Williams, J. (1992) 'Planning, discourse marking, and the comprehensibility of international teaching assistants', *TESOL Quarterly*, 26: 693–711.

Yule, G. and Hoffman, P. (1993) 'Enlisting the help of US undergraduates in evaluating international teaching assistants', *TESOL Quarterly*, 27: 323–7.

12
Local and Dialogic Language Ability and its Implication for Language Teaching and Testing

*Marysia Johnson Gerson**

Introduction

In this chapter I will describe the fundamental principles of a dialogically based philosophy of second language acquisition (Johnson, 2003) that is based on Vygotsky's Sociocultural Theory (SCT) and Bakhtin's dialogized heteroglossia. Vygotsky's SCT combined with Bakhtin's dialogism as an epistemology for human sciences offers the field of second language acquisition a unique opportunity to develop a new framework that unites rather than separates the learner's social environment from his/her mental functioning.

Vygotsky's and Bakhtin's theories examine learning processes from a holistic perspective where the two opposite parts of human existence, mental and social, merge together in a dialectical relationship. The external world affects and transforms the individual's mental functioning that, in turn, affects and transforms social, cultural, and institutional settings.

In this new model of second language acquisition (SLA), the origin of second language competence lies not in the Language Acquisition Device, or any other mechanism, such as Bley Vroman's (1989) general problem solving system, but in a social reality; social contexts create language and language creates social contexts: one constitutes the other. These contexts are not universal. They are highly localized (henceforth, local second language ability). Since these social settings are locally bound, language ability is also locally bound; language ability reflects all the characteristics of a well-defined sociocultural and institutional context. Second language ability is not situated in the learner's mind but in a multitude of sociocultural and institutional settings and in a variety of discursive practices to which the learner has been exposed throughout his/her life. This is illustrated in Figure 12.1:

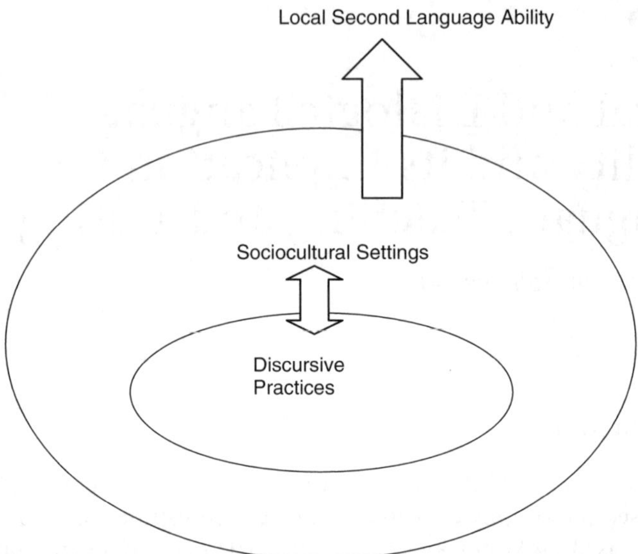

Figure 12.1   Local second language ability (Johnson, 2003:175)

Since the local second language ability model is based on Vygotsky's sociocultural theory and Bakhtin's literary theory, I will first briefly describe their fundamental principles and then discuss their implications for SLA theory and practice.

Key concepts of Vygotsky's sociocultural theory and Bakhtin's literary theory

Vygotsky's sociocultural theory of mind can be summarized in terms of three main tenets (Wertsch 1985, 1990; Johnson 2001, 2003):

1 the developmental analysis of mental processes;
2 the social origin of human mental functions;
3 the role of language in the development of human cognitive functioning.

The first key concept refers to the type of analysis that Vygotsky advocates for appropriate investigations, understandings, and interpretations of the higher forms of human mental functions. Vygotsky (1978: 64–7) claims that 'we need to concentrate not on the *product* of development but on the very *process* by which higher forms are established ... To encompass in research the process of a given thing's development and all its phases and changes – from birth to death – fundamentally means to discover its nature, its essence' (emphasis in original.) Thus, to discover how human mental functions work, we ought to focus on *processes* and changes, their origins and developmental transformations, not on the final product of development.

Vygotsky views the ontogenesis of development of children in terms of two forces: *natural* (that is, biological), which is responsible for the lower level mental functions such as perception and involuntary attention, and *cultural*, which is responsible for higher mental functions such as voluntary attention, planning, monitoring, rational thought, and learning. What distinguishes these two forces is a degree and type of regulation. The lower (elementary) functions are regulated by the environment and the higher mental functions are self-regulated.

The ontogenesis of development of the child may be described in terms of three stages delineated by the degree of control over the mental processes. In the first stage, the object-regulated stage, the child is controlled by the environment; in the second stage, the other-regulated stage, the child's mental functions depend on the assistance of and collaboration with other people; and in the final stage, the self-regulated stage, the child takes control over his/her higher mental development. The object-regulated stage is the result of the operation of natural forces, and the self-regulated stage is the result of the operation of cultural forces.

The second tenet of Vygotsky's sociocultural theory claims that higher mental functions originate in a social activity. This claim is captured in the *genetic law of cultural development*:

> Any function in the child's cultural development appears twice, or on two planes. First it appears on the social plane, and then on the psychological plane. First it appears between people as an interpsychological category, and then within the child as an intrapsychological category. This is equally true with regard to voluntary attention, logical memory, the formation of concepts, and the development of volition. We may consider this position as a law in the full sense of the word, but it goes without saying that internalization transforms the process itself and changes its structure and functions. Social relations or relations among people genetically underline all higher functions and their relationships. (Vygotsky 1981: 163)

According to the *genetic law of cultural development*, individuals internalize many patterns of social activities, which they observe and participate in on the social (that is, interpersonal plane). However, the process of internalization should not be viewed as the mere coping of the social activities observed on the social (interpersonal) plane because 'internalization transforms the process itself and changes its structure, and functions' (Vygotsky 1981: 163). Recall that the internal and external processes are in a dialectic relationship. Vygotsky here was influenced by Engels's dialectic philosophy, which stresses the importance of change as the main factor in human social development. For Engels, this change is brought about by a constant conflict between opposite forces.

The transition from the interpersonal to intrapersonal plane is a dynamic and gradual process that takes place within the Zone of Proximal Development (ZPD). Vygotsky develops the notion of the ZPD to address the problem of assessment in education and the problem of teaching practices. According to Vygotsky, the existing forms of assessment and teaching practices focus solely on the individual's actual level of cognitive development, and they neglect to take into consideration his/her *potential* level of development. Vygotsky (1978: 86) defines the ZPD as 'the distance between the actual developmental level as determined by independent problem solving and the level of potential development as determined through problem solving under adult guidance or in collaboration with more capable peers'.

Vygotsky is more interested in the individual's potential level of development than in the individual's actual level of development. Two individuals, for example, may be at the same actual level of development as determined by their final test scores, but their ZPDs may differ, reflected by their differing ability to solve problems during collaboration or interaction, with a more capable peer or an adult. Vygotsky views mediation (that is, a form of assistance) within the ZPD as the key element for the individual's mental development. He calls the individual's potential level of development 'the buds' or 'flowers' of development rather than the 'fruits' of development' (Vygotsky 1978: 86). These 'buds' need to be cultivated and nourished in the zone of proximal development by providing appropriate assistance to the learner.

Vygotsky claims that 'an essential feature of learning is that it creates the zone of proximal development; that is, learning awakens a variety of internal developmental processes that are able to operate only when the child is interacting with people in his environment and in cooperation with his peers. Once these processes are internalized, they become part of the child's independent developmental achievement' (Vygotsky 1978: 90).

The third fundamental tenet of Vygotsky's sociocultural theory pertains to the role of language in the development of the higher mental functions. For Vygotsky, the transition from the interpersonal (social) plane to the intrapersonal (mental) plane is dependent on the mediated function of language. Vygotsky views language as speech rather than a system of abstract morphosyntactic rules. Speech plays a crucial role in the transition from the interpersonal to the intrapersonal plane.

To summarize, Vygotsky's sociocultural theory accounts for the role of society and culture in the development of human higher mental functions. An individual's mental functions reflect the social, cultural, and institutional settings to which the individual has been exposed during the course of his/her life.

As Wertsch (1985, 1990) points out, the short life of Vygotsky did not allow him to pursue the investigation of the effect of various social and institutional settings on mental development. The works of his contemporary, Bakhtin, fill this gap.

Mikhail Bakhtin (1895–1975) worked in the field of literary criticism and his literary theory includes such concepts as speech genre, voice, and dialogue. Similar to Vygotsky, Bakhtin (1981, 1986) refuses to view language as an abstract system of signs that is devoid of social, historical, cultural, and institutional contexts. For Bakhtin, language is a living thing, and as a living thing, it reflects and defines at the same time the various contexts in which it used. Language always lies on:

> the border between oneself and the other. The word in language is half someone's. It becomes 'one's own' only when the speaker populates it with his own intention, his own semantic and expressive intention. Prior to this moment of appropriation, the word does not exist in a neutral and impersonal language (it is not, after all, out of a dictionary that the speaker gets his words!), but rather it exits in other people's mouths, in other people's contexts, serving other people's intentions: it is from there that one must take the word, and make it one's own. (Bakhtin, 1981: 293–4)

When we speak, we speak not with one language; we speak with many 'languages,' we speak with many voices. These voices reflect the social, cultural, and institutional environments we have been exposed to in the course of our lives. Only through the exposure to these various contexts can we acquire different voices, which are essential for human communication.

Although we speak with many voices, which Bakhtin calls *heteroglossia*, these voices can be studied because they are associated with a given type of speech genre. Bakhtin (1986: 78) claims that we only speak in 'definite speech genres, that is, all our utterances have definite and relatively stable typical *forms of construction of speech genres*', and we may not be even aware of it: 'Like Molière's Monsieur Jourdain who, when speaking in prose, had no idea that was what he was doing, we speak in diverse genres without suspecting that they exist' (ibid).

Despite the fact that there exists a diverse number of speech genres, speech genres can be divided into two major groups: primary and secondary. The former includes daily conversations, narrations, diaries, letters; the latter includes novels, dramas, all kinds of scientific research. They represent 'more complex and comparatively highly developed and organized cultural communication (primarily written) that is artistic, scientific, sociopolitical and so on' (Bakhtin, 1986: 62). Secondary, more complex, genres arise from primary genres that have been internalized and transformed into secondary genres.

In Bakhtin's view, not only do we speak in speech genres, but we hear in terms of speech genres as well. Thus, without speech genres, human communication would not be possible. Bakhtin (1986: 79) writes:

> We learn to cast our speech in generic forms and, when hearing other's speech, we guess its genre from the very first words; we predict a certain length (that is, its approximate length of the speech whole) and a certain compositional structure; we foresee the end; that is, from the very beginning we have a sense of the speech whole, which is only later differentiated during the speech process. If speech genres did not exist and we had not mastered them, if we had to originate them during the speech process and construct each utterance at will for the first time, speech communication would be almost impossible.

Bakhtin's voices and speech genres are always in a dialogic relationship. Bakhtin places a dialogic relationship at the core of his literary theory. According to Bakhtin, we only 'speak' in a form of a dialogue; even if we speak to ourselves, as in a monologue, we speak in a form of a dialogue. For Bakhtin, dialogue is not synonymous with the conventional meaning of a dialogue, which presupposes the presence of two interlocutors who take turns at producing utterances. For Bakhtin, every voice stands in a multiple dialogic relationship with other voices in a text, but since every utterance, every word, is 'half someone's', this dialogic relationship extends to the original owner of the utterance, to the social, cultural, and institutional context in which it was originally situated. Language for Bakhtin is always in a dialogic relationship to other voices (henceforth, dialogic language ability).

To summarize, Bakhtin's concepts of speech genres, voices and dialogues present an important contribution to Vygotsky's sociocultural theory. They explain the effect of speech genres characteristic of a given sociocultural and institutional setting on human mental development; that is, the exposure and practice within various social, institutional and cultural settings are crucial for acquiring many different voices. These voices affect the pattern of higher mental functions.

The application of the view of language, which is local and dialogic to SLA theory and research would require that we abandon accepting theories that proclaim the existence of a general language ability. Also, we would need to eradicate the assertion that second language acquisition progresses along a predetermined mental path that cannot be altered no matter how much exposure to the target language the learner has experienced either in naturalistic or instruction-only contexts.

Such an approach to SLA would require that we view language not as an abstract system of morphosyntactic rules and structures, but as speech. In this new paradigm, the heterogeneous nature of speech is homogenized under the term speech genres; that is, many different voices captured in Bakhtin's heteroglossia are united within discursive practices that reflect a variety of sociocultural and institutional settings.

Within this new paradigm, the focus of SLA research would be on identifying, describing, and explaining all possible discursive practices one may encounter in a given sociocultural and institutional context. Here, current advances in corpus linguistics as well as in discourse analysis should provide essential tools for conducting authentic discourse analyses of a variety of speech genres.

In addition, the focus of SLA research would be on investigating the effects of various discursive practices on the learner's second language ability. For example, how do discursive practices typical of a university context affect the learner's language ability? How easily is the language ability acquired in one sociocultural setting transferable to other sociocultural and institutional contexts?

It is important to note that discourse analyses of speech genres typical of a given sociocultural and institutional context would not be conducted in terms of linguistic code, but in terms of utterances, speech acts, turn-taking mechanisms, repair mechanisms, topic patterns, and nonverbal signs such as gestures, and facial expressions. According to Bakhtin, we are all a product of the appropriation of the many voices we encountered in a variety of sociocultural and institutional contexts, such as educational, family, political, economic, justice, healthcare, and religious institutions. New voices of the target language's sociocultural and institutional settings need to be experienced, absorbed, and appropriated by L2 learners so L2 learners can become active participants in the target language culture. The local and dialogic approach to SLA can be summarized as follows (Johnson, 2003: 179):

> Language learning is not universal or linear but localized and dialectical. Language performance and language competence cannot be separated because they are in a dialectical relationship.
>
> Language is not viewed as a linguistic code but as speech embedded in a variety of local sociocultural contexts.
>
> The learner is not viewed as a limited processor that cannot attend to both form and meaning at the same time. Therefore, information-gap tasks such as structured input activities or spot-the-difference-in-pictures tasks are not considered to be useful for the appropriation of new voices or for the appropriation of language viewed as speech.
>
> To acquire the target language is to acquire discursive practices (speech genres) characteristic of a given sociocultural and institutional setting.
>
> Discursive practices typical of a given sociocultural setting are not limited to verbal signs. They also include nonverbal signs such as gestures, facial expressions, and other semiotic signs such as computers, graphs and maps.
>
> Cognitive and second language development are not separated in this model. They are in a dialectical relationship; one transforms the other.
>
> Interaction between new voices and old voices is essential for the learner's language and cognitive development.
>
> The development of second language ability is viewed as the process of becoming an active participant in the target language culture. The participation metaphor should replace, not complement the existing acquisition metaphor.
>
> The responsibility of researchers within this new approach is to investigate the processes that lead to becoming an active participant in locally bound social contexts. Such investigation requires that qualitative research methods be acknowledged as appropriate research methods for the field of SLA.

New research methods need to be developed to capture the fundamental processes of the participation metaphor. These new research
methods need to investigate L2 learners who were successful or
unsuccessful in their boarder-crossing endeavors. The ultimate goal
of this investigation is to develop a prototype of an active participant in the target language culture. (Johnson, 2003: 179)

The acquisition of local second language ability through the process of
active participation in local discursive practices is illustrated in Figure
12.2:

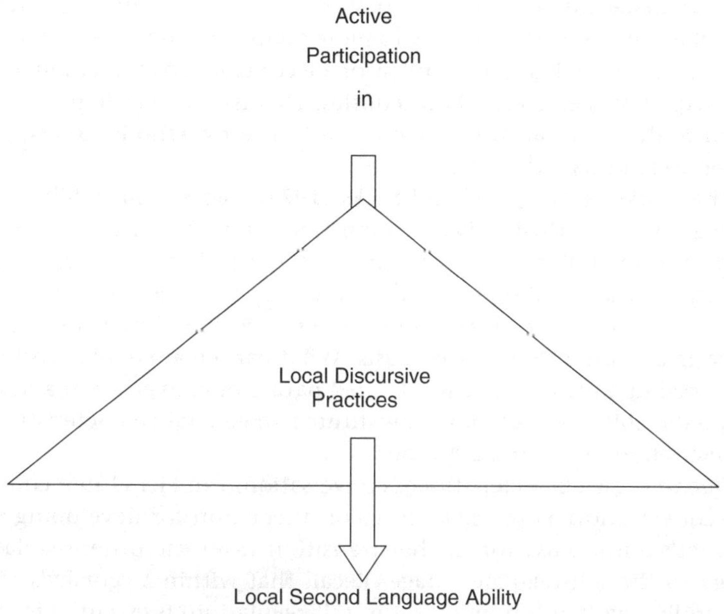

Figure 12.2   Local second language ability acquired in the process of active participation in local discursive practices (Johnson, 2003:177)

Some implications of local and dialogic language ability for language teaching and testing

The classroom in this approach would have to be viewed as a real
sociocultural setting where an active participation in the target language culture is promoted and taught. The classroom would need to
reflect as closely as possible the outside sociocultural and institutional
realities. Also, in such a classroom, we would be expected to create the

ZPDs for each individual student, in which through dialogized inter-actions the learner would have a chance to appropriate a variety of speech genres relevant to his or her individual needs.

Interaction within these individually created ZPDs may take on many forms. For example, it may be expressed in the format of a collaborative dialogue. A collaborative dialogue is a 'knowledge-building dialogue' (Swain, 2000: 97) where 'language use and language learning can co-occur. It is language use mediating language learning. It is cognitive activity and it is social activity' (ibid.). Or it may be realized in the format of an everyday conversation (van Lier, 1996; Johnson, 2000).

Van Lier advocates the usage of conversation in the second language classroom because symmetry of power is one of the main characteris-tics of a conversation. Contrary to more asymmetrically oriented forms of interaction such as an interview or a lecture, in a conversation, each participant has equal rights and duties. That is, each participant has a right to decide what to talk about, for how long, who is to talk, and when to terminate the talk.

The works of Schegloff and Sacks (1973), Sacks *et al.* (1974), and Schegloff *et al.* (1977) advanced our understanding of the nature of conversational discourse. According to these authors, conversation is locally managed and is produced on a turn-by-turn-basis. The turn size, turn order, and turn distribution are not specified in advance; they vary greatly on a case-by-case basis. What participants say is also not specified in advance. 'The unplanned nature of conversation and the unpredictability of outcomes constitute two general characteristics of conversation' (Johnson, 2001: 50).

Due to these characteristics of conversation, van Lier (1996) consid-ers conversation as the ideal form of interaction for developing the learner's autonomy, for his/her transition from the other-regulated stage to the self-regulated stage. Recall that within Vygotsky's SCT, the individual's autonomy (that is, self-regulation) is essential for the development of the individual's higher mental functioning.

Conversational interaction should not be limited only to a collabor-ative interaction with more capable peers or tutors; it should include interactions with learners who are at the same level of actual develop-ment. Van Lier (1996: 193) points out that 'conversational interaction among language learners of roughly equal ability might be particularly useful, perhaps more so, in certain circumstances, than interaction with more capable peers or with native speakers'.

The knowledge and skills acquired in interactive classroom activities within individualized ZPDs should be relevant to the L2 learner's individual needs and goals outside the classroom. The classroom should provide a context for drawing the learner's attention to different discursive practices. It should reflect the social reality that exists outside the classroom.

Such a new approach to teaching a second language would require the development of many different videotapes and internet programmes that describe a variety of discursive practices. Also, new textbooks should be written to promote the view of language as speech genres and the view of second language ability as the process of becoming an active participant in the target language culture.

In my book, *The Art of Non-Conversation: A Re-Examination of the Validity of the Oral Proficiency Interview*, I developed a model for testing second language speaking ability which I called the Practical Oral Language Ability (POLA). Since the POLA model falls under the dialogically and locally based approach to language testing, I will first summarize its main principles, and then I will elaborate on some issues that are relevant to our discussion of the application of the local and dialogic approach to language testing, such as the relationship between the traditional testing method of assessment and the new testing method of assessment – Dynamic Assessment (DA). The fundamental principles of POLA (based on Johnson, 2001: 199–205) are:

Major interactive oral events typical for a given sociocultural or institutional setting should be clearly identified and described. For example, in a hypothetical university context with the International Teaching Assistant (ITA) as a targeted audience, the following interactive oral events could be identified: office hours, group discussions, lectures, etc.

Each selected interactive oral event ought to be carefully analyzed in terms of its main functions, tasks, abilities, and skills.

The format of each interactive oral event should resemble as closely as possible its real-life format.

Each interactive oral event should be rated separately and independently of the other interactive oral events.

If possible, there should be a group of evaluators who would be responsible for rating the candidate's performance.

Not only should the candidate's performance be rated, but the tester's performance should also be evaluated. Recall that within this new framework, interaction is viewed as a social, not a cognitive, issue and therefore the candidate's speaking language ability is dependent on the tester's performance.

Within this system, language competence is locally situated. Although language competence is viewed as being locally situated in well-defined sociocultural and institutional settings, some local competencies are more universal than others. For example, the language competence to conduct a conversation in a cafeteria will not differ that much from a conversation in a bar or a restaurant. However, these similarities cannot be assumed automatically. They need to be supported by careful discourse analyses of a given sociocultural setting.

The issue of assessing the learner's potential development is at the core of Vygotsky's theory, and thus at the core of a dialogic approach to testing. In traditional testing, the focus is on measuring the learner's actual level of development as precisely as possible. To assess the learner's actual level of development, usually a series of tests are administered to the student at different points in time. These tests consist of a series of tasks that are arranged in a linear and sequential fashion (Newman *et al.* 1989). For example, if at one point, the learner was not able to perform a task, but later on the learner was able to perform the same task, then it may be inferred that the learner's actual competence has improved.

The question arises: How would the learner's potential level of development be measured? I suggest that a scale be developed utilizing the two principles of Aljaafreh and Lantolf's (1994) study: how much assistance and what type of assistance is required on the part of the tester? Based on these two principles a regulatory scale, similar to Aljaafreh and Lantolf's (1994: 470) scale, would need to be developed locally. The main theoretical assumption behind such a scale is that the more explicit assistance the candidate requires, the less advanced is the candidate in his/her potential development within the ZPD. It is important to note that the assessment system, which I advocate here, falls under the category of *Dynamic Assessment* (DA), more specifically a *hybrid* type of DA.

According to Poehner and Lantolf (2003), the central theoretical underpinnings of DA are: (a) Vygotsky's ZPD; and (b) mediation understood as a form of instruction offered to the individual during the process of assessment. The individual's responsiveness to assistance or feedback 'is an indispensable feature for understanding cognitive ability because it provides an insight into the person's *future* development. That is, what the individual is able to do one day with assistance, s/he is able to do tomorrow alone. Importantly, potential development varies independently of actual development, meaning that the latter, in and of itself, cannot be used to predict the former.

Moreover, the former is not an a priori prediction but is derived from concrete activity mediated by others or by cultural artifacts' (Poehner and Lantolf, 2003: 2).

Poehner and Lantolf (2003) discuss methodological differences between statistical approaches to assessment (SA) and DA. They claim that SA focuses on the learner's actual development, 'on the product of past development while DA foregrounds future development. Said in Vygotsky's terms, SA taps into already matured abilities but DA promotes functions that are maturing' (Poehner and Lantolf, 2003: 5).

Another difference between SA and DA is that the tester in SA is expected to play a neutral role (that is, s/he is not allowed to offer any assistance to the individual). Such a behaviour is required of the interviewer in the Oral Proficiency Interview (OPI), for example.

Assistance or mediation is not allowed due to the fact that SA relies heavily on psychometric analyses, which require that potential sources of error be eliminated to increase test reliability. 'Traditionally, test reliability derives from a commitment to standardization whereby all sources of potential error should be minimized to ensure that the observed score on a test is as close to the true score as possible. Reliability assumes that what is being measured is more or less stable' (Poehner and Lantolf, 2003: 15–16). Contrary to SA, in DA the trait being measured is viewed as being less stable.

Poehner and Lantolf (2003) describe two types of DA: interventionist DA and interactionist DA. Interventionist approaches to DA adhere more closely to a psychometrical analysis and quantification: they are concerned with the elimination of measurement error 'through reliance on standardized form of assistance' (Poehner and Lantolf, 2003: 16). In addition, interventionist approaches to DA are interested in observing how much learning is developed in the process of providing feedback to the individual and what kind and how much intervention is needed to foster learning. Interventionist approaches focus on 'helping individuals to become more efficient in their learning' (Poehner and Lantolf, 2003: 22).

Interactionist approaches to DA are more concerned with psychological processes involved in human mental development. Interactionist approaches adhere more closely to Vygotsky's preference for 'qualitative assessment of psychological processes and dynamics of their development (Minick, 1987: 117 cited in Poehner and Lantolf, 2003: 8). They are less preoccupied with the assessment of the individual's learning potential or identifying the most efficient learning tools.

Contrary to interventionist approaches to DA, there is no restriction on the amount and type of assistance provided by the examiner to the individual. In sum, interactionist approaches to DA strongly favour a one-to-one-dialogic interaction between the examinee and the examiner and are interested in uncovering psychological processes involved in human mental functions.

According to Poehner and Lantolf, interactionist approaches, because they are more labour intensive, are more suitable for a classroom setting and interventionist approaches with their focus on some of the psychometric properties of more traditional assessment are more appropriate for the assessment of a larger number of learners.

As indicated above, local and dialogic second language ability falls under the category of DA. More specifically, it represents a hybrid type of DA due to the fact that it contains within its boundaries some features of both approaches: interventionist and interactionist. A one-to-one format, and a dialogic relationship between the examinee and examiner point in the direction of interactionist approaches to DA; however, the application of a regulatory scale describing different degrees and types of explicit assistance points in the direction of interventionist approaches to DA.

In sum, local second language ability would require that we develop DA; however, since most of DA in second language contexts focuses on helping the individual to improve his/her learning efficiency, I would lean towards including some principles of the traditional testing method such as a regulatory scale. Assistance in the format of a face-to-face interaction, however, would be absolutely essential for assessing the learner's potential level of language development.

One may ask whether this new testing method of assessment would replace the traditional testing method. In my opinion, the new testing system would not eliminate or replace the traditional testing method. However, what would be required of the traditional testing system is that it openly admits what it measures. The traditional testing method measures the learner's actual level of language development; what the learner can do without any assistance at a particular moment in time. To assess the learner's potential language ability a new type of test needs to be implemented. These testing instruments need to be built on a different theoretical foundation. DA offers a unique opportunity for the SLA community to experiment with new measuring tools that may provide valuable insights into the working of human mental functions.

Note

* The ideas presented in this chapter are based on my two previous books: Johnson (2001) *The Art of Non-Conversation* (New Haven and London: Yale University Press) and Johnson (2003) *A Philosophy of Second Language Acquisition* (New Haven and London: Yale University Press).

Bibliography

Aljaafreh A. and Lantolf, J.P. (1994) 'Negative feedback as regulation and second language learning in the zone of proximal development', *Modern Language Journal*, 78: 465–83.

Bakhtin, M.M. (1981) *The Dialogic Imagination*, Michael Holquist (ed.) (Austin: University of Texas Press).

Bakhtin, M.M. (1986) *Speech Genres and Other Late Essays*, Trans. Vern McGee (Austin: University of Texas Press).

Bley-Vroman, R. (1989) 'What is the logical problem of foreign language learning?', in S.M. Gass and J. Schachter (eds), *Linguistic Perspectives on Second Language Acquisition* (Cambridge: Cambridge University Press) 41–68.

Johnson, M. (2001) *The Art of Non-Conversation: A Re-examination of the Oral Proficiency Interview* (New Haven and London: Yale University Press).

Johnson, M. (2000) 'Interaction in oral proficiency interview: problems of validity', *Pragmatics*, 10, 2: 215–31.

Johnson, M. (2003) *A Philosophy of Second Language Acquisition* (New Haven and London: Yale University Press).

Minick, N. (1987) 'Implications of Vygotsky's theories for dynamic assessment', in C. Schneider Lidz (ed.), *Dynamic Assessment: An Interactive Approach to Evaluating Learning Potential* (New York: Guilford Press).

Newman, D., Griffin, P. and Cole, M. (1989) *The Construction Zone: Working for Cognitive Change in School* (Cambridge: Cambridge University Press).

Poehner, M.E. and Lantolf, J.P. (2003) 'Dynamic assessment of L2 development: bringing the past into the future', *CALPER Working Papers Series*, 1, (Pennsylvania State University, Center for Advanced Language Proficiency, Education and Research) 1–26.

Sacks, H., Schegloff, E. and Jefferson, G. (1974) 'A simplest systematics for the organisation of turn-taking in conversation', *Language*, 50: 696–735.

Schegloff, E.A., Jefferson, G., and Sacks, H. (1977) 'The preference for self-correction in the organization of repair in conversation', *Language*, 53, 2: 361–82.

Schegloff, E.A. and Sacks, H. (1973) 'Opening up closings', *Semiotica*, VIII, 4: 290–327.

Swain, M. (2000) 'The output hypothesis and beyond: mediating acquisition through collaborative dialogue', in J.P. Lantolf (ed.), *Sociocultural Theory and Second Language Learning* (Oxford: Oxford University Press) 97–114.

Van Lier, L. (1996) *Interaction in the Language Curriculum: Awareness, Autonomy, and Authenticity* (London: Longman).

Vygotsky, L.S. (1978) *Mind in Society: The Development of Higher Psychological Processes* M. Cole, V. John-Steiner, S. Scribner, and E. Souberman (eds) (Cambridge, MA: Harvard University Press).
Vygotsky, L.S. (1981) 'The genesis of higher mental functions', in J.V. Wertsch (ed.), *The Concept of Activity in Soviet Psychology* (Armonk, NY: Sharpe) 144–88.
Vygotsky, L.S. (1986) *Thought and Language*, Trans. Alex Kozulin (Cambridge, MA: M.I.T. Press).
Wertsch, J.V. (1985) *Vygotsky and the Social Formation of Mind* (Cambridge, MA: Harvard University Press).
Wertsch, J.V. (1990) 'The voice of rationality in a sociocultural approach to mind', in L.C. Mall (ed.), *Vygotsky and Education: Instructional Implications and Applications of Sociocultural Psychology* (Cambridge: Cambridge University Press) 111–26.

Index